COMPAGNIE GÉNÉRALE AÉROPOSTALE

Toulouse-Casablanca ..	1.845 km
Casablanca-Dakar	2.850 —
Marseille-Perpignan ..	275 —
Casablanca-Oran ...	755 —
Alicante-Oran	305 —
TOTAL....	6 030 km

Paris
Bordeaux
Toulouse
Marseille
Perpignan
Barcelone
Alicante
Tanger
Malaga
Rabat
Oran
Casablanca
Fez
Agadir
Cap Juby
Villa Cisneros
Port Etienne
AFRIQUE
St-Louis
Iles du Cap Vert
Dakar
Fernando Noronha
Natal
AMÉRIQUE DU SUD
Pernambouc
Maceió
Bahia
Caravellas
Victoria
Rio de Janeiro
Santos
Florianopolis
Porto Alegre
Pelotas
Asuncion
Valparaiso
Montevideo
Buenos Aires

Saint-Louis-Iles du Cap	760 km
Iles du Cap Vert.... } Ile de Noronha .... }	2 320 —
Ile de Noronha-Natal...	370 —
Natal-Buenos-Aires.....	4.650 —
TOTAL....	8.100 km

otal du Réseau... 14.130 kilomètres.

Saint-Exupéry

Other books by Marcel Migeo

LES ROGNEURS D'AILES,
Debresse, 1941

BATAILLES DANS LE CIEL,
Editions Colbert, 1942

POUR L'HONNEUR DES AILES,
Editions de la Nouvelle France, 1945

FILOUVILLE,
Editions de la Nouvelle France, 1946

HENRI GUILLAUMET,
Arthaud, 1949

MARYSE BASTIÉ,
Le Seuil, 1952

Saint-Exupéry

by Marcel Migeo

translated from the French by Herma Briffault

McGRAW-HILL BOOK COMPANY, INC. NEW YORK TORONTO LONDON

Library of Congress Catalog Card Number: 60-10600
FIRST EDITION 41908

Part one

1

Whence come I? I come from my childhood. I come from childhood as from a homeland . . .

—*Flight to Arras*

The national highway beyond Toulon in the direction of the Gulf of Saint-Tropez gradually leaves the coast and, shortly after passing Hyères, clings sinuously to the side of the Maures Mountains. It is a rather melancholy route, deserted at certain hours. For miles the Forest of the Dom borders it with dusty pines and cork oaks half stripped of their bark. The continuous chirring of cicadas fills the burning air in summer but does not enliven these desolate landscapes, where only the creaking of an oxcart occasionally exhibits human life in a region unamenable to progress. It is a land for monks or poets. True, another sign of life is there, below the road—the river flowing between its embankments. But the murmur of La Môle, as it tirelessly wears away its rocky bed, is inaudible in late summer; nothing can be heard above the insistent chanting of the cicadas. For miles there is not a hamlet or a clock tower to greet the traveler; there is only a forest ranger's house, where a dog barks, aroused by the passing of a stranger.

It was along this road that I went toward Congolin, on the first stage of a pilgrimage to the scenes familiar to Antoine de Saint-Exupéry in his childhood. I was gathering notes for the life of the man who had at one time been my flying comrade and whose life had been incomparably deep, rich, and intense, although it lasted less than half a century.

When at last I stood before the bulky little Château de La Môle, its two round towers lending it a melancholy charm and making it so intimately a part of the Provençal landscape, I pictured that day in 1906 when the six-year-old Antoine had his first glimpse of the house, which belonged to his maternal grandmother, Madame de Fonscolombe. He had been brought here from Lyons to live. And I tried to visualize Antoine's mother, the Countess Jean-Marie de Saint-Exupéry, a pretty young woman in widow's weeds, surrounded by her five children: Marie-Madeleine, nine years old; Simone, eight; Antoine, six; François, four; and the three-year-old Gabrielle. Left almost penniless at her husband's death two years before, she had returned to live with her mother in this house where she had been born and had spent her childhood.

Surely she must have been heavy of heart. But Antoine and the other children were never to remember a young mother crushed by grief and care: they recalled only her profound piety, serene courage, proud and easy manner, lively and inventive mind. Perhaps her smile had something of sadness in it, but nothing more. They remembered her with pride, too, for she was a talented painter, it would seem, since the French government bought one of her paintings and the city of Lyons purchased three others. She was a lenient and indulgent mother, they recalled; a woman who gave no great importance to material things. Fortunately—for her husband's family, which traced the title back to the thirteenth century, had fallen upon hard times, and toward the end of his life, Count Jean de Saint-Exupéry had kept his wife and children largely on his pay as a public health officer in Lyons. When he died, at forty, his wife had nothing to fall back upon except her own meager resources and the generosity of her mother and her aunt, Madame de Tricaud, whose home was also opened wide to receive the young widow and her brood.

As I stood before the closed and shuttered Château de La Môle, the cicadas fell silent and the shadows of night gradually filled the valley, enclosing La Môle and the nearby forest, darkening the sky. An intense silence descended upon the Maures Mountains. Not a sound could be heard; there was nothing to disturb the serenity. Not even a breath of air stirred the branches of the pines and eucalyptus.

Now I imagined the family that had gathered within those walls on that night long ago. Dinner was over; the family had trooped into the drawing room, where the lamps were carried, "Real lamps, heavy lamps," Saint-Exupéry described them. Time and again in his writings he refers to those lamps and how, transported from room to room, they stirred into motion "great wondrous shadows on the walls." When you picked one up you displaced "bouquets of light and great black palms. Then, the lamps finally set down, there was a settling into motionlessness of the beaches of clarity and the vast reserves of surrounding darkness, in which the wainscoting went on creaking." [1] In those shores of light the children played until the beloved old Austrian housekeeper, Paula, came to take them to bed.

Paula was one of those devoted servants whom modern life, two wars, and the emancipation of the working classes have practically banished to the realm of memory. The children regarded her as one of the family, expected her to join their games, and tyrannized over her. They forced her to take long walks with them and their pets, which included a tortoise led on a leash, a cat, and several dogs. She was a great storyteller. Austria is a land of mountains and forests, and children's stories seem to have their source in the darkness of forests and mountain ravines. The children were all bright, and Antoine had a fertile imagination; his taste for the marvelous and strange manifested itself quite early. He often spurred Paula to greater flights of fancy by persuading her to tell them what it had been like when, in her other life, she had been a lion, an elephant, or a monkey.

Paula made a lasting impression upon him; time and again he refers to her, often at crucial moments, as when flying a reconnaissance mission over the burning city of Arras. The enemy antiaircraft guns were peppering his plane, when suddenly her image flashed through his mind. "Paula, they are firing at me!" he exclaimed, as long ago he had cried, "Paula, they're being horrid to me!" He addresses himself to her in a long passage in *Flight to Arras*, as though she were close at hand. Yet long before he had piloted his first plane, she had returned to her house in the Tyrol which the children fancied "deep in snow and looking like the toy chalet on a Tyrolean barometer."

As the darkness deepened, I imagined that bedtime hour over which Paula had often presided. Perhaps the children insisted that she tell them still another story, although it was time to sleep. Sometimes she yielded. Then, after tucking them in, off she would tiptoe, taking the lamp with her. And night entered the room, soon to be peopled with dreams.

At Saint-Maurice-de-Rémens, not far from Lyons, stands another old château where Saint-Exupéry spent some happy childhood years. It is the house most often referred to in his writings, especially when, in *Wind, Sand and Stars,* he wrote of the lasting effect a childhood home can have upon the mind. "The marvel of a house," he tells us, "is not that it shelters or warms a man. . . . It is that it leaves its trace on the language." For a home such as this lays down layers of sweetness, forming "deep in the heart that obscure range from which, as waters from a spring, are born our dreams."

The Château of Saint-Maurice, somewhat eclectic in style, is situated almost in the heart of the village of Ambérieu. One approaches it through a courtyard where, to the right, is what was once a chapel. Above the door, carved into the stone, is a motto taken from the Gospel of St. John: *Eamus et Nos*—"Let us also go." Beyond this is a quaint old moss-grown well which has tumbled into ruin. The château is no longer a private home, but houses a vacation colony of schoolboys, and the one-time chapel has been converted into a laundry.

Entering the château from the courtyard one passes through a great dark vestibule into the dining room; these remain as they were in Saint-Exupéry's childhood. The park, too, is as he remembered it; everything else has changed.

The château's façade, wide and low, is toward the park—a vast lawn surrounded by tall trees. Crossing the park, between a double row of scaly pines, one reaches an iron grilled gate leading to a vista of fields and pastures above which, in the distance, loom the blue and cloud-hung Jura Mountains.

It was to this old mansion and park that Saint-Exupéry turned his thoughts for relief that night when his plane crashed in the Sahara. Lying on the sand, gazing at the stars, he recalled in his solitude "a park dark with firs and linden trees, and an old house that I loved." Isolated from it by space and time, he was still "filled with the memory of its odors, with the cool breath of its vestibules, with the voices that had animated it." [2]

Would he have been glad to know that this old house was now bringing joy and health to crowds of boys from Lyons? Recalling how he sought to relieve the misery of the urchins in the desert, of the old slave at Juby, I believe he would.

When I arrived, the boys were playing in the park. I waited until their shouts died down and until, their games over and the noon hour sounded, they entered the refectory for their midday meal. I wanted to hear what the ancient stones and trees had to say, in their turn, about that life I was recalling from his books and conversation.

Antoine's memories of the place were bathed in summer light. There were the games on the sunny lawn, the deep shade cast by the linden trees, the attic where the children assembled when storms threatened. For years this was the house where the children spent their summer holidays. After a short stay with her mother at La Môle, Mme. de Saint-Exupéry had moved to this more spacious domain, the property of her aunt, Madame de Tricaud, from whom she eventually inherited it. We can reconstruct those summer holidays not only from Antoine's recollections, but from those of his sister Simone.[3]

Of all the five children, he was the most wild and fearless. It was he who directed the games, tyrannizing over the others, interrupting them whenever a new idea struck him, quarreling with his rebellious younger brother François, keeping up the quarrel even at mealtimes, until he had won his point. Simone, two years older than Antoine, liked to take part in some of the noisy games, but Marie-Madeleine, the eldest, was quiet and contemplative. As gentle as a doe, she had won the nickname "Biche." Biche loved birds and became distressed when the boys' shouts drove the frightened creatures away into the nearby woods. Biche loved flowers—to such an extent that she never picked them because it made them suffer. Returning from a walk one day she pronounced the outing "ugly . . . there were no flowers." (This gentle girl was destined, like a flower, to have a brief life; she died at the age of twenty-three.)

However, when more than three were required for a game, Biche could be induced to join the others, and even the youngest, the delightful little Gabrielle (nicknamed "Didi"), would sometimes play with them. One of these games is described in *Flight to Arras*. The clouds and flames above Arras made Antoine recall it, for the game of "Aklin the Knight" was one he had invented on days of thunderstorms. As the black clouds piled up and threatened to break after the first flashes of lightning, the children assembled at the farthest end of the park, facing the château. When the first big, far-spaced raindrops fell, they raced at top speed across the lawn to the house. The one first touched by the raindrops was "out," as were the second and third and fourth. "He who survived longest was acknowledged the darling of the gods, the invulnerable. Until the next storm came, he had the right to call himself Aklin the Knight."

The attic was the children's refuge when rain inundated the park. Only those who have similar memories of an enchanting attic with mysterious corners lost in shadow, slanting rays of sunshine where motes dance, can understand the pleasure of the Saint-Exupéry children. Grownups rarely entered the attic; it was the children's impregnable domain, a treasure-trove of costumes, hats and boots, stuffed birds, of clocks whose old hearts could be made to throb once or twice when shaken. And strange objects whose uses were matters for investigation. Recalling this particular attic, Saint-Exupéry once said that attics were "life's back-stage." Curious and questioning as a child, he remained so all his life. Even the most enigmatic objects possessed a meaning for him, if only a partial one, and he could never rest until he had plumbed their mysteries.

In *Wind, Sand and Stars* he describes a discovery he made when his plane was forced down on a wild desert plateau in Spanish Africa. The place was so isolated, the sides of the plateau so steep, that it was, he realized, inaccessible except from the sky. Night came, and as he gazed at the first star he was struck by the idea that the land he stood upon had never before been trod by man, that "this pure surface had lain here thousands of years in sight only of the stars." Just then, he kicked against a stone. Picking it up, he perceived that it was hard and black, shaped like a tear, as if carved by some mysterious hand. And he reflected, "A sheet spread beneath an apple tree can receive only apples; a sheet spread beneath the stars can receive only stardust. Never had a stone fallen from the skies made known its origin so unmistakably." For the moment, forgetting his mission and the Moorish interpreter who accompanied him and was waiting to be flown to a place from which he could set out on foot, Saint-Exupéry began to search the plateau for other aerolites. He did find others—"at about the rate of one stone to the acre." The child eager to know everything still existed in the man.

While Antoine explored the attic, Biche, who hated the stoved-in old trunks, the broken objects, the accumulation of dust, played in her "Chinese bedroom," as she called one corner where no one could enter except with stockinged feet. François, for his part, sometimes stopped playing in order to "hear the music made by the flies." Handsome, dark-eyed François had musical talent and was very imaginative. Everything to him was music—the humming of the flies, the wind whistling in the dark pines, the strident chant of the cicadas in the olive trees at La Môle. Only two years younger than Antoine, he could be not only his elder brother's playmate but also classmate. They attended the same schools in Le Mans and at Fribourg. However, the two boys often quarreled, for Antoine was a tyrant and François was not easily subjugated.

In 1917, while they were both boarding pupils at the Collège de St.-Jean in Fribourg, François fell seriously ill with rheumatic fever. He was taken back to Saint-Maurice, where he died.

Antoine felt the shock of this premature death—François was only fifteen—in his own curious way. Writing to his mother from Fribourg at the time of François' illness, he said, "I saw Madame de Bonnevie, who told me about François' disease. Poor boy!" But he did not grasp the fact that François was fatally ill, for at once he continued, without transition, "She also told me he was sure to pass his exams, and I was glad to hear that." At the time of François' death there is no evidence that Antoine suffered greatly. But years later he wrote some very moving passages on this death. Such delayed reactions were typical of him. Events had their impact long afterward, when he had had time to meditate upon them. From this sifting of events, this decantation, came unexpected moments of illumination. Thus, in *Flight to Arras*, published fourteen years after François' death, there is a description of the deathbed scene. It is when he himself is risking his life and is meditating upon death that suddenly he recalls how his fifteen-year-old brother left life, left family, quite serenely, accepting the uprooting—indeed, trying to console his mother. "You know, Mamma," François had said, "some of the things I've seen or guessed in life were too ugly. I'd never have been able to tolerate them. I'll be better off in the other world to which I'm going." Most poignantly he recalled what François had said to him. "Lying in pain, he waved his hand as if saying 'No!' I did not understand. I thought it was death he was rejecting. The pain passed, and he spoke again. 'Don't worry,' he said, 'I'm all right. I can't help it. It's my body.' "

We find an echo of this in the Little Prince's character and words. Just as François had heard the music made by flies, so the Little Prince hears the music made by the rope, the pulley, the bucket, when drawing water from the well. And when he prepares to "go home," as he puts it, he explains to his friend: "You understand. It is too far. I cannot carry this body with me. It is too heavy." [4]

Throughout his life, Saint-Exupéry was demanding, immoderate, unsatisfied. These are the usual defects, if indeed they are defects, of people who are dynamic, enterprising, never contented with things as they are. Such people—and Saint-Exupéry was one—are often inventive. Even as a schoolboy, he was constantly contriving ideas for new kinds of engines and mechanical things. At this period, automobiles were a rare sight and the first airplanes were only beginning to leave the ground. Antoine would sketch his inventions and would explain, "This is a piston, this is a ball bearing," as he forced his classmates to look, listen, and admire, even though they would have much preferred to go on with the game the young inventor had interrupted. When they showed their annoyance, Antoine would flare up and sometimes use his fists.

But this domineering boy was capable of very generous impulses —another aspect of his contradictory nature. His sister Simone has recounted how one evening, after they had spent an exhausting day in the mountains, negotiating hard climbs, scratching themselves on brambles, and getting lost, she was about to take the train back to Saint-Maurice when she noticed that she had lost her gold watch. Doing as he advised her, she sadly went to the railway station, while he returned toward the mountain, climbing again each path, descending again a steep slope covered with treacherously slippery pebbles, stopping once more in the little grove where they had had their picnic lunch—sparing no pains in looking for the lost watch. Very late that night a carter picked up the tired boy on the road leading to Saint-Maurice. At the house, he merely said to her, "Monot, I'm frightfully sorry, but I didn't find your watch."

The Saint-Exupéry children may have had their quarrels, but no quarrel ever lasted long. For one thing, they enjoyed too many things together, especially their private jokes and mystifications. "When I was a child," Saint-Exupéry said in *Wind, Sand and Stars,* "my sisters had a way of giving marks to guests who were honoring our table for the first time. Conversation might languish for a moment, and then in the silence we would hear the sudden impact of 'Sixty!'—a word that could tickle only the family, who knew that one hundred was par. Branded by this low mark, the guest would all unknowing continue to spend himself in little courtesies while we sat inwardly screaming with delight."

Antoine had his baptism of the air in 1912, at the age of twelve, thanks to the kindness of one of the aviation "aces" of the period.

Only a few miles from Saint-Maurice was an aviation field—it still exists—to which Antoine often went on his bicycle, following a narrow yellow dirt road that wound between rocky fields of weeds and brambles. There he would wait for an airplane to take off. Sometimes the wait was long, for the engines of those days were unpredictable. Much simpler than they are today, less was known about them, even by the aviators who flew the machines. So Antoine would wander about the plane, examining its fragile wings, its varnished tail-booms held by crisscrossed piano wires. One day toward sunset, the aviator kindly took the boy up with him.

Jules Védrines was the flyer's name. Forgotten today, his exploits once classed him as among the greatest pilots of the world in the pre–World War I period. By 1912 he had broken several records and won several prizes. His plane, in a famous Paris-to-Madrid race, not only bore off the prize but was the only one to complete the course, and broke the world speed record by flying at 104 miles an hour. In 1913 he succeeded in flying his plane from Paris to Cairo, via Turkey, Libya, Syria, and Jerusalem—an extraordinary feat for the period. During World War I, Védrines was entrusted with some dangerous missions flying spies into enemy territory, which often meant having to land in very unfavorable terrain, wooded and hilly. In 1919 he performed a trick landing that was sensational at the time, bringing down a Caudron G–3 on the roof of the Galéries Lafayette store in Paris—a space 92 feet long by 39 feet wide and surrounded by a balustrade. Three months later Védrines was killed, with his mechanic, in a crash at Saint-Rambert-d'Albon on a flight to Rome.

That summer day in 1912, Védrines had no way of knowing that the boy he took up in his plane was to emulate him and enjoy a greater fame. Nor did Antoine seem to carry away with him a profound impression of that first flight—unlike the experience of the aviator Henri Guillaumet, who had his first flight at the age of fourteen and never ceased from that time onward to bend his energies toward a career in aviation. But this flight above the fields at sunset did inspire Antoine to write a poem—something about "evening breeze, heart at ease," and so on. Already at the age of twelve he was beginning to set down impressions and aspirations in verse, which he liked to read aloud to the assembled family. And there again he was domineering, for he would often insist upon reading his poems at bedtime when his brother and sisters were dying for sleep. But forced they were to listen, while he draped himself in a tablecloth and declaimed.

At about this same time, Antoine fabricated some kind of wings which he attached to his bicycle, demonstrating their use with no great success. But he would not easily admit defeat, and continued to expound his plans excitedly: "You'll see, one day I'll fly and crowds of people will shout, 'Bravo, Antoine de Saint-Exupéry!' "

After a long summer day of games, races, fist fights, the children were ready for bed quite early at night. But their great-aunt, Madame de Tricaud, the chatelaine of Saint-Maurice, was very devout and an autocrat. Beginning to intone her prayers while they were still finishing the dessert, she would rise from table and leave the room, motioning to the resigned servants and sleepy family to follow her to the chapel for evening prayers.

The children's rooms were on the third or top floor, overlooking the park. Iron grilles had been attached to the windows to prevent excursions on the roof. Paula had returned to her native Tyrol and been replaced by "Mademoiselle," quite a different sort of person—tiny, wizened, always on the go. Saint-Exupéry affectionately recalled that old housekeeper when he was lost in the Sahara. "Ah, I owe you a page, Mademoiselle!"—with these words he begins one of the most moving passages in *Wind, Sand and Stars*. He recalls how she continually trotted from cupboard to cupboard and how at night they went upstairs to bed, leaving Mademoiselle to "burn out her eyes under a lamp" interminably mending the sheets and tablecloths.

After the epoch of Paula and her storytelling had ended, it was Mme. de Saint-Exupéry who went upstairs to tuck in the children and bid them good-night. "Oh, mother, I recall how you bent over us, intent on making easier this departure of angels," Antoine wrote many years later, "and how you effaced any sign of rough weather from our beds, flattening out a wrinkle, smoothing that ridge, banishing that shadow. For a bed can be pacified, like the sea, by a divine finger." [5]

From the affectionate way this mother speaks of her world-famed son, it appears that she gave him preference over the other children —using the word in its true sense, "to put before," and by no means implying that she loved him more. Unconsciously, she did "prefer" him, and for two reasons. First, he clung to her more than the other children did. As a quite small boy, he followed her everywhere, carrying with him a little chair which he placed near her when she sat down. Then, he displayed his affection for her and was more demonstrative than they were. This was all the more appealing, since he was rather undemonstrative with other people.

Aside from this, Mme. de Saint-Exupéry had always had a presentiment of Antoine's high destiny. Presentiments cannot be disproved, especially maternal ones, and particularly when they have been justified by events. She was confident that this son would be a great and famous man; yet there was nothing in the child or youth to indicate an exceptional career. Because a boy attaches wings to his bicycle does not necessarily mean that he will be an aviator; because a schoolboy writes poems or short stories does not necessarily indicate that he will be a famous writer of talent. Certainly there was no evidence that he would be remarkable either as writer or aviator or man. But exceptional he was; he was a genius among the great men of his epoch. And nothing foretold it. At school he was not an outstanding student. Apparently he made little impression on others at his first school in Le Mans—at least, not according to one of his classmates who is now a priest. Mme. de Saint-Exupéry met this former classmate two years after her son's death and questioned him. "Father Barjon," she said, "you must surely have guessed that my Tonio would be a great man." "No, Madame," he replied frankly. And, speaking for myself, when I first met Saint-Exupéry at the age of twenty, I never suspected to what heights he was destined to ascend.

To those who knew him in his youth, he appeared intelligent and sensitive, of course, and to have a strong personality; but the total impression he gave was that of an eccentric. His brother and sisters were also unusual. Marie-Madeleine, the gentle Biche, wrote charming stories about flowers and animals; a collection of these was published by Lardanchet, in Lyons, under the title *Les Amis de Biche*. Simone was a brilliant student at the École des Chartes; François had a strong personality and was very imaginative; Gabrielle was also a child of exceptional intelligence and sensitivity—in her later married life, as the Countess d'Agay, it was to her and her family that Antoine went for comfort and understanding. If Antoine, in his manhood, emerged as more noteworthy, the explanation may perhaps be found in his own words. Time and again in his various books he examines the factors in "man's gropings toward self-fulfilment"—indeed, that is one of the main themes of *Wind, Sand and Stars*. In his frequent tributes to the courage and grandeur of his comrades of "the Line" he reminds us that it was their craft which cast them in its mold and recognizes that he and they had "had the luck" to find their vocation, which enabled them to be "transformed into men." Time and again he compares the evolution of the individual to the unfolding of a seed which develops according to whether or not it falls upon the right soil. Gazing upon the face of a Polish refugee's child, he reflected: "This is a life full of beautiful promise.... Protected, sheltered, cultivated, what could not this child become?"

His childhood environment could not have been more favorable for his development as a writer. At Reims in 1953 I heard his mother read a paper which she was later to use as preface to the letters he wrote to her through the years [*Lettres à sa mère*]. In it she describes the bedtime stories she told her children. The terrible Bluebeard, in her version, explained to his wife, "Madame, here is the chest where I keep my dimmed sunsets." And she asks, "Was it here that the Little Prince found them?"

In 1909 the children were of an age to make the problem of their schooling of prime importance. Mme. de Saint-Exupéry therefore took them to Le Mans, where relatives of her late husband lived, and entered the two boys in the Collège de Nôtre-Dame de Sainte-Croix, a Jesuit school which their father had attended when his own father had been prefect of the Sarthe department.

It was hard to leave Sainte-Maurice even temporarily, and the children reluctantly said good-by to the big house, the park, the mysterious attic, the rooms high up beneath the roof where they had accumulated so many memories.

At school the boys accomplished nothing remarkable. Antoine excelled in French and made merely passable grades in other subjects. And the two boys continued to argue and fight. Antoine was a tormentor, François was more or less the same, and Antoine could not stand ridicule. Because of his turned-up nose and his gaze directed skyward, his classmates dubbed him *Pique-la-Lune,* and this drove him wild. He hated such sarcasms, hated irony. He may have been recalling his schooldays when he wrote in *The Wisdom of the Sands,* "irony is not the habit of a man but of a dolt."

Mme. de Saint-Exupéry frequently stayed at Saint-Maurice, leaving the children in the care of their Aunt Marguerite, but every winter she paid them a long visit. Antoine still clung to her, still demonstrated great affection, but was ever more demanding. The other members of the family remarked her preference for Antoine, and his skill in playing up this preference to his advantage.

The summer vacations brought the family together again at the Château of Saint-Maurice, where life continued much as before, with games and fights and excursions filling the days and with Antoine making new experiments and discoveries. The children even continued to insist upon having their story hour at night and hearing the same old stories told over and over again. Their mother complied, and the tales she told again filled their nights with dreams. Mademoiselle was growing ever more wizened and old, but she still continued to trot back and forth from cupboard to cupboard and to wear out her eyes mending the linen.

The summer vacation of 1914 passed in a tense and ominous atmosphere. The children may have continued to play as gaily and noisily as ever, but they noticed the solemn faces of the grownups and heard their apprehensive remarks. The talk was all about war; and finally the war broke.

To the children the war represented, as the teachers at school depicted it, a fine adventure, with bugles sounding attacks, with battles and of course battlefields strewn with dead, but with a glorious dead. To the grownups it meant all this too, but it also stood for wrongs to efface and vengeance to take. The soldiers went off to war with bouquets in the barrels of their rifles, and at the railway stations they sang patriotic songs as they boarded the trains. The trains soon returned, filled with silent and suffering men. Mme. de Saint-Exupéry had a diploma as a hospital nurse, and soon she was in charge of the ambulance at the Ambérieu station, tending the war wounded who arrived from Alsace, and she continued this work during the four years of the war.

The boys were sent to a boarding school in Villefranche-sur-Saône. They complained about conditions at the Collège Montgré, and said repeatedly that they were unhappy. They were not ill treated, nor did the school have a prisonlike atmosphere. Life in a simple boarding school was just not grand enough for the Saint-Exupéry boys. They were too used to beautiful surroundings and to being waited upon by servants. Finally, at the end of the first term, their mother came to their rescue and took them to Fribourg in Switzerland, where they entered the Collège de St.-Jean.

Fribourg is a university city. Students from all over the world are drawn to its many colleges; not only are French students to be found there, but Italian and English, Hungarian, Polish, and Egyptian pupils abound, and there are even some from the Far

East. The city also happens to be a stronghold of Catholicism in a country whose population is sixty-five per cent Protestant.

The Collège de St.-Jean, directed by the Marist Fathers, is an aggregate of houses, very bright and clean, as are all houses in Switzerland, with gay window boxes of geraniums. Each house has its name—"The Elms," "The Pine-Woods," and so on. The cluster of houses, situated on the Perolles plateau, overlooks the picturesque little town and the narrow gorge where flows the Sarine River. There is no cloister. Flowering fields and calm, dark forests partially enclose the school. Here the French boys found a natural landscape, untamed by man, quite different from the rigid plantings of pruned chestnut and linden trees to which they were accustomed. At dawn the songs of birds and the fresh forest smells came into the boys' rooms through the open windows.

Discipline at this school is very relaxed; the fathers believe that young people may be brought to love discipline and that it should not be imposed upon them, that strictness leads only to a semblance of obedience, with the students trying by every means to evade rules. The fathers appeal to the students' sense of honor; conscience, they say, is God's voice within us. The teachers live with their students, participate in their games, have informal talks with them. There are tennis courts, a football field, a swimming pool, a fencing school, and in winter the snowy slopes are used as ski runs and toboggan slides where the youngsters get their fill of invigorating air and exercise. Everything is done to make the students feel as much at home as possible and never to feel that they are part of a herd. The lodging of boys in separate houses accomplishes much of this desired result. In addition, some pupils may occupy separate bedrooms. Antoine enjoyed this privilege, which gave him privacy for study and enabled him to surround himself with family photographs and souvenirs—and also to smoke a cigarette or prepare a cup of hot chocolate when he liked.

All this was obtained for the boys at a cost far beyond Mme. de Saint-Exupéry's means. But she had been brought up in the aristocratic tradition, and her family still managed, they said, to maintain their rank. This was becoming ever more difficult in that period of war and social revolution; already many people who had formerly lived on private incomes were taking paid jobs and earning their livings. The children, of course, were unable to comprehend their mother's financial situation and continued to make unreasonable demands, while she bent all her energies to fulfill their desires. Every week end she paid a visit to Fribourg, making a tiresome journey of more than three hundred miles, counting the distance both ways. She once wrote to tell François that she would have to cancel one of these visits, and to this letter Antoine replied characteristically.

Villa Saint-Jean, Fribourg
February 21, 1916.

Dearest Mamma,

François has just received your letter saying you cannot come here again until the first of March. And we always look forward so to your Saturday arrival! Why do you have to postpone your visit? Think how happy it would have made us.

Now, you will receive this letter on Thursday, or perhaps Friday. Perhaps you'll be able to send us a wire telling us that you'll take the Saturday morning express train and will arrive here in the evening. How happy we would be! You can't imagine how disappointed we were when we read your letter telling us you would not be able to come here until the first of March. Why don't you want to see us before that?

We're hoping so much that you'll come, after all. Perhaps, if you still decide not to come—painful thought—you will be so kind as to telegraph your reply Friday evening, at the latest, so we can make our plans for Sunday. But surely you'll want to come?

Au revoir, dearest Mamma, I send all my love, and am waiting impatiently to see you.

Respectfully your son,
Antoine

The letter reveals not only how much Antoine loved his mother but also how demanding he was and how obstinately he tried to have his own way. And how dictatorial! It is Antoine who replies to a letter addressed to François. His mother is given a short delay to send a wire—he was always insisting on having telegrams sent. The letter is dated February 21—she has promised to come at the beginning of March. But Antoine could not wait, and he completely disregarded the time consumed by those weekly visits and the energy his mother expended in caring for the wounded. It was wartime; trains were scarce, were often delayed. These demands seem childish. And Antoine was no longer a child, for he was then sixteen.

At the end of three years at Fribourg, he matriculated in 1917 and went to the École Bossuet in Paris to prepare for the entrance examination into the French navy. The turbulent, absent-minded, and untidy schoolboy was about to enter a new phase of life. But the years at Fribourg were more than an interlude, since among his books and papers of this period are to be found sketches and descriptions of inventions he was planning to make, other drawings, and poems he had composed. He had been studious, but not brilliant. His character had begun to assert itself in the philosophy class. He was becoming more thoughtful and meditative. He was also subject to inexplicable changes of mood.

It is odd that, living in a religious community, his faith was shaken, although in his childhood he had been rather devout. Had the death of François made him doubt God? Had he perhaps wondered why that young brother should be snatched away and why his mother should be plunged into grief? Or was it merely his persistent dissatisfaction with things as they are, his constant search for something more, his need to examine and dissect? Whatever the cause, he seems to have rejected dogmatic teaching at the age of seventeen, and from then on groped toward the truth in his own way. There was no vanity or conceit in this, but merely his natural bent for investigation and research.

Saint-Exupéry's writings or the writings of anyone near to him do not reveal an explanation for this spiritual crisis. But at this period it is evident that he turned away from Christianity and toward a philosophical search for truth.

Up to this time the life of Antoine de Saint-Exupéry had been relatively smooth and easy; the education he received at the Villa Saint-Jean was excellent, differing little from what he had been accustomed to at Sainte-Croix in Le Mans and at home. But his existence in Paris, and in the army while doing military service, in no way prepared him for the difficulties he would soon encounter.

"Once you have grown to manhood, the Good God lets you walk alone." Saint-Exupéry was about thirty years old when he wrote that, but he was thinking of himself at the age of eighteen when he was a pupil at the École Bossuet in Paris and then, later, taking a special course in mathematics at the Lycée Saint-Louis, studying for the French Navy entrance examination.

For the first time, he was turned loose in the world, alone, and feeling his solitude, which he could not endure except occasionally for writing and meditation. And he did not make friends easily. During the three years at Fribourg he had made but one real friend, Louis de Bonnevie. At the École Bossuet he was fortunate enough to have three or four friends, among them Bertrand de Saussine and Henry de Ségogne. Saussine's two sisters, Renée (Rinette) and Laure sometimes went out with their brother and his friends to some favorite cafés in the Boulevard Saint-Germain and the Saint-Germain-des-Prés quarter, which were beginning to be popular with noisy young people. Saint-Exupéry particularly liked the Brasserie Lipp, but he did not disdain the little pastry shops where he and his friends went to stuff themselves with cakes.

At times they had stormy arguments. Sometimes Saint-Exupéry, after a prolonged and inexplicable silence, would suddenly become enraptured with a subject and expound his theories in such a positive and dictatorial way that no one dared contradict him; he would quash all arguments ruthlessly, and often the friends parted in the street rather coolly. However, their quarrels did not last; next day they would meet again.

At night he wrote stories and verse which next day he would theatrically declaim to his small audience. He was already smoking too many cigarettes, and of course favored the more expensive Virginia tobacco.

It was not a life calculated to satisfy a youth who had always been spoiled and wanted to go on being indulged. His letters to his mother at this period are filled with complaints: he is sad, he is cold, he has chilblains. And he wants her to write to him every day. In these letters he tells her about his studies, about his marks, with which he seems satisfied, gives amusing descriptions of classmates in math, tells about the fellows cramming for the École Polytechnique, the "suckers" studying for the École Centrale, the "baggy-pants" who are preparing for the Navy, and the "Cyriards," future cadets at the Saint-Cyr Military Academy—"fellows you never hear talked about." He relates how, in his class, "as a result of intrigues and counter-intrigues, exactly as in the Chamber of Deputies, the government was forced to resign" and how, in the new government, he had become "the P.D.M."—*Prefet des Moeurs,* roughly translated "the policeman of morals." He also tells her of his readings in the Bible: "Throughout, the moral laws burst forth in all their usefulness and beauty; it is splendid." Or he questions her: "Have you read Proverbs? And the Song of Songs? How beautiful!" He acquaints her with his plans for the future: "If I pass the exams in August, I'll be an officer in February at Cherbourg, or Dunkirk, or Toulon. I'll rent a little house and you and I will live there; you'll see, we're going to be very happy." [6]

But in these letters he also asks her frequently for money, and his need is always urgent. Once he has to buy a bowler hat, then he must have toothpaste or shoe laces, or a sailor's beret is an absolute necessity. He also asks for addresses of relatives or friends upon whom he could call. He is often invited out and enjoys himself, no doubt being reminded by the houses he visits of the home he misses.

One day he writes exultantly to his mother: "I've done it, I've lunched with the Duchesse de Vendôme . . . the sister of the King of the Belgians!" (His aunt, Anaïs de Saint-Exupéry, was lady in waiting to the Duchess.) The Duc de Vendôme had also been present, and the young man comments, "I'm absolutely delighted with the Duke and Duchess. They're charming, and the Duke seems to be very intelligent and witty."

As may be seen, the "poor student" over whose sad lot so many commentators have grieved, was not greatly to be pitied. He could even indulge his sin of gluttony, as he quite frankly confesses. In the letter describing his visit with the Duchesse de Vendôme, he ends by saying: "I had an excellent luncheon, and a no less excellent tea. That's something to appreciate." The postscript to another letter is a request for a favorite sweet: "Have some chocolate truffles made for me and send me things like that in quantity, they'll just fit into my digestive landscape." His letters sometimes contain Rabelaisian references to food: "Aunt Rose is still delightful, but what is most delightful about her are the luncheons she gives. I lunched with her on Sunday, and I assure you I consumed enough butter to last me a week. What butter! Exquisite, fresh, melting. . . ."

Debauchery and corruption reigned in wartime and postwar Paris, but Saint-Exupéry seems to have escaped them. The boulevards were thronged with fast young women—*poules,* they were called—and all women enjoyed a greater liberty than ever before. The war had emancipated women, who replaced men in offices, factories, and on trams and autobuses. Skirts were at the knee, hair was bobbed *à la Ninon,* feminine decorum had been cast off with the furbelows, and women expressed themselves more freely. Temptation lurked in the shadows, and not only for the soldier—the *poilu*—but for young students entering upon an ardent period of sexual life. There were risks, but the risks did not always restrain, as Saint-Exupéry's letters to his mother clearly show. In one he mentions that "some of the fellows here behave themselves because carousing in Paris is dangerous and they prefer to keep their good health. As for me, everything is quite all right from the moral point of view. Be assured, I'll always be your Tonio who loves you."

He crammed mathematics. But this did not keep him from

flunking his exams. In the written tests he passed, but he failed the orals. For a time he was bewildered. He had been so sure of success. He had written to his mother, "I'm going to make it," or "I'm full of hope"; he had mentioned the little house where they would live together when he would soon be a naval officer. Now, where to turn, what to do? He had looked forward to leaving Paris, the life of the city did not suit him in any way. "Tonio is a provincial" the poet Léon-Paul Fargue said of him in later years. And it was true. Atavistically, perhaps, or because the country and the sea were an ineradicable part of his childhood memories, or perhaps because of his love of independence, he always preferred wide horizons to the perspective of city streets. And now he was stuck in Paris. Without much enthusiasm, he registered at the École des Beaux-Arts for a course in architecture.

It has been asserted that the following year (1919–1920) was for him a year of misery, but this is a great exaggeration. True, his way of life had changed; it was a student's life, in which he had to be content with a modest bedroom, meals in second-rate restaurants, shortage of pocket money—the difficulties most young people cope with while learning a craft and growing up. And most young students do not have, as he had, mothers to send them money orders, or invitations from relatives to dine.

His chief problem that year was perhaps uncertainty over his future. His aspirations at this time were vague, but he felt the need to do something, to have a profession, which would be out of the ordinary. The demon of adventure lay dormant within him, and when that tyrannical demon fastens upon a man only Heaven knows in what direction it will drive him. The demon waits. Events, chance, perhaps Providence, will inspire him.

2

But life withstands disorder and natural inclinations, and it is from the dust that it draws forth the cedar tree....

—*The Wisdom of the Sands*

World War I produced a new type of hero: the aviator. For the first time in history battles were fought in the air, sometimes above the clouds, and these air battles were often fierce and terrible duels with escape impossible and death the only alternative to victory. The survivors of these single combats were everywhere regarded with something close to awe, and nowhere were they given a more thrilling welcome home than in Strasbourg which, with the Allied victory, became a French city again. While marching soldiers filled the streets, the modern knights of the air flew their planes low over the town, grazing the roofs, filling the sky with the thunder of their engines. The faces of the people as they watched the soldiers and planes reflected a kind of grave joy. And the insignia on those planes could not but affect the Alsatians: it was the stork, that great bird which always returns to the house where it first lived; the stork, symbol of fidelity. From every window floated a tricolor flag, fabricated in secret during the long German occupation. The *Cigognes* finally ended their triumphant circling over the houses and in a massed formation headed toward the southern suburbs, where they touched down in a field bordered by green woodlands extending to the banks of the Rhine.

This was the field of Neudorf, to which I came two years and three months later. At that epoch, events did not succeed one another with cinematic rapidity, as they do today, each fugitive image thrust into oblivion by the succeeding image. When I arrived in

Strasbourg, people were still talking about that victory parade, and still remembered those first heroes of the air: Brocart, Nungasser, Guynemer, Dorme, Navare, and so many others. And I remember all this as clearly as my first months at the Neudorf airfield, for I was then only twenty.

Spring was just beginning, with early morning frosts stiffening the dew on the grass, transforming the myriad crystals into flashing jewels in the sunshine, and I remember how one trod upon them with regret.

We were four young fellows waiting to begin our flight training. The first thing we had to learn was the handling of weapons—and I recall how hard we tried not to learn. The greater part of our time was spent on the ground watching the flight of other planes. The pilots of the Spad and Hanriot machines were often extremely daring. They were volunteers who had asked to serve in fighter planes, and had trained at the aero-acrobatics school at Pau, where standards were ruthlessly high. After only a few hours in the air, the young pilot had to climb to an altitude of 6500 feet and kick his plane into a spin. The tailspin always terminates a badly carried off flying stunt but greatly impresses the neophyte, and it is indispensable that he learn how to do it. The young trainee was rapidly told how to perform the feat. "Kick everything over"—that is to say, rudder-bar and stick pushed all the way in the direction the pilot wants to spin. "Move both back to center"—or, back in the opposite direction from the spin, the rudder on level, the stick directly in front of you, but still pushed forward to maintain the dive. Then "pull back slowly on the stick and gradually give it more throttle." And so the young aspirant at 6500 feet put his machine into a spin. He then maneuvered to pull out of it. If he succeeded, he became a full-fledged pilot. If he failed, he became a corpse. There were several failures each week.

Sometimes, looking down, the trainee glimpsed a formless mass of wreckage from which they were pulling out the horribly mutilated body of a comrade. Whereupon, losing heart, after hesitating and cutting off the engine, he simply glided down.

In that case, he would be washed out of the fighters and would be assigned to the bombers or observers.

Many of those pilots whose audacity we admired had still been in training when the war ended; the Armistice had cheated them out of an opportunity to fight. In these exercises of trick flying, they were satisfying a frustrated urge to risk their lives and were working off surplus energy. But some of them had been in battles, and their *Croix de guerre* ribbons were embellished with palms. We regarded these aces in respectful silence. These seasoned pilots were not as impetuous as the youngsters; their style of flying showed greater restraint. It was a style they had acquired when facing an adversary who would be either their victim or their executioner.

Among us newcomers was a tall, broad-shouldered, rather hulking young fellow, with a turned-up nose and a strange expression in his brown eyes. He was Antoine de Saint-Exupéry, second-class private, not handsome, about my own age. For some mysterious reason he made a lasting impression on me—as he always did on everyone. His round face, which became lined with two long dimples when he smiled, usually wore an expression of concentrated thought. The odd look in his eyes was due to the fact that the iris was placed rather high on the eyeball, revealing a rim of white below, which made him seem to be always gazing upward. He was reserved and shy. But in conversation he became very animated and his voice, generally muffled and grave, soon rose in argument, or when he spoke dramatically or played the clown. His looks changed little with the passing years, except for added weight; and apparently the first impression he gave people in later years was much the same as when I first met him and we were both only twenty.

The regulation uniform of the French soldier at that time was, I believe, the most grotesque ever worn in the history of war, and Saint-Exupéry was particularly ill-favored in it, for no suit ever seemed to fit him. His round face was comic beneath that absurd two-pointed forage cap, his broad shoulders were constricted by the tunic which was too tight, the sleeves were much too short, disclosing a great length of wrist, his puttees were frayed, his heavy boots were enormous, his trousers were always wrinkled. Twenty years later he apparently had about the same aspect, for Jules Roy describes him, in *La Vallée Heureuse,* as being "got up in strange clothes, a mixture of civilian and Air France dress, bearing little resemblance to the uniform of the Air Force. His cap always looked as if it were on the point of falling into three separate pieces: the badge with its gold braid, the peak, and the crown." Somewhat earlier than this apparition described by Jules Roy, Saint-Ex had already become famous in South America for his battered caps, which his comrades said always looked like the shapeless headpiece worn by Louis XI. But beneath his weird outfit, he was endowed with such keen wit and subtlety that even in his youth he baffled those in the army who measured intelligence according to the number of stripes on the sleeve.

The Second Air Regiment had as squadron leader Captain Garde, an admirable person who had entered the Air Force from the Infantry and had flown combat planes during the war. Indeed, all the officers were fine types. Life would have been entirely agreeable at the Neudorf airfield, where the routine of the squadron continued but with slightly relaxed discipline, had it not been for the presence of the inevitable rampant sergeant. This "loud-mouthed bastard" was the bane of Saint-Exupéry's existence, and he took his revenge upon the petty officer by a show of infuriating listlessness and by remarks which tickled only his comrades.

There was the time, for instance, when Saint-Ex had been assigned to "potato duty." Instead of getting down to work peeling the spuds for the soup, he sat staring vaguely at them, his hands in his pockets. The sergeant pounced upon him from the kitchens, his bovine eyes flaming, and began shouting, as Saint-Ex stared at him with malicious calm—or rather, looked through him.

"What?" said the sergeant, "so you just sit there doing nothing?"

"As you see."

"You don't want to work?"

"I ask nothing better."

"Then why don't you begin to peel the potatoes?"

"Because I don't have a knife!"

"No knife! Why not?"

"Because they didn't give me one."

"How did that happen?"

"I'm sure I don't know. When I came here, they gave me a pan, a mug, a fork. But no knife."

The sergeant, nonplused, stood there frowning, no doubt pondering the reason why young recruits were not given a knife. Saint-Ex stared blandly at the sergeant, saying nothing.

"That's neither here nor there!" growled the sergeant. "Do what you're told to do! Peel those spuds!"

Saint-Ex leaned over, took up a potato, and began slowly to peel it with his fingernail.

Reveille was sounded by a factory siren, and the corporal of the week, his eyes still puffy with sleep, opened the dormitory doors one by one shouting the traditional *"Debouts, là-dedans!"*—a rough equivalent of "Rise and shine!"

Saint-Ex had been detailed to the S.O.A. [*Section d'Ouvriers d'Aviation*], the Air Force Workmen's Platoon, under the command of the extremely likable Captain de Billy. Characteristically, Saint-Ex wrote to his mother asking her to do what she could to commend him to Captain de Billy. In the past he had asked similar favors of her: in 1918, when the pupils of the Saint-Louis lycée were evacuated to Bourg-la-Reine because of bombardments, he wanted her permission to request a private room for himself.

To have a room of his own and not be obliged to mingle with others had always greatly preoccupied him. But in the army such a thing was nonexistent, barrack life was the rule, with thirty or forty men sharing a dormitory, a concentrate of humanity, with all the good and bad, superior and vulgar men, intelligent and stupid men living a life in common. It was certainly not the select group of the Villa Saint-Jean epoch. Saint-Ex was plunged up to his neck in brackish smells and would simply have to get used to it, as would other young fellows who suffered as he did. But not at all! He immediately looked for a room in town. He found one, and described it to his mother as "marvelous, luxurious, with a bathroom and central heating; it's in the most fashionable street in Strasbourg." The rent was only one hundred and twenty francs a month (the equivalent of about six thousand today). There the humble second-class private Saint-Exupéry went at night to enjoy solitude, to read, drink tea, take a bath. Moreover, when he went out in town, he usually wore civilian clothes. He returned to barracks only for the morning roll call, at nine.

He had no close acquaintances, established no friendships. He did not take his meals in the company mess, but at the canteen or in restaurants. Money was needed for such things, and the pay of a second-class private was fifty centimes a day, barely the price of a pint of Kronenbourg beer. Saint-Ex was therefore asking his mother continually for money, and his letters of this period are filled with cries of distress. "I haven't a sou," he wrote her. "I haven't a sou and I want a cup of tea, and here I sit, staring miserably at my alcohol stove, which I can't light because I'm out of matches." In another letter he tells her he will doubtless need to buy a motorcycle, because the barracks are at such a distance, and he would like to have more time for his "work"—he does not specify what work. But he adds, speaking of the motorcycle as a certainty, "When I have it, I'll be able to tour Alsace!"

With each letter his wants vary. Now he needs money to buy textbooks; he is studying or means to study internal-combustion engines and aerodynamics. "I'll need quite a few expensive books for this, could you send me some money on receipt of this letter?" But a few days later he asks her to buy in Lyons a book which dealt comprehensively with both subjects.

He himself settled the amount of the "allowance" she should give him: five hundred francs a month (about 25,000 today). "I believe that will cover my expenses," he writes. But shortly afterward he was asking for two thousand francs to enable him to train for a civil airline pilot's license.

To this letter his mother replied cautiously, asking him not to make such a decision without due reflection. But he insisted. His mind was made up, he wanted to begin training immediately, and he wanted the money without further delay. If he did not receive it at once he would be in "a most embarrassing situation"—embarrassing in regard to the commercial airline company where he would get his flight training. He was sometimes sad in the evenings, he confessed, for he longed to have an occupation he could enjoy, and thus not be tempted to "hang out in bistros." And when his mother delayed sending the necessary sum, he did not hesitate to ask her to *bring* him the money.

This twenty-one-year-old, intelligent and sensitive, was unable to comprehend that his mother was not rolling in wealth. She had always satisfied his desires in the past, so why could she not continue doing so? He seemed to forget that she was also burdened with one daughter who was ill and another daughter who was studying in Paris, while the third lived with her at home—and they also needed money, while he, her grown son, was helping her to ruin herself.

However, he continued to demonstrate his affection, and his letters were filled with tender phrases: "You are so exquisite, you are the most subtle of all mothers. You so deserve to be happy, you so deserve not to have a big untidy son who is always grumbling and complaining."

Why must he have a civil aviation license at such cost, since he was doing military service in the Air Force and was waiting, along with his comrades, to train in military planes without having to spend a penny? He had come to Strasbourg to learn to pilot a plane, and he could not endure waiting. The daily spectacle of the planes soaring over the airfield, the thunder of the Spads climbing the sky, filling the air and the very onlookers with their vibration, the skillful maneuvers of fighter pilots doing loops and rolls, impressive tailspins—it was all too exciting, and his impatience grew.

One day a pilot took Saint-Ex up with him in a Herbemont biplane. He came down from his flight in a daze, his limbs weak, but his heart thudding with emotion. It was a kind of test: after such an experience, one either resolves never again to fly or one wants to begin anew—naturally, with mingled apprehension and desire, something like being led by the devil into temptation. Saint-Ex wanted to begin all over again.

It was still not the passionate but contained vocation of a Guillaumet. With Henri Guillaumet, the desire to fly was implanted like a seed in his subconscious where it put forth roots and sprouted, then suddenly burgeoned in all his being, animating and inspiring him, dictating all his actions. With Saint-Exupéry this vocation came into being by a slower and more complicated process, maturing only in the exercise of the craft and linked with his writer's vocation; it was inseparable from his intellectual development. But for the time being, he had a liking for adventure which might equally well have turned him into a sailor or explorer. He was manifesting the adventurous bent of one of his ancestors, that Georges Alexandre Césarée de Saint-Exupéry who, a hundred and forty years earlier, had set out with La Fayette to fight for the American colonists in their War of Independence and had taken part in the siege of Yorktown.

Saint-Exupéry, along with three other soldiers, of whom I was one, was allowed to train at Strasbourg while doing military service. It was an exceptional privilege, since at Istres there existed a training school for pilots, to which Air Force aspirants were supposed to go. To escape Istres was a favor, since it had the reputation of being a hard-labor camp where one served "an apprenticeship to Death"—we had heard some pretty demoralizing stories of the place. Our group was the last to enjoy the privilege, however, after a serious accident occurred at Neudorf, which made the government frown on flight training on the regimental level—although accidents were more numerous at Istres. A trainee cadet in dual instruction had his engine stall on him at the take-off. In the crash, the instructor was killed and the trainee badly injured. A Council of Ministers handed down the decree that a soldier wanting to obtain a pilot's license must remain in the army for at least two years after getting his wings. Since Saint-Ex was not a volunteer but had merely been drafted for his two years of military service, he was out of the picture unless he took the step of enlisting in the army.

He was at first bitterly disappointed. Then, thinking it over, he decided that he might become a machine gunner, and thus be able to fly anyway. This idea did not last long. He had decided to be a pilot and so he must be a pilot. But how? Finding a solution to the problem was suddenly very difficult. He could of course enlist for one year, but the prospect was far from tempting; two months of military service had been enough to make him detest this profession "in which there is strictly nothing to do." Nothing, that is, except physical exercise—which he hated. He preferred the idea of "three years of flying to two of this degrading military life." Another alternative was to wangle an assignment to Morocco, where flying instruction was still available on the military level. At last he discovered a third solution, which was to obtain a civil air pilot's license. This could only be achieved at a training school for civil air pilots—and there happened to be one, of sorts, at Strasbourg.

Right on the Neudorf flying field, beside the road leading to the hangars that sheltered army fighter planes and where the regiment's headquarters had been established, a patched-up old canvas hangar had been installed; it was one of those dirty old gray "Bessoneau" army hangars which had gone through the war being transported the whole length of the front to accommodate the planes of a fighting squadron in their occasional hours of rest. But now beneath the canvas were two small planes, a workshop for repairs, and an office. Here, in miniature, was the first stage of one of the first air-transport lines in the world.

At the end of the war some farseeing men had realized that the airplane could be put to some use other than as a mere instrument of destruction. They imagined the plane as a means of communication between peoples, a means of tracing, above the fields and roads and rivers and mountains, air routes between nations. Commercial airlines sprang from the will and imagination of a few men of incorrigible faith, condemned by many of their contemporaries as madmen, and finding only with difficulty men of their own caliber who believed in them. The first airline linked Paris with London; the second, Toulouse with Casablanca; the third, Paris with Bucharest. From this point of view, the little civilian flying school at Strasbourg was the first phase of the great adventure.

Pilots and mechanics who had known each other in the Air Force squadrons met again at the ports of call of these early airlines and compared notes on the glorious and terrible war years, swapped stories of the pioneering days of the airlines, the accidents they had suffered, the comrades whose broken bodies had strewn the routes they traveled. These men had not been able to resume their humdrum, earthbound lives or to renounce the airplane; they had refused to abdicate. At these airfields one also met men and women making their first trip by air to Prague or Paris or Bucharest. And in what a plane! An old Salmson biplane, used during the war for reconnaissance and artillery-range practice. The pilot sat in front of the wings, near the engine. Behind and separated from him by the fuel tank, the passengers sat in what had once been the gun turret—two passengers at most, and these had to be lightweights! Wearing helmets and goggles, muffled up in greatcoats, their bags between their feet, their faces whipped by the wind or pelted by the rain, these travelers were admirably stoical.

Accidents were numerous, a horrifying percentage which today would soon ruin an airline. Newspapers did not feature them: accidents were a forbidden subject. The planes had not been built for carrying passengers and luggage, and were therefore often overloaded; aside from this, the pilots flew without radio and without meteorological information; there was no way of knowing what kind of weather could be expected on a given flight. But these pilots had gone through the war, they had survived worse tests, and they accepted it as their destiny to disappear one day in a storm or to crash against a peak in the Vosges or the Carpathians. As for the passengers, their courage was harder to explain; it puzzled even the men who piloted them on their dangerous voyages. The story is told of a Latécoère Line pilot who, after battling through a storm for more than an hour, apostrophized his two passengers upon landing: "You certainly must be keen on breaking your necks!"

More than once Saint-Ex had been on the Neudorf airfield when a plane on the Franco-Rumanian run returned to base. He had seen those heroic—or oblivious—passengers, their faces reddened by the wind and splattered with engine oil, shaken to their very depths by the emotions they had experienced and impatient to reach the end of their rough journey through the air. He admired them, but admired and envied even more the men responsible for bringing these people safely to their destination. He began to prowl about the old canvas hangar, watching the mechanics at their work, getting acquainted with some of the men. One day he talked with a mechanic who was working on a valve stem of the biplane remaining at the field. He admired that plane, with its great, wide-spread wings, standing high on its landing gear, more attractive and more accessible, somehow, than the army Spad—less thoroughbred-looking, too.

"Could a fellow learn to pilot that?" he asked.

"Naturally," said the mechanic.

"And a fellow could get his pilot's license?"

"For Heaven's sake, why not?"

"And how much would it cost?"

"I'm not sure," the mechanic replied. "Why don't you talk to the manager?"

Saint-Ex saw the general manager, explained his situation and his plans. The manager accepted him as a trainee, and a pilot who was in Strasbourg was assigned to be his instructor. The fee—to be paid in a lump sum—was two thousand francs (the equivalent, today, of 100,000). After payment of that sum, training could begin immediately. There was a less costly course of instruction, but in that the trainee agreed to pay for any damages and Saint-Ex considered this too risky.

He now began to beg his mother for this considerable sum, asking that she send it by telegraph or bring it in person, putting his demand in an ever more insinuating and affectionate way. He was behaving like a little boy again, but he was also a young man capable of reasoning, despite everything. This child–man duality occurs in many people, but in Saint-Exupéry it was very pronounced and continued to be so, even at a much later period. He had become aware that his mother had others depending upon her and now he wrote her more diplomatically: "I beg of you, Mother, do not speak of this to anyone, but send me the needed money. I will reimburse you little by little, if you like, out of my pay." This would indeed take a long time, for even if he were to become an officer after obtaining his license, his pay as second lieutenant would barely suffice to meet his personal expenses.

Mme. de Saint-Exupéry finally yielded and produced, at great self-sacrifice, the necessary two thousand francs.

Private Second Class de Saint-Exupéry was authorized by his squadron leader, Captain Garde, to train on a civilian plane. He could begin at once, since he had already passed, along with his three future pilot-trainee comrades, the physical examination. This was given in two parts: the first one, very summary, took place before a kindly old army doctor who put some rather odd questions.

"Now, tell me, young man," he quavered, "what color are my trousers?"

Saint-Exupéry stared. The doctor was wearing the very bright red trousers with black braid of the French army before World War I. Pretending great uncertainty Saint-Ex asked the next in line, "What color are they?"—speaking in a low voice but not so low as to be inaudible to the old doctor, who immediately rapped out: "Color-blind, unfit for service."

This jest of Saint-Exupéry's did not prevent him, however, from taking the second physical exam, a more serious one, at the military hospital of Kronenbourg, although his love of a joke might well have cost him his career.

He began at once his period of dual instruction. Now, no longer a mere passenger, he held the vibrating stick in his hand, and his feet were set on the rudder-bar which swung crazily before departure, but which steadied and became taut when the plane was airborne.

The instructor, with a slow wave of the hand toward the empty field ahead and then toward the sky, gave the signal. Simultaneously the trainee pulled the ignition lever toward him and pushed the stick toward the instrument panel. The machine shuddered, gave a bound, ran, hopped, and—suddenly losing weight—freed itself from the earth, sat on the air, climbed into the sky. Intently, Saint-Ex imitated all the instructor's movements. The stick inclined to the left, the left foot pressed on the rudder-bar, and the landscape below slowly tilted. The cathedral spire emerged from the brown tile roofs, seeming to be rigidly fixed in the transparent disc of the propeller, then it swayed to the right and the whole city turned with it, the houses, the streets, the river Ill. And faster and faster they swung past as the stick was brought toward the pilot and his right foot pressed on the rudder-bar. The right wing rose, stretched out in the sky, hiding a great patch of blue where light clouds floated. The city disappeared, hidden by the wing, and now ahead of the cowling lay the countryside with its multicolored fields, and the shining steel plate of a lake, and the forest's light spring green; the Rhine, whose muddy water was transformed and made dazzling by the altitude and sunshine, flowed between gray and green banks of fields and woods. Again the hand and foot accompanied the movements of the stick and the rudder-bar. Once more the plane tilted, once more the wing stretched into the sky, obeying the pilot. When it lowered, it revealed a view of bright villages and dark forests and bluish mountains: the Vosges Mountains. The pilot, traversing the sky, could survey all this and at his leisure could fill his mind with the landscape and often, despite its diversity, fix it in his memory and recognize each landmark when he next flew over.

Saint-Exupéry, pupil pilot, filled his soul with that vision, unique at the time. Detached from earth, he dominated the earth, not like the mountain climber who still clings with all his weight to a rock but like a bird—liberated, free.

The instructor laid his right hand on the side of the fuselage, and with his left hand made a signal. Saint-Ex slightly inclined the stick and pressed on the rudder-bar. The wing did not tilt up into the sky, and the plane sped through the air, veering off in the desired direction. And the pupil was invaded by a sweet pride, a thrill as of physical possession.

Any sensitive person who has learned to fly a plane has experienced that feeling of carnal possession, but this was particularly so at a time when the plane was not the heavy machine it now is with complicated mechanism, a veritable ship plowing through the air, but was a very light apparatus of which the aviator felt himself to be a part. Indeed, every least vibration was transmitted through his body as he sat there, incorporated in it. And when an engine stalled—fatal to so many aviators when the plane was half airborne and about to go into a sideslip—it was the pilot's bottom that felt the danger first and gave the warning to the brain—often too late, but still in time to avoid complete disaster. The life of the plane and the life of the pilot were closely knit together, united as if by bonds of love or kinship.

Saint-Exupéry may not have analyzed these sensations on his earliest flights, but they left an indelible trace. Passage after passage in his books describes this feeling of union between pilot and plane, and the sudden metamorphosis of the plane which, one moment inert and cold, springs to life through the pilot's action—"the mystery of metal turned to living flesh" is the way he puts it in *Night Flight*. Or, in the same book, we find Fabien at the controls of his plane "snugly ensconced," and upon touching a steel rib receiving the sensation that "the stream of life flowed in it . . . it was alive. The engine's five-hundred horsepower bred in its texture a very gentle current, fraying its ice-cold rind into a velvety bloom."

After the run above the countryside, when the trainee had to hold the line of flight correctly and neither climb nor dive, when he had to make shorter and shorter turns faultlessly, the next step was to learn how to approach the ground, how to land. The stick was pushed completely down so that the plane headed toward the earth, the roar of the engine gradually diminished, the cut-out propeller made a sound like rustling silk which mingled with the whistling of the wind in the struts. The sky vanished from in front of the cockpit and the earth seemed to be lovingly pulling the plane toward her. The green runway which at a distance looked like the smooth turf of a croquet field came nearer, grew bigger, along with the well-lined-up army hangars and the solitary Bessonneau hangar of the Franco-Rumanian line; the little men on the road leading to headquarters became bigger, and everything seemed to be rising toward the plane.

The contact with the ground was another pleasure, a triumphant conquest which could be enjoyed many times, like a game. The field flattened out, the grass became visible, and the men who had been running came to a standstill there, to the right. Again the pilot pulled the stick slowly toward him, as the instructor regulated the rhythm with his voice. "That's right, that's right. . . ." Suddenly the plane seemed to float in space. "Here we are! Steady, steady. . . . Level off. . . . Now!" With a jerk, the stick was pulled against the pilot's stomach. A muffled sound, a great shuddering of the whole machine, then immobility.

Then the instructor turned toward the trainee to criticize or advise. "Relax! Don't be so tense on the controls," he would say. Or "In the short turns, when you're beyond 45 degrees, equalize the rudders. Watch those feet! And don't dive so much in the approach. Come, let's go up again!"

And once more the plane climbed the sky.

Saint-Ex made rapid progress. The fearless little boy at Saint-Maurice had wanted excitement and adventure; now, as a young man, he was finding satisfaction in this apprenticeship. But, as usual, his need of the absolute as much as the desire of any student to be liberated from school made him ardently want to fly alone. He did not wait for his instructor to authorize him to make a solo flight.

At this point, it is customary to tell the oft-repeated story of

Saint-Exupéry's first solo flight. According to this tale, the young neophyte was so impatient to fly on his own that, after only one hour and twenty minutes of dual instruction, he decided not to wait any longer. And so, when the instructor was absent, he went to the hangar, hauled out the plane, started up the engine, climbed in, and took off. He circled over the airfield, very proud of himself at first, but soon felt rather anxious about landing, for he was not at all sure he knew how to manage it without the instructor's help. However, he had no time to waste on such questions, for suddenly he noted smoke issuing from the plane beneath his feet, then flames. The plane was on fire! So he cut off the engine and brought the plane down on a field where bewildered spectators had assembled, among them Captain Garde, the squadron leader, who pronounced—in this version—the memorable sentence: "It's clear, Saint-Exupéry, you'll never kill yourself in a plane—otherwise you'd be dead this minute!"

As it happens, this story is pure fiction. Told by Saint-Exupéry, it could have had credibility, if he told it to the uninitiated, as he did. But never did he repeat the tale to his aviator friends. And indeed, embellished by those uninitiated, it is stupefying to anyone who knows a thing about piloting a plane.

J. G. Fleury, in his book *La Ligne,* was perhaps the first to set the fable down in black and white—he was to learn to fly a plane himself later on. In his version Saint-Ex, once in the air, perceived that "the planks of the fuselage were burning," which implies that the flames were already extensive and were about to consume the highly inflammable machine, constructed mainly of wood and painted canvas.

The story was taken up by René Delange in his biography of Saint-Exupéry and improved upon. In his version the young pilot circles over the field, not knowing how to land, and below him are "some pilots and mechanics waving their arms, signaling instructions to him." One wonders what kind of gestures gave such instructions. Finally, according to Delange, "the plane was brought down by a miraculous improvisation of its pilot, who, as he touched the field, cut off the fuel and jumped from the machine, which rolled another fifty yards or so. His shoes were scorched by the flames." This detail of the scorched shoes had also been mentioned by Fleury, which proves that the flames had already reached the cockpit.

R.-M. Albérès, in his biography, devotes five whole pages to this sensational event. He too pictures the pupil pilot in the sky after having managed to set the propeller in motion from the cockpit. According to this version, the flight over the countryside was almost idyllic. And the pilot, sitting there between his wings, was as calm as an old-timer, as calm as a pilot who had won his stripes, while on the ground the spectators were in a panic. But the cool-headed young trainee was to be put to a severe test, for suddenly "a white flame spurted right in his face." Albérès adds: "Saint-Exupéry did not flinch." In that one sentence we see the hero, and nothing he could subsequently do would astonish us. He did not flinch but "the blood rushed to his chest, constricted his heart, and then ebbed. . . ." The author goes on to analyze the feelings of the pilot—he is not even referred to as "future pilot"—in his flaming machine.

Pierre Chevrier, who knew Saint-Exupéry well, did not want to omit this anecdote from his life of the aviator, a work otherwise well documented. But he provides Saint-Ex with an accomplice, a mechanic, who swings the propeller. He also adds a surprising detail: the apprentice pilot "managed to sideslip to lose altitude." There is an echo here of an expert aviator; Saint-Ex himself must have used the phrase. In the event of fire on a one-engine plane, the sideslip from one wing to the other was the only means of getting out of the fix, if the pilot were not too high. By making the flames bend to the left or the right, he could prevent them from reaching the cockpit. But this maneuver was one that Saint-Ex was incapable of putting into practice at that time. He might manage, after only an hour and a half of dual instruction, to take off and to land without accident—more than one trainee has managed this—but he certainly did not know how to pull off a *glissade,* a sideslip. That maneuver requires a certain amount of training and even then is hard to effect when the plane is nearing the ground.

In Chevrier's version no mention is made of scorched shoes, but Saint-Exupéry's puttees were on fire—which is near enough. He does quote the immortal phrase of Squadron Leader Garde—but in his version Garde is not on the field; instead, he calls the soldier Saint-Exupéry to his office next day. And before quoting the phrase, Chevrier writes, "This exploit was to decide his future."

So much for history and the way it is written. An effort is made to explain, by an exploit that never took place, an entire life of heroism. The preposterous myth was accepted because anything seemed possible to Saint-Exupéry, whose courage and cool-headedness were well known and who never seemed to have to learn anything but to know everything in advance. However, there is a true account, much simpler, and much less moving too.

The plane in which Saint-Ex made his first solo flight was a Sopwith equipped with a rotary engine—the cylinders of which, arranged in a star, turned with the propeller around the same axis. The engine was fed with gasoline by a Tampier "block tube," the most rudimentary carburetor imaginable: the gas flow regulated by a valve which was in turn controlled by a throttle placed in the cockpit to the left of the pilot. In the same section of the cockpit another throttle permitted the pilot to regulate the amount of air. The pilot, with the aid of these two throttles, had to adjust by hand the required mixture of gas and air, an adjustment automatically made in ordinary carburetors and which controls the gasoline explosion. To do this, he constantly regulated with his index and middle finger the position of the two throttles. Once in the air, with the engine leveled off at cruising speed, these throttles could be released, provided they were secured firmly enough to remain in place. This was rare on the planes at the flying school, which were subjected to hard treatment. Sometimes, as a result of the plane's vibration in flight, they came out of balance. If the air-feed throttle shut more slowly than the gas throttle the mixture would soon have an excessive amount of air, which caused backfiring in the exhaust. But if, on the contrary, the mixture became overbalanced with gas, there were muffled explosions and the exhaust was a black smoke. This is what happened to Saint-Ex on his first solo flight. It represented no least danger of a fire, but was very impressive for a young trainee. He was most certainly afraid and most certainly thought his plane was on fire.

For Saint-Exupéry, it was easy to start with this basic fact and end up by telling his friends that his machine had caught fire on his first solo flight. He was a poet, with a great deal of imagination and a tendency to exaggerate. As a child, he had transformed Paula's stories into something else. In the same way, he sometimes recited certain Biblical stories, giving them a personal twist.

There is another apocryphal tale about Saint-Exupéry's school-days; it has been told again and again that he flunked his exams for the École Navale because he refused to write the French composition that had been set—the subject displeased him. But he gave credit to the legend, which flourished in his lifetime; he never denied it. And in this case the story could only have originated with him; it is hard to see who else would have invented it or for what reason.

His imagination, desires, and regrets all impelled him to relate certain events not exactly as they happened but as he wished they might have happened. Some of these fables were repeated and exaggerated by others and became part of the general legend. This is so with many great men: their childish or youthful gestures are soon amplified and transformed beyond recognition.

Some of the tales told about Saint-Exupéry are wildly improbable. Pierre Chevrier, who no doubt had it from Saint-Ex himself, refers to a serious accident that he had when his plane crashed in Guatemala in 1938. For several days his life was in danger. "Every evening he ran a high temperature, the cause of which could not be ascertained. Then, upon examining the still open wounds on his right arm, he discovered a pretty little green plant flourishing there, a plant that must have got wedged into the wound at the moment of the accident." This is incredible, since for several days physicians had been dressing the wounds and having X rays made of the fractures.

Other fanciful legends have been circulated about him, but there are some real incidents which no one has described, not even Saint-Ex himself. For instance, the time he was involved in a collision on the Neudorf airfield.

In his apprenticeship he had reached the stage where he was making one landing after another to acquire precision. One day he had brought his plane down several times at a given point when, upon landing, he shut down the engine too suddenly and it stalled. He therefore waited for the mechanic to come from the hangar to swing the propeller and set the engine going again. It meant a real wait, for the mechanic, busy at some work, must first see that Saint-Ex was stalled in the middle of the field. Saint-Ex, who had a horror of making any physical effort—the least exertion fatigued him—remained seated in the cockpit, staring at the sky where some woolly little clouds were drifting. Suddenly he heard the roar of an engine, the powerful roar of a plane about to take off. He unbuckled his belt and raised himself to look round the field. To his amazement, he saw a plane running straight toward him at top speed. Saint-Ex jumped to the ground and, waving his arms, stood to one side of the runway. But it was too late. The plane, which was one of the Franco-Rumanian line and carried four passengers, crashed into the Sopwith and rolled over on its side. Fortunately its pilot had time to shut off his engine, thus avoiding a fire.

What had happened was quite simple. The old Salmsons of the aerial transport line had been replaced by some Spad Herbemonts, four-passenger planes copied mainly from the Herbemonts used as fighters by the Air Force. They were handsome and graceful machines with good lines. But piloting them was a very delicate operation. The engine was not powerful enough to carry with maximum security its full load of gas plus the pilot and passengers. To become airborne, these planes had to run a great distance, and at the Neudorf field they required the entire length of the runway. Very often the pilot managed to raise his plane only at the end of the field, where it skimmed the adjacent road. On this particular day, while Saint-Ex was bringing in his Sopwith, the Herbemont was running toward the far end of the field to have the greatest possible space in which to take off. And as the Sopwith landed, the pilot of the Herbemont was making a wide turn in order to set its nose in the direction of departure. On a Herbemont, the pilot was seated quite far back in the body of the plane, in the open air, but he had in front of and slightly above him the enclosed passenger cabin and the long cowling of the engine. When running along the ground and about to take off, the pilot could not see an object lying directly ahead of him unless it happened to be at some distance. Before starting to run down the field, the pilot had leaned to right and left, had seen nothing, and had stepped on the gas . . . with the results we have noted.

Saint-Exupéry's pilot's license cost his mother a great deal, but it was to cost the Alsatian Transport Company even more. The future pilot had chosen well when he decided to pay the higher fee for his training, the aviation school paying for damages.

Having obtained his civil pilot's license, Saint-Ex was granted his request to be sent for a period to Morocco, where he could train as an Air Force pilot, since this was the only way to get his civil license transformed into a military license. He remained for a few months in North Africa, first at Rabat, then at Casablanca. At Rabat he met some "wonderful young fellows, well-bred and well-educated," he wrote to his mother. He also met there a former classmate of his at Fribourg and another classmate from the Lycée Saint-Louis. With these friends he was welcomed to the residence of a captain whom he described as being "disgusted with his colleagues." In that house—white, gay, hospitable—Sabran, the Fribourg classmate, played the piano while the others indulged in card games and Saint-Exupéry, "in an adorable little Moroccan sitting-room, reclining among big cushions," drank tea, smoked cigarettes, listened to the music, lost himself in revery, or wrote letters to his mother.

The letters written from Strasbourg were nostalgic, gloomy.

Those from North Africa expressed a kind of euphoria. He was happy with his lot. Rabat, as he described it, was an enchanting town, with its white houses, its sunny and colorful little streets. In the native quarter, between the shops selling golden slippers and silver belts, he saw an assassin being driven along and tortured to make him confess his crime. His description of the scene is fancifully poetic. "It was barbarous, it was splendid. The little golden slippers and the silver belts were quite oblivious." He lingered to gaze at the golden babouches, some of which were so small that, he said, "they'll wait a long time for their Cinderella. But then, while the little golden slippers told me their dream," he continued, "such slippers, you know, need a mosaic floor to walk upon, a veiled woman dickered over the price of the slippers and finally bore them away. I could see nothing of her but her immense eyes. . . . I hope, O golden slippers, that she may be the youngest of princesses and that she lives in a garden full of enchanting fountains."

His descriptions of the North African country over which he was flying show that he was wistfully remembering the more familiar scenes of France, the green meadows, the flowering apple trees. For this was not yet the true desert he was to know and passionately love a few years later and which, with the airplane, was to inspire some sublime pages.

He was filling his sketchbook with drawings. "I've discovered what I was made for," he told his mother. "I was made to use a Conté lead pencil." He would make other discoveries before he found his true vocation; at this period he was again actually thinking of taking up architecture.

After six months in Morocco, he was detailed to the airfield at Istres in southeast France for advanced training. This was in January 1922.

Istres represented everything he had wanted to escape; it was the central training post for military pilots. But at this flying school disorder, incompetence, and brutality reigned. It had been dubbed a "prison for apprentice-corpses" and this was, alas, no exaggeration. The discipline resembled that of the harsher types of concentration camp. Aside from the training, which lasted many months, the student pilots were set to gathering stones on the immense fields in wind, snow, or sweltering sunlight; they were made to scrape the cement walls of the hangars; although they had no mechanical knowledge, they had to repair their own engines. The pilots trained with Caudron G–3, supple-winged planes dating from World War I. These machines, ill maintained, were often completely out of order. The result was that the morgue, a sinister room with shutters always closed, often held a crude pine box from which seeped a brownish liquid drop by drop, while some soldiers watched nearby, smoking cigarettes in silence. The wooden box served until a lead coffin arrived, which would be loaded upon a freight car with a few faded flowers to be taken away for burial. Before the open door of the van, the squadron leader would make a speech—always the same speech, in which he talked about the heavy tribute demanded by progress, mentioned fate, mingled the name of the victim with those who had gone before him, and usually ended with an *au revoir* which sounded to the listeners like a "Who's next?"

Fortunately Saint-Exupéry was spared a long stay at Istres where, moreover, the life of pilots completing their training was less hard than that of beginners. During his stay in Morocco he had passed his exams and had received his call-up papers as a reserve officer in the French Air Force, and had been detailed to the Avord flying school, where he would take a still more advanced course of training. In October 1922, with the grade of second lieutenant, he set out for Avord.

At Istres he had made no more friends than at Strasbourg or at Casablanca. Yet on the flying field at Istres he had more than once rubbed shoulders with the man who was destined in later years to be his best friend: Henri Guillaumet.

Given Saint-Exupéry's contempt for the military, it is surprising that he sought to become an officer. In fact, he had hesitated a long time. From Morocco, he had written to his mother of his uncertainty. "I'm none too keen about having passed the exams, for I'm none too keen over having to stupefy my mind for a year in a horrible school of military theory. I have a poor opinion of such dull, mechanical work. Even if I win my wings, I sometimes think I might resign my commission." But after Morocco there had been Istres, military discipline, and the gregarious barrack life he hated. And when he wrote his mother a few months after demobilization that he had never liked anything as much as "the life of a private soldier, and the pleasant friendliness of the mechanics and the others," we find it hard to believe this, for it runs counter to everything he had said in letters written as a second-class private. He had found his comrades "not unlikable" and recalled with melancholy his "luxurious room" in Strasbourg where he could have a bath and a pot of tea whenever he liked. His taste for comfort, for a room of his own, would represent some of the advantages of being a second lieutenant and would help him overcome his distaste for the army.

So he passed the examinations and did not resign, but spent the required time at the Avord airfield, after which he was appointed to the 34th Aviation Squadron at Le Bourget. By that time there remained only five more months of his military service.

At Le Bourget, Lieutenant de Saint-Exupéry was able to renew relations with some friends in Paris, although many of his former classmates were away from the capital. However, friendship soon took second place, for he fell in love. He fell passionately in love with a charming, intelligent, and distinguished young lady, who is now well known in literary circles. The affair did not last long, for his fiancée soon broke off the engagement. But for a short time Lieutenant de Saint-Exupéry's life was bound up in hers. They went out together, they visited Saint-Maurice together, a happy interlude at the old home, where he found his mother and sisters—Didi, of whom he was so fond, and Biche, still absorbed in flowers and birds—and old Mademoiselle, who was all admiration for her little Antoine now grown up to be an officer in the Air Force. When he made the poor woman tremble with fear as he recounted his exploits as a pilot, she matched his stories with recollections of his bicycle to which he had attached fragile wings, and said she preferred that. But now he had wings, real wings, and was flying in the sky. *Mon Dieu!* He must be cautious. Up there, he'd have nothing to catch him if things went wrong, and he'd crash to the ground. At this thought Mademoiselle shuddered.

And she was right. The daring little boy had become a daring pilot who often risked his life. One day his engine stalled over Le Bourget field. They pulled him out of the wrecked plane with a fractured skull. It was his first serious accident. There would be others later on, still more serious, which he would miraculously survive.

The accident did not diminish his ardor and audacity. But oddly enough, when the time came for his demobilization, he did not seem to be upset. No doubt an army career was not suited to him. But the airplane? It seemed that, in 1923, flying was for him nothing but a sport—the only one he would ever engage in—and a means of evasion, as well. He had experienced the ineffable joy of solitude in the sky. He loved airplanes, loved flying. But as yet it was not the great passion for which one sacrifices everything.

3

For in the end man always gravitates in the direction commanded by the lodestone within him.

—Flight to Arras

"I've taken a dingy little room in a dingy little hotel at 70-bis Boulevard d'Ornano. My life is far from amusing. And to cap everything, the weather has been dreadful." Thus Saint-Exupéry described his life in Paris shortly after demobilization from military service. But this description, in a letter the twenty-three-year-old Antoine wrote to his mother, reflects more accurately his state of mind than his actual material condition. The hotel was dingy, the weather dreadful, and there he was, all alone in a small hotel room, humble and characterless with its plain pinewood furniture and faded counterpane. In one corner an open trunk displayed a fantastic disorder. On the table before him, a few books and an overflowing ash tray. It was a far cry from his room at home or at Fribourg or even the "luxurious room in the most fashionable street of Strasbourg." But if he had had nothing worse to complain of, his situation would not have been deplorable. The room merely added for the moment to his melancholy, or rather to his uncertain state of mind.

His feeling of discontent is understandable. Needing to earn money and not finding anything better, he had come to Paris and had taken a job as bookkeeper at a tile firm, the Tuileries de Boiron, a job that suited him, he said, "like a dress with a train."

But what kind of employment would suit his tastes and abilities? He was still uncertain, had turned over various ideas, had seized upon this and that plan or proposition, then discarded it as worthless next day. He was still searching. Journalism, perhaps? There was an opening on the big newspaper, *Le Matin*. But it turned out to be a humdrum job, editing the news items. Again, he was offered work with an insurance company, but decided against it. What he would like to do, he believed, was to go to China as a flying instructor. As director of a flying school he would have, he told his mother, "a magnificent situation from the pecuniary point of view." Then he had another idea. Once, while flying a plane, he had taken some photographs for his group; he now suggested that they found an association of aerial photographers which would cater particularly to factories. It was a new idea at the time, and the French Aviation Company eventually developed this enterprise, taking aerial views not only of big factories but also of some towns in France and abroad, useful to city planners. But already Saint-Exupéry was imagining himself as director of such an enterprise and was pulling wires. The Boiron tile firm was quite content with one photograph of the factory and preferred to continue to manufacture tiles.

In the midst of all these uncertainties, Saint-Exupéry also began to think of getting married, but the urge was faint and he did not even have any particular girl in view.

He was, indeed, at loose ends. Not surprising, when we recall his grandiose dreams. He had studied for the École Navale, already imagining himself in a naval officer's uniform and voyaging over the seven seas, discovering distant lands. Frustrated in that ambition, he had compensated by training to fly. Aviation had satisfied both his thirst for adventure and his need for evasion, exaltation, and discoveries as well. But now he was chained to an office desk, filling an ordinary job. He suffered not only from lack of air but lack of light; he felt as if buried. By nature a nomad, he had been forced into a sedentary career; born a globetrotter, he was obliged to become a bureaucrat. He was therefore looking for a way out, a peephole of light, employment suited to his temperament.

This period of his life, between his demobilization in 1923 and his employment by the Latécoère Airline Company in 1926, was hard; but it is wrong to depict it as a period of struggle against almost overpowering material difficulties. Biographers have exaggerated his sufferings, for compared with those of the average young man alone in Paris and trying to get a start in life Saint-Exupéry's was a very good life indeed. Another great aviator, Jean Mermoz, almost literally starved in Paris and had to sleep in flophouses. Whereas Saint-Ex had a room of his own, no matter how dingy, and received many invitations to luncheons and dinners. Thanks to his Aunt Anaïs, lady in waiting to the Duchesse de Vendôme, he lunched at the home of the Duchess "every Wednesday," he writes in one letter, and with Aunt Anaïs "made a tour of the Parisian restaurants." Captain Priou—the same captain who had entertained him in Rabat—invited him to dine, and lent him his comfortable apartment for a time. He often dined with his uncle, Jacques de Fonscolombe. And with his former classmates Bonnevie, Salès, Ségogne, Saussine, he was often seen in the brasseries and pastry shops of the Boulevard Saint-Germain. But of greatest importance to him at this time were the people he met at the house of his cousin, the Duchesse de Trévise (Yvonne de Lestrange), who took him under her wing, introducing this aspiring young writer to some of the most eminent people in the Parisian literary world. At the home of this beautiful and distinguished woman (whom he called his "best pal"), he met his future publisher, Gaston Gallimard, and that publisher's most brilliant writers: Jean Prévost, Charles du Bos, Ramón Fernandez, Drieu la Rochelle, André Malraux, Henri Michaux, and André Gide—Gide was to write a preface to Saint-Exupéry's second book, *Night Flight,* in 1931.

Saint-Exupéry states in his letters that he sometimes refused Yvonne's invitations, feeling that "a man who doesn't earn his living hasn't the right to eat." A noble sentiment, perhaps, but rather farcical when expressed by Saint-Ex, who was still continually asking his mother for money.

But his requests were expressed in a less imperative way than formerly, although with the same type of arguments. He had moved to another house, which meant "a number of tips to the cleaning woman, the concierge, and so on, the carting of books, trunk, and suitcase, and on top of all this, three hundred francs that I owe the dentist, who refuses to wait. . . ." He still appealed to his mother's sympathies with phrases such as "my situation is grim" or "my room is so depressing that I lack the courage to tidy up my things and I haven't yet even separated my collars from my socks. . . ."

When his mother suggested opening an account for him at the Crédit Lyonnais bank, he said the sum she proposed to deposit was insufficient. "Why, Mother, we talked about this at Saint-Maurice and I told you that 20,000 francs [about a million today] was barely enough, because I need to take out some insurance [for a car he was hoping to buy] and I must have some new clothes, since everything I own, except my topcoat and evening suit, date from my demobilization." The remainder of this letter is rather curious. After having said that twenty thousand francs was barely enough—and he underscored the word—he added: "But after all, you owe us nothing"—the *us* apparently including his sisters who were not as demanding as he was—"so send me whatever you like. But send it as soon as possible, because working at Suresnes is ruining me in taxis which I have to take when they wake me up too late in the morning."

Yes, he occasionally refused his cousin Yvonne's invitations to dine, saying he wasn't earning his salt and therefore could not impose upon her generosity, but he took a taxi to work, he continually asked his mother for funds, and on one occasion at least, he struck a cousin for a loan—a provincial cousin whose wedding he was attending. What a mass of contradictory behavior!

A great deal has also been said about Saint-Exupéry's contempt for money. Rather, he felt little attachment to money: it ran through his fingers. He never learned how to economize or how to deny himself. However, he seriously wanted to earn money. He was beginning to have scruples at being dependent upon his poor mother, and he needed the feeling of independence that earning his living would give him. He wanted to have an apartment to which he could invite friends; he wanted to be on the giving end rather than always on the receiving end.

Thus, the minute a seemingly lucrative position came along, he immediately recovered his zest for life and all his illusions. He was offered a job as salesman for Saurer, the motor-truck firm, and accepted it, estimating that he would earn, in salary and commissions, "somewhere between 30,000 and 40,000 francs a month, plus a small car in which I will take you gallivanting over the country," he told his mother. After holding down various jobs at the home office of the Saurer firm, he was sent out to "prospect" the departments of central France—the Allier, Cher, and Creuse regions—where, he wrote his mother, "Saurer trucks are apparently greatly appreciated." And he rejoiced: "At last I have solved the problem of paying my way."

In the beginning he enjoyed this job because of the travel it entailed. In his letters he described the remote little hamlets he passed through, the country inns at which he stopped, the people he saw and heard—one fop, a local lord of the manor, he described as "stupid and useless, a noisemaker." He even enjoyed a "mechanical piano grinding out sentimental tunes" and he noted how "the woman at the cashier's desk swayed from right to left. The inn proprietor, all his desires fulfilled, yawns sleepily, and the waiter hovers over me because he, too, is sleepy, and I am his last customer." A friend of his came to join him in a village and together they went to the town hall where the young people of the region were putting on a show, a kind of pageant. "Crowded in between a fat grocer woman and the pharmacist," he wrote to his mother, "we learned in five minutes the first name of the tenor, heard about the escapades of the deputy mayor's daughter, and picked up the local accent. What open-heartedness!"

The agent for Saurer trucks discovered some remote little subprefectures over which he exclaimed in delight or melancholy, depending upon his mood or the weather. But he sold no trucks. Saint-Exupéry would never be a success in commerce; he had none of the talents of a salesman. He needed to create. And so he wrote. He told his mother of a novel he was working on. No doubt it was the never finished *L'Evasion de Jacques Bernis*, a portion of which, called *L'Aviateur*, was published in 1926 by Adrienne Monnier in *Le Navire d'Argent*.

In these letters he reveals his method of writing. The novel "ripens from page to page." There is no frenzy of inspiration, but unfolds a kind of gradual decantation, as of wine. "I am making considerable inner progress, through observation; I force myself to observe at all times, every second. I am storing up things." This explains his long silences, his mute presence in society when the conversation failed to interest him. He was observing. Then, alone in his room or in a café surrounded by indifferent strangers, he matured his thought and wrote it down.

It has been remarked that Saint-Exupéry, in all his writings, abstains from quoting any author. He would write of Conrad, whom he greatly admired and to whom he has sometimes been compared, but he would not quote from him. He had no master, really; he imitated no other writer; he was under no influence. Hence the original and personal quality of his work.

One of his flying comrades was also a writer, and Saint-Exupéry gave him advice, which he describes in one of his letters to his mother, after the young fellow, referred to merely as "X," had gone to Morocco. "I have to a certain extent made a human being," he wrote, "by bringing him into contact with the outside world. I am rather proud of my ideas on the cultivation of the art of thinking. We learn everything in school except that. We learn to write, sing, speak, be affected emotionally, but never to think. And words lead us astray, they even falsify our true feelings. I want thought to be human, not bookish. And I've noticed how, when people talk or write, they immediately abandon all thought and draw artificial conclusions, using words as though they came out of a calculating machine that manufactured Truth. It's idiotic.... I detest those people who write to amuse themselves or to show off. The main thing is to have something to say. And so I pointed out to X...

how artificial and futile were the words he lined up on paper, and showed him that the fault was not in a lack of hard work—a deficiency easy to correct—but went deeper, was in his vision, which is at the base of everything, and I told him that what he had to re-educate was not his style but everything within himself—intelligence and vision—before he began to write. . . . At first he was discouraged, disgusted with himself—a healthy stage of growth through which I myself have passed."

At about the same time, he gave similar advice to Renée de Saussine, whose brother had been a classmate and who was therefore one of "the gang" of his Lycée years. She had written a story which she asked Antoine to read and criticize. The story was returned, accompanied by a long letter, which she published in a collection of Saint-Exupéry's youthful letters, *Lettres de Jeunesse*. The very night before writing the letter Saint-Ex had attended a lecture given by a former classmate at the Lycée whom he refers to as Eusebio, a name which conceals that of a well-known Alpine climber, and he began by criticizing the lecture severely. Eusebio "bestows the sweetish colors of lollipops on sublime mountain peaks, the sky, dawn, and sunsets. . . . He gives us an edible landscape. . . . It is the method that is wrong, or rather, the vision that is lacking. One should not learn how to write, but how to see. Writing will come as a consequence."

The young man who had evolved these ideas was only twenty-three years old; he had still not published anything, yet he was able to sum up in a lapidary phrase his concept of an art in which he was destined to shine.

As he observed what went on around him, he was storing up, as he put it, thoughts not only about other people but about himself, and it was this introspection which enabled him to judge himself and strive to improve. He made a truly praiseworthy effort. However, he continued to be withdrawn from his fellows and to be difficult and demanding. Intelligent people were so rare! He was not content merely with the surface polish acquired by education; what he sought in human beings was "substance." He confessed, "It hurts me when I do not find what I look for in someone, and I am always disappointed and disgusted when I discover that a mentality I had believed to be interesting is nothing but a mechanism easy to take apart. I have a grudge, then, against that person. I'm eliminating a lot of people from my life, men and women; I simply can't help it."

These remarks are to be found in a long letter to his mother, written in a little hotel sitting room at Montluçon, a letter in which he defends himself against certain reproaches that had been made. "The family still regard me as a superficial creature, a talkative pleasure-seeker," he writes, "whereas what I seek in life, and even in pleasure, is some additional knowledge."

Talkative pleasure-seeker he certainly was not. Perhaps he was merely distorting and exaggerating something that had been said. But he could be reproached for his love of luxury, his inability to deprive himself, and his willingness to impose upon his mother's generosity to obtain superfluous creature comforts. He himself was beginning to be aware of these defects, for he had discovered how hard it was to earn a living. When he thought about himself he felt, he wrote to his mother, "very different" from what he had been. "But I am rather hard on myself," he adds. "For how could you expect me to fill my letters with such things as 'I've taken a bath,' or 'I've had dinner with Uncle Jacques and family?' " Not so long before this, his letters had contained just such phrases; indeed, in a quite recent letter he had written "Dined last night at Uncle Jacques.' "

By a roundabout road, Saint-Exupéry was journeying toward the life to which he was secretly called.

The agent for Saurer trucks was as little successful as the accountant for the Tuileries Boiron had been. As a result, typically, his enthusiasm soon died down. He who had thought he had solved the problem of existence was once again obliged to hunt a job.

Weary at not finding a career suited to his tastes, aptitudes, intelligence, and discouraged at finding himself relegated to a mediocre rank, he was sometimes overwhelmed with melancholy. There was one sure way of dispelling depression, and that was to go to Orly for a few hours of flying, as did many of the reserve pilots of the Air Force. It was also a way of keeping in training. Once in the air, he was happy; nothing weighed him down, nothing depressed him, he felt renewed and without burdens again. Altitude meant something more than flying in the air above the earth; it meant, for him, leaving behind the meanness he often encountered in his fellow men, banishing all the scurvy tricks and intrigues and demeaning acts, big and little, of daily life. The reserve pilots all experienced this; their occasional flights banished care, calmed their nerves, provided an elation that nothing else could procure, so purifying and revivifying was the solitude of the sky.

Beneath his wings, Saint-Exupéry contemplated the little suburban houses that had sprung up haphazard among their gardens because city dwellers were already seeking a freer and purer air. Here and there, too many people had felt this need and even the suburbs were crowded rows of houses where the air was vitiated. In the sky it was otherwise. We can imagine Saint-Ex consulting his altimeter, observing that the needle registers 6500 feet, and climbing still higher. Now, his circular gaze embraces space, the sky is his, the earth remote. Paris is left behind, in its perpetual halo of mist, where men swarm like grubs. To the left stretches the plain of Brie, with its motley of grain fields and meadows and woodlands, while ahead of him the Forest of Fontainebleau spreads its immense tapestry of every shade of green. On the roads, antlike creatures crawl, seeking their livelihood, passing each other without recognition. He leans out beyond the windshield and receives a breathtaking slap from the wind. Suddenly he has a happy urge to do battle, to impose his will, to test his brain and muscles. He pushes his foot against the rudder-bar and the stick first to the left, then toward him. The plane banks, all the earth tilts, the forest vanishes, the villages disappear as if by magic, and the ants behave as if quite insane. Soon, he cuts off the engine and the plane comes down to earth, where Saint-Ex rejoins his comrades and recounts the details of his flight. They all do this, embroidering the facts, imagining much, even the pilots not gifted with imagination. Saint-Ex will say, "My engine overheated, I was scared." But later on he will write to his mother "The weather is gloomy, but even so I went to Orly on Sunday to take up a plane and I had a fine flight. Mother, I adore this métier!"

Flying had now become a real passion and he would not be satisfied until he landed a job as pilot for an established airline. His old friend and former schoolmaster, the Abbé Sudour, director of the École Bossuet, was able to help him satisfy this ambition.

When Saint-Exupéry first told the Abbé Sudour that he now wanted to make his career in flying, the abbé was shocked and surprised. At that period the profession of airline pilot was considered so dangerous that it could only appeal to young men of a reckless nature. The abbé therefore began by urging Saint-Exupéry to reconsider, to think of his other vocation, writing. But his arguments did not shake Saint-Ex's resolution, and finally the abbé agreed to recommend him to an old wartime friend, Beppo de Massimi, managing director of the Latécoère Airline Company and one of its creators.

In Massimi's book, which is a well-documented history of "the Line," he tells about the first interview he had with Saint-Exupéry on October 12, 1926, describing the young man as "a tall, shy young fellow who seemed to be very conscious of his size and annoyed at taking up so much room in his armchair."

The managing director, after some preliminary questions, told Saint-Ex that he would have to undergo some flying tests at Toulouse, and that if he came off well in them he would be taken on as pilot on the Line for a period that would be fixed later.

"And after that?" he asked anxiously.

"After that.... Well, you see, our director needs an assistant."

"Sir, I only want to fly," said Saint-Ex, flushing and speaking in a supplicating voice. "I want to fly."

Monsieur de Massimi was moved at this display of emotion.

"When do you want to leave for Toulouse?" he asked.

"Tonight, this very night, if you like!"

"Agreed. You will ask to see Monsieur Daurat, our general manager. I'll telephone him to warn him of your arrival."

Two days later Saint-Exupéry arrived in Toulouse. The sky was gray and gloomy, but the young man was oblivious of everything except his own emotions of mingled joy, apprehension, and uncertainty. For the first time he felt he was headed toward a sure and definite goal, although he still did not know exactly what it was. He was completely rapt in thought as he settled into the jolting and jingling old omnibus which carried him to Montaudran and the famous airport of the Latécoère Airline Company.

The plane carrying the first airmail had taken off from this field in 1919—seven years before Saint-Exupéry's arrival. The newspapers had described the event in a few brief lines that were doubtless soon forgotten by the people who chanced to read them. But to the group of men assembled that morning on the Montaudran airfield, it was a world-shaking event. Those men gave themselves wholly to an achievement which it is still difficult to evaluate as to its amplitude and importance in the history of aviation.

Among the officials present on that epoch-making day, according to Beppo de Massimi's account, were "three gentlemen in black suits and bowler hats; they were the Prefect of Police, the Mayor, and the Postmaster." But the most remarkable man among the onlookers was Pierre Latécoère, that intelligent if cold and autocratic industrialist, whose proud face, nearsighted eyes, and slender figure would set him apart in any crowd. Incontestably he was the creator of the South American–France Airline, which the initiates have always referred to simply as "the Line," the very mention of which suggests the audacity, grandeur, and spirit of self-sacrifice that characterized everyone who had a part in it. For the Line was the rootstock from which the great and flourishing tree of French commercial aviation was to spring.

From the sawmill owned by his father at Bagnères-de-Bigorre, through a period of manufacturing railway cars and then (in

1914) munitions, Pierre Latécoère in 1917 launched out into the manufacture of airplanes. The war was not over when this lively and positive mind began to think of the beneficent uses to which the airplane could be put at the end of hostilities. He was one of the first to see that the airplane, because of its speed and ability to leap over obstacles, was destined to bring nations closer together. While he was still manufacturing munitions, Latécoère was thinking of peace, almost the only one to do so. He looked toward Morocco, to which France had for many years been bringing her civilization. By air, via Spain, one could reach Morocco in thirty hours. Looking at the map, Latécoère envisaged a line uniting Morocco to another French center farther south, Dakar, accessible by a long hop over the Sahara. From Dakar, across the southern Atlantic one could fly to South America, where France enjoyed an enormous prestige. The cultural and commercial relations between Europe and South America occasioned a yearly exchange of two thousand tons of letters—while the amount of mail to and from the East Indies totaled seven hundred tons. A reply to a letter sent from Paris to Buenos Aires required fifty days. The average Atlantic liner took twenty-three days to sail from France to Argentina. A plane could make the trip in seven days, in four days when night flying would become possible.

Pierre Latécoère brought to the realization of this dream a ruthless drive, a singleness of purpose that made him appear almost inhuman at times—a false impression, for this graduate engineer of the École Centrale read Plato, Bergson, and Stendhal in his spare time and enjoyed the music of Bach, Schumann, and Berlioz.

To appreciate the temerity and vision of his project, we must recall the epoch in which he conceived it. In those days planes flew at a speed of about eighty miles an hour and had a range of action covering only five hundred kilometers, roughly three hundred ten miles. Moreover, an engine rarely turned for a hundred hours without needing to be overhauled. His ideas therefore smacked a little of Jules Verne's fancies, they were an anticipation of the future; small wonder that many of his contemporaries, among them intelligent men, regarded these ideas insane.

Latécoère's tenacity overcame all resistance. He was able to convince the skeptics and to force public authorities, always so slow to grasp innovations, to see the importance of his plans. This was not easy, since the practical purpose of the enterprise was not very apparent in the midst of the atrocious war which was engaging everyone's attention almost exclusively.

Despite all these difficulties, by the time the war ended Latécoère was ready to launch his airline. All he lacked was the manpower, and this would not long be an impediment. One by one his aviators arrived on the Montaudran airfield, some of them still wearing their French Air Force uniforms. There they were: Moraglia, Beauté, Rodier—who was destined to head the list of one hundred martyrs of the Line—Genthon, Cabanes, Dombray, Delrieu, Vanier, Bonnetête, Daurat. They had hailed the Armistice with joy, of course, but also with a note of sadness—they would fly no more. Their excursions into the sky had provided their minds and bodies with a satisfaction they could never forget, an ecstasy close to that of love, for under its sway a man is able to give himself utterly, to the point of self-sacrifice. Despite his tenacity, Latécoère could never have realized his vision without such men. Would they please report to Montaudran to fly the mail? They were still not quite sure what that implied, had no idea what would be expected of them by that Monsieur Latécoère, with his impassive face, piercing eyes, and glittering monocle. They knew he had spent the war in his factory, far from danger, making money. But this did not bother them unduly, since he was now going to enable them to continue to fly.

It is important to realize what kind of men these pioneer flyers were, for it was in them that the grandeur of the Line germinated, through them that "the men of the Line" attained a reputation of having such profound humanity that they were sometimes regarded as supermen. This applies to Saint-Exupéry as well. Yet they had come to Montaudran merely to fly, or as Saint-Ex put it in a letter to his mother, "to take a job that represented a solid start in life." Those young men who reported for work at the Latécoère airfield outside Toulouse had not come there with a great urge to serve others or impressed with the idea of unifying the nations of the world through closer communications. Not at all. The spirit of the Line, the total devotion, the mystique of the Line that made the delivery of the mail an almost sacred mission, had to be created, shaped, molded, out of the lives of these young men who regarded flying as a profession. The man who created that mystique was Didier Daurat.

When Daurat first joined the Latécoère company, he was twenty-eight years old and, like the three or four pilots who preceded him, fresh from his war experiences. As pilot and then squadron leader, Captain Didier Daurat had flown with Beppo de Massimi, who had served as pilot and observer. Daurat knew how to command, and despite his youth also knew how to size up men, how to gauge their powers and weaknesses. In combat, when the aviator finds himself isolated and without the moral support of a company of men fighting shoulder to shoulder, Daurat had seen how the instinctive, animal shrinking from danger must be overcome. On his first flight over the Pyrenees, he had also noted that the same reactions held true in this type of flying. He had at once apprehended the difficulties and grandeur of the airmail enterprise. Rapidly he emerged as a leader from the small group at Montaudran and was put in command of the crews and the actual ordering of the flights.

He had all the qualities, physical and mental, of a man used to wielding authority. Massively built, with an energetic face and penetrating eyes, he made few gestures and spoke in a slow, measured way, the words falling from his lips as if made for the occasion. He had an unusual understanding of how other men's minds worked. He had rid himself of all sentimentality, one almost might say of all sentiment. The war had taught him to do without it, and the life he was to lead as the working manager of the Line reinforced him in his willful hardness. Tremendously serious, he was also endowed with a great sense of responsibility; he not only accepted it but sought it out, for he had a need to devote himself completely to a hard task and overcome difficulties. As a result, Didier Daurat had a substance and maturity rare in a man of twenty-eight.

The organization, when he came to it, was at the fetal stage; it was a potentiality, and a still unstable one. Neither the machines nor the men seemed to be made to carry out what was going to be expected of them. Didier Daurat would shape the men to the task and they in turn would shape the enterprise. It would become, thanks to them, both a gigantic and a very human project.

No matter how brave these young men were, they sometimes balked at the tasks demanded of them. We must keep in mind that aviation was still in its infancy, and that the air was still far from being conquered. One of the best pilots handed in his resignation after only two or three routine flights, saying "This is a job for madmen; we will all end up in a crash!" He was both right and wrong: right to leave, if he was unwilling to transcend himself; wrong in losing faith in himself and the enterprise. Daurat molded the characters of his men, but he needed, to start with, men of an unusual stamp.

Didier Daurat commanded the respect of those under him, even of men his own age. His comrades found it natural to address him as "Monsieur Daurat." Envy did not even faintly stir in their minds, nor any feeling of servility. The men accepted the true hierarchy of worth. And those who came later to reinforce the phalanx or fill in the gaps, "the young ones," such as Mermoz, Guillaumet, and Saint-Exupéry, at once adopted the formula; even when speaking among themselves, they said "Monsieur" Daurat and Latécoère. Saint-Exupéry dedicated his *Night Flight* in 1931 quite simply "To Monsieur Didier Daurat."

The working team that crystallized around the chief was composed of men he himself had chosen. He did not take on any and all who came to offer their services, but chose them with swift and sure judgment. He also knew how to keep a man of quality, as when, for instance, he kept on Jean Mermoz after a display of acrobatics and a lack of discipline that would have earned dismissal for a less gifted man.

Mermoz, on his first test flight above the Montaudran field, a test imposed upon all new recruits, indulged in some spectacular stunts. Mermoz was by nature quarrelsome, artistic, impulsive, not at all a type congenial to Daurat. But when the new recruit brought his plane down, Daurat merely said, "We don't go in for acrobatics here. That sort of thing is for circuses." And when Mermoz shrugged with impatience, Daurat let it pass, commenting drily, "Don't worry, we'll tame you!" For he saw beneath the foibles and eccentricities of Mermoz a flyer of the quality he needed.

Daurat had no delusions about the difficulties ahead. He knew the goal was distant, but knew also that it could be reached. "If I had not had faith in the ultimate success of the venture," he has said, "I would have given up at once. I'm no gambler." But in a way the achievement was largely due to his faith in it, his will to succeed, and the will to succeed with which he inspired his men.

No one ever thought of questioning his orders or taking offense at his remarks. Mermoz, for instance, grew tired of working in the machine shop and made it clear one day that he was chafing at the bit. "When am I going to be allowed to fly?" he asked the general manager.

Daurat's steely eyes surveyed Mermoz as he calmly but categorically replied: "Such questions are not asked here."

Mermoz, who for three years had never been able to yield to military discipline without protest, said not another word but again bent over his work.

Daurat's ascendency over his men was indeed so great that they would submit even to an injustice from him, or what seemed to them an injustice. An incident in which Guillaumet figured illustrates this.

Having stopped over at Montaudran between two routine flights, Guillaumet was asked by Daurat to try out a Laté 28 plane that had just been overhauled. Guillaumet asked nothing better than to fly, so at once happily took the controls, let the engine warm up a bit, and then, in a rather strong wind, opened the throttle to take off. While the machine rolled down the runway against the wind, he noticed that the controls were not responding normally and at once cut off the gas—but not soon enough to avoid crashing into a mass of wreckage that happened to lie just beyond the field.

Daurat, who had been watching from his office, went down toward the scene of the accident. Guillaumet had jumped out and was trying to discover what had happened. Then, after some reflection, he climbed up on the wing, held on to the fuselage with one hand and with the other worked the throttle while observing the wingtips. The aileron wires had been crossed by mistake.

"Well," said Daurat, arriving beside him at that moment, "I see you've forgotten how to fly!"

"Why, M'sieu Daurat," Guillaumet replied, again working the control column, "just look: the aileron wires have been put on in reverse."

Daurat did not look, he had already seen. He lit a cigarette and went back to his office. But at the end of the month, when he received his pay, Guillaumet noticed that he had forfeited his "no-crash" bonus.

This story was told to me one evening by Mme. Guillaumet in the presence of Didier Daurat. She ended by asking in a tone of friendly reproach: "Now, M. Daurat, why did you do that?"

"All this was twenty years ago," Daurat replied in his usually slow and serious way, "and you're still talking about it. Whereas Guillaumet forgave me immediately." Then he turned to me. "You see, a pilot should always make sure that everything is in order before taking off. I could not let any slackness go unpunished, even if it was committed by one of our best men. At that time any least weakness in our fragile edifice might have made the whole thing collapse."

The edifice was, indeed, fragile. Meteorology was far from an exact science, and the planes had not been built to endure what was demanded of them. Compasses frequently got out of order. Engines, soon worn out, were apt to fail suddenly, without warning. There was no radio. The pilot—not always accompanied by a mechanic—might run into a storm over Spain or into a fog that would bury him in its woolly depths, hiding the mountain peaks where the terrible wind sometimes dragged the frail man-made bird into the abyss.

But the mail must be delivered. The pilot struggling in the sky, isolated from the world, was responsible for it.

Such, then, was the man Saint-Exupéry encountered shortly after his arrival at Montaudran. One cannot help wondering about that first meeting of two men who were so unlike. What was the first impression of the young writer whose rude life as a pilot was so to enrich his mind, as he confronted this leader of men for whom he was soon to feel deep respect and admiration, a man whom he was to turn into a legendary hero five years later? For there is little doubt that Monsieur Daurat, to whom *Night Flight* was dedicated, inspired Saint-Exupéry to write this book, which brought him fame.

Massimi had advised Daurat by telephone of the arrival of the new pilot, but it goes without saying that he had not "recommended" the new recruit, since he was all too well aware how useless such a recommendation would be to the general manager of the Latécoère airline: Daurat liked to judge for himself.

All we know of that first interview is that Daurat looked the new pilot up and down, then glanced through Saint-Exupéry's flight book. It was not a very big or important book, and only one accident was recorded in it. But at sight of that notation, Daurat knitted his brows and dropped his cigarette butt into the ashtray before questioning the young man who stood there as if intimidated.

"My engine stalled," said Saint-Exupéry. Then he added, in a lower voice, "The accident was inevitable."

Daurat muttered something which Saint-Ex did not catch, but

was too shy to ask to have the words repeated. Then, after a silence, during which he felt the eyes of the chief leveled upon him, Saint-Ex recovered his aplomb and said eagerly: "Sir, above everything else, I want to fly."

"Do as the others do. You will have to take your place in line," said Daurat, and proceeded to roll another cigarette.

Taking his place in line meant going every day to the freezing-cold hangar for lessons in meterology or navigation and helping the mechanics in their work. It meant entering into the communal life, participating in all the work, even that of the mechanics who toiled unceasingly on the planes which had to take such rough usage. For Saint-Exupéry it was truly an apprenticeship; for the first time he had to take all the hard knocks of life. Up to this time, he had never really tried to escape from the aristocratic milieu into which he had been born, not even when doing his military service. While he accepted this training period without complaint, getting used to the new conditions was hard, and he did not immediately enter into a close relationship with his comrades. It was all so different from anything he had known before. And he could not overcome his shyness which sometimes made him silent; his absent-minded look seemed to put a distance between him and the others, as if he felt above them—as perhaps he really was.

There were all kinds of men in this little nucleus of pilots and mechanics that comprised the Latécoère airline. Some had fought in the war. Others had experienced the rude life of the desert. Two of the men, Lécrivain and Mermoz, came from Syria. There were distinguished men and common and coarse men. But under the ferule of Didier Daurat, confronting the same dangers and spurred by the same ideal, this group became completely welded together in a homogeneous whole. Soon Saint-Ex felt a part of it.

Besides working with the mechanics in the hangar, he took up rehabilitated planes for trial flights. This, too, was taking his place in line. What he was longing for was "to take a Bréguet to pasture on the clouds," and he envied those who made the long flights.

With mingled hope and regret he watched the departure of the mail plane at dawn. M. Daurat was always there, smoking a cigarette in silence, nothing escaping his sharp scrutiny. When an accident had occurred or was feared, he remained in his office at all hours, waiting for news, sometimes leaving Montaudran at one o'clock in the morning, accompanied by his faithful secretary-chauffeur, Bouisset. (Bouisset's devotion was proverbial, and twenty years later he was still at the side of his chief, who was then director of the Orly airport.) Being a faithful attendant of Daurat meant going without much sleep. "Good-night, Monsieur Daurat," he said as he stopped the car before Daurat's lodgings in Toulouse, late at night. "Good-night, Bouisset. Come for me at four in the morning. . . ."

In the evenings, after work, Saint-Exupéry took the bus back to Toulouse, where most of the pilots lived at a pension, the *Grand Balcon,* which they eventually made famous, for it became associated with many heroes of the Line. It became their second home, the scene of some gay evenings when no doubt one of the pilots was hiding a secret premonition that he was spending his last hours among men.

At the *Grand Balcon,* Saint-Exupéry listened to the talk of the veterans, "gruff, not particularly approachable, and inclined somewhat to condescension when giving us the benefit of their experience," he tells us in *Wind, Sand and Stars.* From their stories he learned what the line to Morocco via Spain was like, heard about the fogs, the rain, the snow, the storms that had to be faced. And he tells us of the return to base of one of these veterans, "Bury, he who was later to die in a spur of the Pyrenees." He had seen Bury come in, his face reddened by the wind, his leather jacket streaming with the rain, and had seen how wearily he sat down to eat, bending over his plate, wolfing down his food. After a moment of silence, Saint-Ex plucked up the courage to speak to him and "ventured after a bit to ask if he had had a hard flight." He knew it had been hard, but wanted to hear the details. "Finally Bury looked up, seemed to understand me, to think back to what I was referring, and suddenly he gave a bright laugh." This burst of laughter, his only reply, was more eloquent than speech.

His own turn came at last. One evening, M. Daurat called him to his office. Saint-Exupéry had been in the machine shop, working. Hastily cleaning his oily hands, he was soon standing before the general manager's desk.

"You leave tomorrow," said Daurat. Then, after a short pause, "You're acquainted with the regulations, of course?"

The regulations were not posted but were passed from one pilot to another, verbally; they were the results of experience, an experience that had cost many lives. In those days engines stalled with dreadful frequency. When, with a crash as of broken crockery, the engine stopped suddenly, the pilot had no recourse but to make a forced landing, without having time to choose a landing place, and sometimes having to come down on rocky mountainsides. Only the sandy beaches offered an occasional flat space. For this reason the pilot was forbidden to fly above the clouds, since, flying blind, there was a greater risk of crashing against a mountain peak.

M. Daurat quietly recalled this regulation. "Navigating by the compass in a sea of clouds over Spain is all very well," he said, "it is very dashing, but . . ." He paused, then spoke with still more deliberation: "but you want to remember that below the sea of clouds lies eternity."

As Saint-Ex left Daurat, he was "filled with a childish pride" at the thought of the responsibility that would soon be his. And as he stepped out of the bus and walked toward the *Grand Balcon*, he was feverishly concerned with his next day's duties. At dawn he would already be in the sky, at the controls of a plane, carrying the African mails over Spain, which was "poor in emergency fields." He repeated to himself the names of the landings he would make: Perpignan, Barcelona, Alicante. The fellows had spoken about the lodginghouse woman at Alicante. She was called Pepita, a strapping woman. At Alicante there were date palms, orange trees, warm and luminous nights.

His maps of Spain were inadequate. He kept thinking about the mountains of Spain, and he recalled Daurat's words: "Below the sea of clouds lies eternity." Flying a plane was suddenly no longer merely a game. He decided to have a talk with Guillaumet, and as soon as he arrived at the *Grand Balcon,* he knocked at his door.

Henri Guillaumet had signed on as pilot of the Latécoère airline a year before Saint-Exupéry, and from the beginning had been classed among the best flyers. He had all the qualities needed by these air pioneers who were laying down new routes in the sky: a passion for the craft—that is to say, an unreserved acceptance of all the difficulties and risks—and incomparable self-control. Young, robust, his frank expression and ready laugh made him very approachable. Saint-Ex had immediately been attracted to him, and now he wanted to spend with him what he called "the vigil of arms."

"I know all about it," Guillaumet said at once, giving him a hearty handclasp. "How do you feel?" And he went to a cupboard for glasses and a bottle of port. "Don't worry," he said, as he set these down on the table. "It's much easier than you think."

Recounting this in *Wind, Sand and Stars,* Saint-Exupéry tells us that Guillaumet "exuded confidence the way a lamp gives off light."

They studied the maps, sitting shoulder to shoulder in the lamplight, sipping their glasses of port, Guillaumet talking, Saint-Ex listening. It was the beginning of a rich and deep friendship, one of the rare friendships ever made in the writer–airman's life.

Three years earlier at Istres, Saint-Ex had more than once run across Corporal Guillaumet without noticing him. Guillaumet, like most of the others, ate at the refectory, while Saint-Ex took his meals at the canteen, and did not mingle much with the trainees. But in Toulouse, he was suddenly a member of a team, did the same work as the others, rode in the same bus, ate at the same table, lived as the others did. The two men often met, and were mutually drawn to each other. Yet, at first sight, this mutual attraction seemed very odd, so unlike were their characters and backgrounds: the one was a cultivated aristocrat, the other a peasant's son who had not even gone to secondary school. They had the same vocation, true; but neither this nor their mutual attraction can explain the great, fraternal friendship that was soon to unite them.

In this new life, Saint-Exupéry had soon felt a real need to find and to associate with men superior to those he had known in the past. The men at Montaudran shared his ideals and were far removed from the shabby futility of ordinary lives. Even when he was traveling for Saurer trucks, he had suffered more from the lack of comradeship, the society of congenial people, than he had from his actual work or his "dingy room." He had written to his mother that he was "eliminating a lot of people" from his life because they did not come up to his standards. Now, all his keen perceptions—which were to manifest themselves later in his writings—told him that Guillaumet was the man he was seeking, that here at last was a man he could admire and love and emulate. And in the ensuing years, although often apart, their friendship grew, acquiring such an intensity that it was an indestructible bond. To Saint-Exupéry's mind Guillaumet was unique, and when he introduced his friend to Léon Werth he merely said, "This is Guillaumet."

At the most trying moments of his life he was often to call to mind the dauntless Guillaumet. Lost in the Lybian desert, wandering without food for three days, close to dying of thirst and on the verge of despair, Saint-Exupéry tells us in *Wind, Sand and Stars* that he thought of what Guillaumet would do in a similar situation: "This time we should strike out as fast as we could, leave this cursed plateau, and tramp till we dropped in our tracks. That was what Guillaumet had done in the Andes. I had been thinking of him all the day before and had determined to follow his example."

Guillaumet, lost in the Andes, had trudged for five days and four nights and had saved himself only thanks to his heroic will power. The remark he made when the two friends were reunited after this ordeal has been immortalized by Saint-Exupéry: "I swear that what I went through, no animal would have gone through." And in most of his writings, whenever there is a question of bravery, loyalty, greatness, he names his friend. "Guillaumet's courage," he wrote, "is in the main the product of his honesty. . . . His moral greatness consists in his sense of responsibility . . . Guillaumet was one among those bold and generous men who had taken upon themselves the task of spreading their foliage over bold and generous horizons."

Certainly *Wind, Sand and Stars,* which is without a doubt the greatest of Saint-Exupéry's books, would lack some of its most beautiful pages had the author not known Guillaumet. The American edition is dedicated to the Airline Pilots of America; but the original French edition, *Terre des Hommes,* was dedicated to his comrade. The circumstances in which Guillaumet learned of this dedication demonstrate Saint-Exupéry's tact as well as his affection for his friend.

Whenever Guillaumet had a few days of rest between trips, he liked to return to his native village, Bouy, in the Champagne district. There he re-encountered his childhood friends, peasants who were wresting from the earth its secrets as he wrested the secrets from the sky. He loved to lead the simple life and was content to spend an entire day at his favorite sport, trout fishing, in the little Vesle River flowing between rows of silver-leafed aspens and willows. One evening, upon returning with his wife to Paris after such a day, his concierge told him, "M'sieu Guillaumet, your telephone hasn't stopped ringing all day long."

Scarcely had they set foot in their apartment when the telephone rang again. Guillaumet took up the receiver and at once recognized Saint-Exupéry's voice, raised in anger.

"Well! At last you've come home! You go away without telling a soul, you vanish for an entire day."

"Well, I have a right to do so."

"No," said Saint-Ex, who tyrannized his friends in proportion to his fondness for them. "I've been telephoning you in vain ever since this morning. I need to see you."

"Then come over, old chap, by all means."

"You're not going out?"
"No, we'll wait for you."
Shortly afterward, Saint-Ex arrived, with two parcels under his arm, one of them small and flat, the other one long and rounded. Pouncing upon Guillaumet, his index finger extended, he said, "Swear that you don't know a thing about it!"
Guillaumet, although quite used to his friend's peculiarities, was a little surprised. "Why, what's got into you?" he asked. "What do you want me to swear?"
"That you don't know anything."
"Anything about what? And why?"
"Swear," said Saint-Ex, waving his arms. "Swear, and you, too," he added, turning toward Mme. Guillaumet, "you don't know anything either, do you? Swear to it!"
"You've gone out of your mind, my poor dear Saint-Ex!"
"No. Swear, both of you, that no one's told you anything."
Guillaumet and his wife raised their right hands and solemnly took the oath. Then Saint-Ex, his face beaming with pleasure, held out the flat little parcel to Guillaumet. It was a copy of *Terre des Hommes*, the first copy of the limited edition, just out. In the flyleaf, Guillaumet read through a blur of tears: *Henri Guillaumet, mon camarade, je te dédie ce livre.** The two friends gazed into each other's eyes, then embraced. After which they opened the second parcel. It contained a bottle of champagne.
Saint-Ex had talked about the book to Guillaumet and had even read some passages to him from the manuscript, but he had wanted the dedication to be a surprise. He had thought of presenting the book at a dinner his cousin Yvonne de Lestrange was going to give, had told her of the surprise he had in store for his friend, and had begged her not to tell anyone, particularly Mme. Guillaumet, whom she sometimes met. But then he became panicky, was almost sure the secret had leaked out, and in addition he so wanted to see Guillaumet's reaction that he could not wait, although the dinner was only two days off.

* To my comrade Henri Guillaumet, I dedicate this book.

Sometimes depths of feelings are revealed at the most unexpected moments. This happened at a little celebration in 1939 at Parentis-en-Born, on the shores of Lake Biscarosse, the occasion of Guillaumet's thirty-seventh birthday. Guillaumet, with a select crew, was preparing the hydroplane *Lieutenant-de-Vaisseau-Paris* for a crossing of the North Atlantic. Saint Exupéry had been awarded the rosette of the Legion of Honor. All these events were to be celebrated at Guillaumet's birthday party, and after-dinner speeches were to be made by the two honored guests. Present, besides the crew, were Mme. Guillaumet, Mme. Néri, the wife of the radio operator, and Jean Lucas, formerly director of the Port-Étienne airport in North Africa. As the dinner drew to an end, Guillaumet and Saint-Ex each tried to say his little speech, but, overcome by emotion, neither was able to utter a word. These two brave men, who had confronted violent storms and treacherous seas and mountains, were vanquished, overwhelmed by their very friendship for each other. Their emotion was infectious, laughter died down, tears dimmed the eyes of everyone. The women lit the thirty-seven candles on the cake, and as they were blown out there were cries and exclamations that had nothing to do with the festivity but were a release from tension.

Responsive to friendship, Saint-Ex suffered profoundly from any hostile sign, especially when it issued from his comrades and constituted an injustice. After the publication of *Night Flight*, in 1931, he was aware that some pilots of the Line and some comrades he had worked with for years were avoiding him and openly criticizing him. As usual, he exaggerated the situation, believing that everyone was against him. Guillaumet was in South America at the time and Saint-Ex was in Paris. In the depths of his melancholy, he heard that Guillaumet was returning to France on the *L'Arc-en-Ciel* with Mermoz, and at once wrote to him:

> *Guillaumet,*
>
> *I hear you are coming back, and my heart throbs at the news. If you knew what a terrible life I have led since your departure and what a profound disgust for*

life I have gradually come to feel! ... Still, you are arriving perhaps at a moment when the wind is changing a bit, and I shall be able to live down my shame. After so many disillusions, this unjust legend created about me has prevented my writing to you. Perhaps you, too, think that I have changed. And I could not bring myself to justify myself before the one man whom I may perhaps regard as a brother....

He then continues, offering the hospitality of his apartment to Guillaumet, saying that the keys will be left with the concierge, "so you will be as though at home," and concludes gloomily, "But perhaps, after all, you will refuse! And then I shall have lost my best friend."

All this was purely rhetorical, for between the two there existed absolute confidence. In Guillaumet's account of his heroic adventure in the Andes, his faith in Saint-Ex is revealed. Having rejoined Saint-Ex, who had been searching vainly for him, flying over the mountains, crossing mortally dangerous ravines, almost grazing the cols and snowy slopes, Guillaumet said: "I saw you, but you did not see me." "How did you know I was the one flying the plane?" asked Saint-Ex. "No one else in the world," said Guillaumet, "would have flown so low or taken such risks."

Saint-Exupéry's books are full of references to Guillaumet. He devotes many pages to him in *Wind, Sand and Stars.* In *Letter to a Hostage,* Guillaumet's name appears constantly, beginning with the very first pages. Recalling his short stay in Lisbon in December 1940, while waiting for the boat that would take him to the United States, he heard of Guillaumet's death, and in a lecture he gave, he spoke of his friend who had been shot down at sea while flying an unarmed transport plane. "They must have corpses," he said, referring to the hopeless fight still being waged by the French forces. "I mourn the death of the pilot Guillaumet. But now he will change no more. He will never more be present, but he will also never be absent, either." And in *Flight to Arras* we find this tribute: "... when Guillaumet, the best friend I ever had, was killed in the course of duty, there was no need for me to speak of him. We had flown the same airlines. Participated in the building of the same structures. Were of the same substance. Something of me died in him. Guillaumet became one of the companions of my silence. I am part of Guillaumet, and Guillaumet is part of me."

Thus, the difference in social rank and education did not really exist for them; their craft brought them together and made them equals. They were equals, but different. Guillaumet was simple, Saint-Exupéry was complex; and yet it was the former who exercised the stronger influence, perhaps the only man who ever had much influence over him, for no one else exemplified so perfectly the qualities Saint-Exupéry idealized in man. "What I like to do is to ennoble a man," he had written to a friend. But from Guillaumet, Saint-Exupéry received more than he gave.[7]

On the eve of his first flight toward Spain and Morocco, which was to be his baptism as pilot of the Line, Saint-Ex, before confronting "the black dragons" of danger in the skies of Spain, naturally sought the advice of Guillaumet. The geography Guillaumet taught that night had a very personal slant; it was geography as seen from the air, the viewpoint of a flyer who is looking for a safe landing place in case of danger, the view one might have through masses of clouds that were beginning to hide the mountain peaks.

Recalling this evening in *Wind, Sand and Stars*, Saint-Exupéry exclaims: "What a strange lesson in geography I was given! Instead of telling me about Guadix, he spoke of three orange-trees on the edge of the town: 'Beware of those trees. Better mark them on the map.'... He did not talk about Lorca, but a humble farm near Lorca... or of the Ebro River... but of that brook running secretly through the water-weeds to the west of Motril... I was to remember that serpent in the grass... Given the chance, it would transform me into a flaming candelabra... The crosses I marked to indicate safety zones and traps were so many buoys and beacons."

Next morning Saint-Ex left his bed and dressed while the town was still sleeping and when only here and there rays of light filtered through window shutters, indicating that some early worker was up. By the time the whole town awoke, Saint-Ex would already be far on his way. A fine, cold, misty rain was falling from a gray sky, as he sat on his suitcase at the bus stop, waiting with throbbing heart to be taken to the airport.

This young man in a leather jacket waiting for a bus in the cold drizzle which veils the street lamps is the same man who, only a few months before, took a taxi to his office job at Suresnes, when the streets were already swarming with workers and the sun was high; the same, but different. In the account he gives us in *Wind, Sand and Stars* he makes no mention of his own metamorphosis. He thought chiefly about the workingmen who traveled with him in that bus—customs officers, employees of the airport, inspectors—he thought of their precarious little lives, without high ideals, but still secure and calm and rather to be pitied, for they had, like termites, built their peace "by blocking up with cement every chink and cranny through which the light might pierce." And he pitied them, he who a few hours later would "confront in the lightnings the dragon of the mountains." And he recalled the flyers who had traveled before him in this bus at dawn, and those who had never returned to travel in it again.

That bus was to be associated in his mind with an event he heard of while traveling in it three years later. It was four in the morning and still dark when he heard the voice of the field manager, whose face was invisible, talking to an inspector. "Lécrivain didn't land at Casablanca last night." "Ah!" said the inspector. "Ah?" Torn from his dream, the inspector made an effort to wake up, "to display his zeal," and added: "Is that so? Couldn't he get through? Did he come back?" And in the dead darkness of the omnibus the answer came: "No." The people on the bus waited to hear more, but no word sounded. "And as the seconds fell it became more and more evident that that 'No' would be followed by no further word, was eternal and without appeal, that Lécrivain not only had not landed at Casablanca but would never again land anywhere."

Since Saint-Exupéry speaks of Lécrivain and his disappearance, I would like to say more about this comrade of the desert whose name is mingled with the names of "those hundred pilots who on a day or a night of fog have retired for eternity."

I knew Émile Lécrivain in Mesopotamia; had encountered him several times before that in the Sahara. We had been in the same squadron, and I had immediately been drawn to this young fellow, sensitive and good-humored, who carried his violin with him in his plane, along with a stock of food, drinking water, and a gun. We came to a halt one night in the midst of the desert, camping in the lee of our planes, and he whiled away the time playing some sonatas for us. The voice of the violin in the desert silence drew our little group of men together in a very affecting communion, and some of us had to blink back our tears.

Then there was another evening at Djezireh, that desert formerly inhabited and crossed by caravans laden with wealth for Semiramis or for the sultan of *A Thousand and One Nights*, where small tells, or mounds, jutting up here and there show the site of now-vanished cities. Lécrivain had put away his violin and we were making ready to go to sleep when he began to talk.

"I've a confession to make," he said hesitantly. "I want you to know . . . to know why I am going away."

"You're going to leave us?"

"I don't want to leave you. . . . It's . . ." The confession was obviously a painful one to make. "You see, I don't want to fly any more."

We already knew it. From a word dropped here and there, we knew he had a presentiment of a catastrophe. Then he had begun to make pretexts to avoid going on certain missions: he had a headache, or was feverish, or his engine needed an overhaul. And we had said to each other, "Apparently Lécrivain's had it!" We did not ridicule him, but we pitied him. Then one day he went away, returned to France.

Four years later I heard of Lécrivain's death. He had gone back to flying. And he and his mechanic, Decaud, had disappeared somewhere between Casablanca and Juby. Caught in a fog, they had wandered, lost, and had veered off toward the sea. Their plane and their bodies were never recovered.

Lécrivain had become one of the finest pilots of the Line. In May 1926 he had been the pilot who carried the first mail from Casablanca to Dakar, a dangerous trip, for almost two thousand miles straddling a coast fringed with foam: to the right the sea, to the left the desert, and between the two ports no refuge, no life. No life? Oh yes, in the desert there were the warring Moors, enemies who were ready to kill. Lécrivain had opened this route, one of the hardest; in order that the Line might carry on, become stronger, he had given his life.

At the controls of a Bréguet, Saint-Exupéry flew toward Spain. The machine was the same model as those which, in the years 1916–1918, had been used for bombing the German enemy. Its 300-h.p. Renault engine, surmounted by an exhaust pipe that projected like a chimney, could not exceed a speed of 80 miles an hour. Its range of action had been increased by adding supplementary tanks which weighed down the plane. The mailbags filled the cockpit where at times a passenger might be accommodated—a comrade returning to an airport in Spain or Morocco, an airport inspector, or even one of those daring early travelers.

The air route over Spain did not make a beeline over the Pyrenees, but passed over by way of Perpignan and Port-Vendres. Flying without radio, the pilot had no means of checking his route map except by the landmarks below him—railways, roads, canals, ponds, forests. It required continual attention, and it is unlikely that Saint-Ex on these first dangerous flights for the Line gave himself over very much to the meditations he mentions in his books. Those meditations came later, particularly after the advent of night flying, when the pilot, accompanied by a radio operator, could follow a course and get his bearings from the ground stations. Besides, when Saint-Ex made his first flights to Spain and Morocco, he was a pilot who had traveled very little. He had none of the training of the veterans who had flown during the war or the experience of a Mermoz who had flown over the Syrian desert or a Guillaumet who had broken several long-distance records. Nor had he ever, until now, flown in bad weather, in high winds or thunderstorms. He had heard about but never experienced the eddies and downdrafts of air above mountains—and they are terrible. The pilot had to be firmly attached to his seat or he risked being spilled out. Sometimes this turbulence would create air pockets into which the plane would drop so violently that the straps holding the pilot or the passenger to his seat left marks in the flesh. "This isn't much like flying at Le Bourget," he wrote to a friend, when he had made several routine airmail flights.

But then, nothing in this new life resembled the past. Saint-Ex in flying the mail planes was serving another apprenticeship. Ill prepared though he was for it, he had the essential qualities needed: pluck, hardihood, control. But he lacked certain qualities that make the difference between a merely good pilot and a great pilot. Saint-Exupéry knew fame as a writer. But had he been only an aviator, his name, despite his exploits, would have remained in obscurity.

It is hard to separate the pilot and the writer in him. The substance of his work, its richness and power, derive from his métier as flyer. It was a craft he loved and gave himself wholly to, but he did not excel in it as did Mermoz, Guillaumet, and others. If one were to draw up a list of pilots of the Line according to their merit, a great many would come before Saint-Exupéry.

Yet some people have acclaimed him as an airman. His physician and friend, Dr. Georges Pélissier, in his book surveying the "five aspects" of Saint-Exupéry (*Les Cinq Visages de Saint-Exupéry*) analyzes him as a pilot, a man, a writer, an inventor, a "magician." The author calls Saint-Exupéry a great airman, and quotes Mermoz, who once described a difficult landing which Saint-Ex brought off brilliantly. He also quotes Colonel Alias, Saint-Ex's squadron leader during the campaign of 1939–1940, as saying that Saint-Ex prepared his war missions with meticulous care. And he calls upon other witnesses to support his claim: Captain Israël, a crewmate in the same campaign, describes an acrobatic landing perfectly brought off; and Colonel Gavoille, Saint-Ex's squadron leader in 1943–1944, declares "He was an excellent pilot, very adroit." We have no doubt of it; had he not been so, Didier Daurat would not have kept him long.

But Saint-Ex had one undeniable defect that prevented him from being a truly great airman: his absent-mindedness, which was at times fantastic. All too often, when in the air, his thoughts were far from the work in hand. He allowed himself to become absorbed in an idea which soon monopolized all his attention. His displays of absent-mindedness were so talked about that he became known for them. During the war, he forgot to lower or take up his landing gear more than once. He often lost count of time. Once on a long flight his mind wandered and when he came to himself he found his watch had stopped. Believing that he had been in the air for hours, he brought the plane down in a field. But he had been flying for only ten minutes! He was guilty of many such preposterous lapses. But even worse were the caprices in which he indulged. Sometimes he turned aside from the route to fly into a squall, simply to find out what his reaction would be. A legitimate act of curiosity for an author who wishes to write only about what he has experienced, but a serious misdemeanor for an airline pilot.

In 1927 he was sent to Morocco to take charge of the refueling station at Juby. It has been said this appointment was made because he was diplomatic and would know how to deal with the Moroccan chiefs and get on the good side of the Spaniards in the Río de Oro region. Indeed, he revealed great diplomatic ability at Juby. But how could it be known in advance that he would? Clearly, one reason for his appointment to Juby was that the directors at Toulouse had begun to fear that the absent-minded and foolhardy pilot might one day be responsible for a catastrophe.

In 1932, when the Aéropostale line had gone into liquidation, Saint-Exupéry applied to Latécoère for employment as a test pilot. He would have loved to fly a plane that had never been flown before and feel it come to life in his hands. Latécoère employed him, but not, strictly speaking, as a test pilot. Instead, he was entrusted with trying out model planes with a view to perfecting them. André Dubourdieu has recounted in *Forces Aériennes Françaises* two misadventures of Saint-Ex that he witnessed at this time. One day, Saint-Ex was to try out a prototype plane which already, in chocks on the ground, did not promise much, for the engine on the left side was knocking. He took off. In the air the knocking increased and the engine began to backfire and smoke. After banking, the plane circled down to the field, where, just before landing, the terrified spectators saw a large piece of metal drop off the fuselage and fall, spinning, to earth. It was only the door of the plane, torn off by the wind: Saint-Ex had simply forgotten to lock it. On another occasion he took up a Laté 28 (the prototype of planes that were to be sold to Venezuela), climbed to almost 10,000 feet, and brought it back to the ground. The engineer came forward to ask if everything was quite all right.

"No, not at all!" Saint-Ex exclaimed. "This machine flies with one wing low. It's impossible to hold her in course."

"Which wing does she drop?"

Saint-Ex could not recall, "although he made a big effort," writes Dubourdieu, "turning in all directions, trying to put himself in line with his flight, looking toward the road, toward the setting sun, but he simply could not remember to which side the plane leaned heavily. So he had to take it up again and repeat the test!"

Absent-mindedness brought him close to drowning at about this same time, when he was trying out a hydroplane at Saint-Raphaël. He himself has told the story, or rather, has described his sensations when near drowning. But he did not mention the cause of the accident, which could have been avoided. The Laté seaplane was being tested over the bay, where the water was rather choppy, an added reason for exercising care in touching down. Instead of alighting on the heels of the floaters, Saint-Ex dived steeply as if bringing a plane down to earth. The brutal contact with the waves caused the machine to overturn and Saint-Ex was trapped in the fuselage. And, incidentally, the then director of Air France,

M. Verdurand, refused to entrust the piloting of a hydroplane to him, but kept him on as auxiliary pilot.

To offset these mishaps, we have Pierre Gaudillière's account of how Saint-Ex managed, two years later, in Indochina, despite engine trouble to bring his hydroplane neatly down upon the waters of the Mekong.

His skill as a pilot was indisputable. Many times in the desert, while flying to the rescue of comrades in distress, he managed take-offs and landings in very perilous conditions. The fact remains that his absent-mindedness, a byword among his amused friends, was a serious defect in a pilot. Surprisingly, he was responsible for relatively few serious accidents. Aside from the one at Saint-Raphaël, we know of only one other, a crash that occurred in Guatemala in February 1938, for which he could be absolutely blamed.

The sky routes flown by the pioneers were extremely arduous. Danger beset them all along the line but their zest for flying was unwavering, though they knew fear. Saint-Exupéry described his fear in a letter to Renée de Saussine, included in her collection, *Lettres de Jeunesse*. He wrote the letter at Casablanca one night before taking off at dawn for Dakar, and it is filled with his thoughts on a night of insomnia. He was thinking of what might happen were his plane to crash: "I don't want to have my face disfigured tomorrow." He recalled a comrade whose hands were burned in a plane accident: "I don't want to have my hands burnt. . . . They know how to write, how to tie my shoelaces, how to improvise on the piano. . . . And sometimes they clasp and hold a face. A face. Think of that!" He confessed that he was as nervous as a rabbit over what might happen to a damaged plane beset by hostile tribes of Moors: "I don't want to be massacred by Moorish tribesmen. . . . Massacred by the Moors. I don't like this phrase that monotonously repeats itself through the night."

On one of his first flights for the Line, Saint-Exupéry's engine stalled and the plane, in the crash landing, was badly broken up. On the return journey his plane was so buffeted by the wind that it was "dancing for nine hours," but he landed at Toulouse with a feeling of triumph; he had now, he felt, entered into the community of his comrades, a community like a monastery in its disregard for material comforts, for all thoughts of money and gain, ambitions to have a fine apartment, a place to entertain friends, relative security. He who had come to the Line to have "a solid position in life" was certainly far from that aim. But his combat with the elements united him with his comrades and, like them, he could hear M. Daurat say, "You certainly took a long time to come from Barcelona" without protesting. He was now a pilot of the Line. What nobility in that title! He had won his spurs, had won his new and shortened name. To his comrades he was merely "Saint-Ex."

In *Wind, Sand and Stars* he says that "in the mold of this new profession a new breed of men has been cast" and throughout this book he ponders man's need to find a vocation that will set him free. He recognizes that he was fortunate in finding the vocation that would help him come alive and that many men never have the luck he had in this respect.

This book was written ten years after he had joined the Latécoère airline. By then, he had experienced ten years of perilous flights in the sky over Spain, the rude life of the desert post at Juby, the easier life as director of Aeroposta-Argentina in South America, the tortures of thirst in the Libyan desert, the physical suffering after his crash in Guatemala, and had survived many other adventures and tests. He had met and known intimately those men of the Line who, like Mermoz and Guillaumet, had taken up flying in obedience to "a sovereign vocation." But, paradoxically, flying was not for him a sovereign vocation; it was instead a means to an end, which was the freeing of his mind and spirit. His vocation was living. "The airplane is a means of getting away from towns and their bookkeeping and coming to grips with reality," he says at one point, and at another, "It is man and not flying that concerns me most." The plane, as he saw it, was "a tool" which enabled him to carve out his life. It brought him "deliverance."

That deliverance, begun in Toulouse, would continue over the years and would be finally achieved in the defense and liberation of his native land. To him the liberation of France was a part of the struggle for the liberation of man—still a distant but certain event of the future. He found in this new form of humanism of which he was to be the spokesman a feeling of *being,* and in his case it was fostered by his experience as a flyer.

In *Wind, Sand and Stars* he wrote: "Of what can we be certain except this—that we are fertilized by mysterious circumstances? Where is man's truth to be found?" The fertilizing conditions in his life were found in his profession as air pilot, in confronting danger, but still more in contact with his comrades of the air. At the end of a flight, with what jubilation did he see and mingle with them again! He was no longer a spectator, an outsider, but was a member of a group, submitting to the same rigorous discipline, aspiring to carry out an identical aim. As he puts it, he had discovered that "what constitutes the dignity of a craft is that it creates a fellowship" and that "there is no hope of joy except in human relations."

4

"What makes the desert beautiful," said the little prince, "is that somewhere it hides a well."

—The Little Prince

In May 1925 Émile Lécrivain had flown the first mail plane from Casablanca to Dakar, the westernmost port of French West Africa; the next leap in the extension of the Latécoère airline would be in the direction of South America. The audacious dream was slowly becoming reality. From Toulouse, Didier Daurat was launching his crews farther and farther into the sky; yesterday it was the sky of Spain with its fearful winds, apocalyptic storms, and treacherous mountain peaks cloaked in clouds. Now, it was the sky over the Sahara: ten thousand feet above an arid, desolate, inhospitable land.

It must be kept in mind that at this period the pilot had to guide himself by compass and by eye. Flying south to Dakar, he followed the coast, a white fringe of surf sometimes hidden by fog. Then, if he lost that Ariadne's thread, he had to fly blind and sometimes, as he dropped to a lower altitude to find his way, he might perceive with anguish that he had veered out over the ocean just as he was running out of fuel. The very simple instrument panel had a fuel gauge, where the needle inexorably ticked off the figures which might mark the time that still separated him from eternity. Then there would be one more plane never heard from again—as in the case of Lécrivain and Decaud.

The planes were similar to those which, seven years earlier, had flown the first mail to Spain and Morocco. They flew no faster, and their breakdowns were even more frequent on account of the torrid heat and the sandy terrain. The pilots who at this period were still flying without radio were accompanied by a Moorish interpreter, and they could expect no aid when forced to make an emergency landing in the desert. Then, the propeller motionless in the form of a cross, there was the great silence, the immense solitude, an implacable sun, and if they were not quickly found and rescued it meant death from sunstroke or tormenting thirst. Sometimes too the man who loomed up from the sands and came toward them was not a savior but an enemy. The blue-veiled Moorish tribesman, if he spared the pilot's life, did so thanks to the interpreter's intercession and in the hope of obtaining a substantial ransom. After several fatal desert landings, Didier Daurat had arranged to have the mail plane convoyed by another plane, which could, in an emergency, offer some aid. If repairs could not be made quickly, the two pilots and the interpreter flew out in the unharmed plane to the nearest post, from which a rescue plane with a mechanic and spare parts and a second pilot would be sent to repair or salvage the stalled plane.

Saint-Exupéry's first experience of the desert, in 1926, came during a forced landing in a wild stretch of it south of Port-Étienne, on a flight from Agadir to Dakar. Riguelle, an older pilot of the Line, was flying the mail plane, with Saint-Ex as passenger, and Guillaumet was piloting the convoy, at times flying so close that they were able occasionally to wave at each other. But for the most part Saint-Ex was contemplating "the vast sandy void" below. There was nothing in this landscape to remind him of familiar scenes—the rolling plains of France with the jigsaw puzzle of cultivated fields, the dark tapestry of forests, the silvery veins of rivers and long ribbons of roads, and the snow-capped mountains. Here there was nothing but "a sizzling surface of sand," the bare, worn surface of the planet. This was a part of the desert where he would soon be sent to live; it was fraught with danger and mystery, yet he tells us that he succumbed to it at first sight. He was thrilled. "But the heat was so intense that despite my excitement I dozed off," he writes in *Wind, Sand and Stars*. Suddenly he was aroused by a crash like broken crockery. The connecting rod had broken. Riguelle had no time to choose a landing place, but crashed down against a sand dune, losing both wheels, then a wing against another dune, and jerked to a halt against a third. The two men were unhurt.

Guillaumet had seen the crash and brought his plane down on a smooth stretch of sand not far away. He came forward and, after ascertaining the amount of damage, asked them to help him transfer the mail bags to his plane. Then he turned toward Saint-Ex.

"You will wait for us here," he said, "while Riguelle and I hop to the next outpost for help."

Before they went off, leaving him beside the wrecked plane, Riguelle gave him his gun and cartridge clips, telling him to shoot at anything he saw. Guillaumet then turned back, "as if driven by his conscience," and handed Saint-Ex some extra cartridge clips, saying, "You'll want these, too."

When the two returned a few hours later, Guillaumet saw that Saint-Ex was tensely lying in wait for possible enemies and burst into a great laugh. What was the joke? The plane had fortunately crashed in a part of the desert where the tribes had long since been subdued; they had left Saint-Ex quite safe; putting the gun in his hand was merely meant to give him a harmless fright.

That night they spent at the fort of Nouatchott, "an outpost as isolated as an island in the Pacific," where the old colonial army sergeant wept with joy at the sight of the three flyers—he saw Frenchmen only twice a year, when the Camel Corps brought supplies to him and his squad of fifteen Senegalese troops. Saint-Exupéry was never to forget that first night in the desert, which they spent for the most part on the flat roof of the little stockade, "talking about the stars." There was nothing else in sight, nothing but the starry sky and the dark waste of sand.

I cannot call to mind the desert without a feeling of some sadness, for I remember my own first night spent at the post where I was to be stationed for a year. Despite my weariness, sleep would not come, and I lay on the ground looking at the myriad stars: they were the only lights visible. The comrade who had accompanied me from France and who would be with me for the entire year, had lain down nearby. Suddenly he raised himself slightly and touched my arm.

"It's hard to believe, isn't it?" he said.

"What?"

"Where we are." Then, with a sigh: "I'll never be able to stick it, out here."

And he did not, nor did he ever see his native land again. He died of sheer loneliness and boredom—one can die of such things as one can die for love.

That young fellow was a mechanic with a working-class background; he had never known what comfort was. It was not discomfort he feared that night nor the hardships that lay ahead. What troubled him and almost filled him with despair was the infinite solitude of the desert, the infinite silence of that starry sky. He had left the world, and he could not endure the thought of living far from home in this solitude. Instead of searching within himself for something to sustain him, he looked for something outside, and found only a great emptiness.

There is something instinctive and sensual about people's response to the desert: it is either hated utterly—when it is, indeed, fearful—or passionately loved. Saint-Exupéry not only succumbed at first sight but exulted in the solitude, feeling "a sort of appeasement" and giving himself up to a world of dreams. This was fortunate for him, since he was destined to be transferred out of Europe to the Dakar–Juby division, and would live there almost three years. And it was fortunate for the world, as the desert inspired him to write some of his finest prose.

Someone has said that Saint-Exupéry "chose" the desert. No doubt phrases he used in *Wind, Sand and Stars* gave rise to this notion. The desert had for him a mystique that could only be compared with the mystique of the Line—or of the monastic life. Describing an all-night vigil of a little group of men beside a wrecked plane in a particularly desolate stretch of the Sahara, he writes: "...we were infinitely poor. Wind, sand and stars. The austerity of Trappists . . . a handful of men who possessed nothing in the world but their memories were sharing invisible riches." He fell under its spell but he did not choose the desert. It was his destiny, surely, to live there, for we can no more imagine him apart from the desert than we can think of him apart from the airplane. Both favored his meditations and satisfied a strange combination of needs, providing him with long hours of solitude while still offering adventure and contact with the lives of men. Both the desert and the airplane brought him not only "the warmth of human relations" but also the condition of withdrawal which enabled him "to judge man in cosmic terms." And of course, his last book, *The Wisdom of the Sands,* could only have been written by one upon whom the desert had made a profound and lasting impression.

In October 1927, a year after he joined the Latécoère airline, Saint-Exupéry was sent to North Africa to take charge of the company's refueling station at Cape Juby. Juby was one of ten airfields maintained on the Casablanca–Dakar route, the second to the south after Agadir, and situated almost at the halfway point, the others to the southward being Villa Cisneros, Port-Étienne, and Saint-Louis-du-Senegal. Juby was in the Spanish zone on the Río de Oro which follows the coastline, about eight hundred miles of desert stretching between the Draa *wadi* and Cape Blanc. Flying over this route was extremely dangerous because of the hostile Moorish tribes who attacked grounded crews, pillaged mail-bags, destroyed aircraft, held captive aviators—sometimes for exorbitant ransoms, sometimes to torture and kill them. These tribes launched their raids (*razzias*) in southern Morocco and Mauritania, territories protected by the French Saharan Camel Corps, taking refuge in the Río de Oro, where Spain had no troops other than a few who kept closely within two stockades on the coast, one at Juby, more than three hundred miles south of Agadir, the other at Villa Cisneros, roughly four hundred miles still farther to the south.

Close against the little Spanish stockade at Juby stood the long wooden hut—one of the prefabricated huts of World War I—which served as the airline's office, supply depot, and lodgings for the pilot in charge and his three mechanics whose jobs were to take care of supplies and to fly out rescue planes. A few hundred yards from the hut stood the canvas hangar which permanently housed four relay planes. These fragile edifices and the airstrip were surrounded by barbed wire, and one strayed three hundred yards beyond that barrier only at the risk of losing one's life. The Spanish garrison, comprised of disciplinary troops and commanded by five or six officers, lived within their fort without ever leaving it.

Between the hostile desert and the sea Cape Juby stands, a place of desolation. For nine months of the year the powerful trade winds blow, adding their long plaint to the roar of the ocean. Then the nocturnal mists stretch their damp veil, seeping into every crevice and crack, soaking the canvas hangar. At dawn the mists rise, imprisoning the red disc of the sun just above the horizon, lingering a while, then raveling out in long thin stratus clouds which are soon absorbed by the bright sky. In the summer months the trade winds cease to blow, the fogs disappear, and all day long the sun's burning rays beat down upon the arid earth. Occasionally a wind rises over the desert. Wrathful and ruthless, it swells, rushing along the sands with a sinister whistling sound, tearing up whorls of fiery dust. Juby *is* the desert. Whole years pass at Juby without a drop of water falling from the sky.

It was here that Saint-Ex came to live, replacing the pilot Jaladieu who was fated to crash and kill himself a few months later in the region of Almeria, Spain. Jaladieu had remained only a few months at Cape Juby. Before him, André Dubourdieu had been in charge of the post. A native of Bordeaux and brought up in that world-renowned wine region, Dubourdieu was a total abstainer. Intelligent and calm, he was without a doubt one of the greatest pilots of the between-wars period. His presence appeared to be more useful on the Line than at Juby, hence his transfer out.

Why was Saint-Ex sent to this post? As I have said, it was feared that he might one day be responsible for a catastrophe, since he had earned the reputation of being an absent-minded and unpredictable, though daring and skillful pilot. There was also another reason. Our installations at Cape Juby and at Villa Cisneros were located in a territory governed by Spain, with resulting difficulties. The Spaniards, voluntary prisoners of their stockades, were totally uninterested in what happened to the Latécoère airmen in the Río de Oro region. They were not at all eager to be drawn into conflict with the Moorish tribes. On the contrary, their attitude in regard to these tribes who had been responsible for numerous *razzias* in Mauritania, and even of massacres of French aviators, went beyond the barely admitted standards of neutrality. The Spaniards of Cape Juby had actually entertained the bandit Ould Hadj'Rab the day after he had assassinated two of our pilots, Gourp and Erable.

The Spaniards dreaded conflict with the Moors because they felt they were incapable of policing the Río de Oro region, which was too vast in proportion to their strength. Then, observing our successes in Morocco as well as in Mauritania and Senegal, they feared lest we take advantage of our airfields to evict them sooner or later from the region. This dread was groundless. Juby and Villa Cisneros interested us only as airline installations, since without landing strips our aircraft could not fly over this immense territory which extended in the line of flight for more than six hundred miles.

Beppo de Massimi, in his own account, *Vent Debout*, has told of his difficulties in negotiating with the Spanish government for the airfields we had in Spain and in the Río de Oro region, particularly at Juby. The grant was finally obtained; but every time our crews were involved in an incident with native tribes, there was danger that the authorization might be withdrawn. Besides, the Spanish government in Madrid was being courted and cajoled by Germans who hoped to have their own airlines link Europe with South America.

For these reasons, it was essential that the Juby airfield be in charge of a man who was not only an experienced pilot but who was also capable of avoiding any friction with the Spaniards. Saint-

Exupéry was chosen, it would seem, because he filled both requirements.

When the grant for the airfield at Cape Juby was first obtained by Beppo de Massimi, the Spanish Governor, Colonel Bens, was a charming and prudent man with a fondness for France. But after twenty-two years at Juby, he had been replaced by a quite different type of man, Col. de la Peña, an aristocrat and autocrat who, if not a personal enemy of France, was at least entirely devoted to his own government, which was hostile to the French airline projects. At Toulouse, therefore, they had the bright idea of sending down a titled aristocrat to impress and cope with the haughty Spaniard. Count Antoine de Saint-Exupéry possessed, besides his title, a cultivated and penetrating mind, and the appointment proved to be doubly successful: first, for the Latécoère airline, which is to say for France; then, for Saint-Exupéry himself.

The new commander of the Juby airfield did not arrive without the proper introductions; in fact, they were dazzling and he had soon captured the good will of the officers at the Spanish fort, with whom he frequently played chess and had long talks. This gave him the opportunity to study their behavior and attitude toward the French as well as the Moors—the two attitudes being closely related.

Saint-Exupéry's "Report to Aéropostale on the Río de Oro" has been published several times, either in full or in part. In a few pages he describes the territory, its population, its organization and resources. He shows how the Moors, so dangerous for our crews when in distress, were supplied with arms, and explains our means of action in regard to these primitives whom the Spaniards feared perhaps more than they ruled, since they allowed them to live by rapine, *razzias*, and crimes without exerting the least repression.

Our pilots had been the first to suffer from the Moors' instinct for pillage and their age-old hatred of Christians. In December 1925, the young and daring Marcel Reine, with his interpreter, the devoted Elhomée Ben Admed, made a crash landing between Agadir and Cape Juby. He was taken captive by the hostile tribes and released after six hours of negotiations, on payment of a ransom. A few months later, in May 1926, it was the turn of Mermoz to be forced down on his fourth flight with the mail plane. After a long march in the desert, Mermoz fell asleep, and when he woke up it was not his interpreter Ataf he found at his side, but some blue-veiled warriors. He was liberated after three days of captivity on payment of a ransom of 1200 pesetas (about 50,000 francs).

Twice again in the year of Saint-Exupéry's arrival at Juby, 1927, Reine had to make crash landings and was again taken captive, the second time with his co-pilot, Serre. Reine lived to tell the story (*Chez les Fils du Désert*) with morale unscathed, still able to jest about it in the best Parisian manner. But Serre was tortured and slain. Still other aviators were to experience the rigors of captivity. Stripped of their clothing, maltreated, surviving only if the intervention of a more humane or more calculating Moor persuaded the others that the captive could be turned into money. However, there had been a tragic catastrophe in the autumn of 1926, when the two airmen Gourp and Erable and their Spanish mechanic Pintado were savagely assassinated following engine trouble which forced their plane, a Bréguet, to crash-land only 125 miles south of Juby.[8]

More than ever it seemed vital to rescue airmen brought down in the desert and to protect the mailbags and planes. Carrying out this important job at Juby consumed most of Saint-Exupéry's time and energy; he put into it all he had of pluck and intelligence. A report he made to Toulouse on Riguelle's accident in August 1928, not far from Juby, best shows the talents he employed. The full report reads:

> *Monsieur Riguelle having crash-landed July 18, as the result of a broken connecting-rod, thirty kilometers to the south of Juby, his co-pilot, Monsieur Dumesnil, came to report the accident.*
>
> *Since the region is totally unsafe—a Spanish captain of aviation was captured by hostile tribes a few months ago,*

held captive for sixteen days at a distance of only twelve kilometers from Juby—I immediately organized and equipped a rescue caravan, while a plane was made ready for me.

After the return of Dumesnil and Riguelle, whom I passed in the air, these Moors I had employed in my caravan guaranteed to guard the 232 at a cost of 187 pesetas a fortnight and sustenance for camels and horses.

In order to repair this aircraft I ran into great difficulties of every kind. This type of repair being unprecedented, none of my Moors wanted to guarantee our security or to assume the responsibility of transporting an engine and other material across thirty-five kilometers of a zone that is often impassable.

At last I managed to organize, in two days, the following caravan: 6 armed Moors on horseback; 9 workmen and cameleers on foot (5 weapons); 3 horses for the mechanic, Marchal, and me; 2 donkeys for transporting food and water; 1 camel for transporting the material; 2 camels pulling a four-wheeled cart contrived with wheels of aircraft and loaded with the engine, the pulley tackle, and the jack. This cart negotiated a series of most difficult dunes—it is the first time, by the way, that the camel has been used as a draught animal, at least in these parts.

The day of our departure we reached the stalled plane and found a discouraging situation. It had been half taken apart by the Moors. The connecting-rod had sliced the struts.

It was impossible to drag it over such a terrain to a flat stretch sufficiently long for a take-off [a 2-kilometer strip].

By camel I sent orders to Laubergue to dismount the wing assembly of the 232, whose engine we were using, and began immediately in front of the plane to construct a landing strip eight meters wide and ninety meters long, with a revetment at the end. This consumed two whole days.

The night was interspersed with rifle-shots, for the proximity of a razzia of Aït Toussa rendered the Moors highly nervous. Towards midnight messengers came up at a gallop to notify us that the razzia was racing towards us, and there was panic. We were taken back towards Juby without being given time to carry anything with us (the Aït Toussa have recently killed 12 men of the Izarguin tribe). But then, after fifteen kilometers of march, when I learned that this whole retreat was being carried out by order of the Governor (as we had suspected), we refused to advance farther, feeling that with eleven rifles we could hold out in case of a razzia.

Having managed to damage the Moors' self-esteem, we returned towards the wrecked plane.

Towards nine in the morning, two Spanish planes dropped down a weighted message, ordering us to return to base immediately, because of the presence in the neighborhood of 'an enemy party.'

There was a skirmish towards noon, and shots were exchanged with an unknown group of Moors. We succeeded in maintaining order and aroused our laborers who had flung themselves face downward at the sound of the whizzing bullets.

At six in the evening, the engine being at last put in order and the runway completed, I took off in the plane, flying back to Juby with the mechanic, Marchal.

The expenses were rather high; but consider that in addition to salvaging the plane we have made quite a favorable impression on the Moors. To salvage the engine of the Spanish captain who had crashed on the beach halfway from our plane, the Governor had had a warship sent down. Marchal, the mechanic, and I voluntarily spent *two days and two nights at double the distance from our base.*

I am giving you the expense account in a lump sum, because (1) in the transaction no bills or receipts were exchanged; and (2) the accounts are extremely confused, having given rise to interminable arguments and complications.

Since this expedition was without precedent, I cannot judge whether or not its cost is exaggeratedly high.

—Antoine de Saint-Exupéry
Cape Juby, August 1, 1928

Indeed, the expedition was without precedent, and it is hard for anyone not acquainted with the desert and marauding tribes to conceive of the difficult conditions under which this repair work was carried out. The Moors whom Saint-Ex had armed were by no means inclined to fight other Moors, well knowing that if they managed to come off victors they would not fail to be massacred later on for being tools of the French. Besides, there is a phrase in the report that needs to be explained: his laconic "Having managed to damage the Moors' self-esteem." Let us try to visualize what happened.

While the little troop of six warriors on horseback, nine laborers on foot, three camels, two donkeys, followed by Saint-Ex and Marchal on horseback, were on their way toward the grounded plane, a messenger from Colonel de la Peña had come up, bearing the governor's orders to return to the fort because of a *razzia* in the vicinity. The Moors, to whom the messenger had confided the contents of the letter, immediately started to turn back.

"Where are you going?" exclaimed Saint-Ex angrily. And when the Moors continued marching in the opposite direction without replying, he ironically commented on their courage. "Congratulations!" he sneered. "You turn back the minute you hear of a *razzia!*" And he added, contemptuously, "I'd have done better to ask for an escort of women!"

Whereupon, the Arab called Zin, in command of the warriors,

replied. "You desired it. We will go as far as the plane, as was agreed. And then, once there. . . ."

Once there, the warriors wanted to leave.

"Very well," said Saint-Ex. "I employed you to protect us. If you go away, you shall not be paid." [9]

It was the only valid argument. The warriors stayed.

In his report Saint-Ex mentions shots exchanged with an unknown group. They were the Aït Toussa tribesmen firing at the workers. "We succeeded in maintaining order," he says, and mentions that the workers had thrown themselves face downward. The implication is that he remained upright, coolly presenting his body as a target for the dissidents' fire. This indicates not only bravado and courage, but also great self-mastery. He must have calculated the effect of such self-control, for he knew how much the Moors admire a man of courage. That gesture alone would give the men confidence and spur them to work in spite of danger; more important still, the tale would be spread among the tribes and would increase his prestige with the Moorish chieftains. Indeed, the officer in charge of the Juby airfield was soon entertaining those chieftains in his barrack hut and was in turn being entertained by them in their tents. This ability of Saint-Exupéry to maintain social contacts with the dissident sheiks and kaids marked not only a personal success but without a doubt contributed to increasing French prestige.

Saint-Exupéry did not confine his social contacts to the chieftains, those all-powerful rulers of the desert who arrogate to themselves every right, even the power of life and death over their subjects, but mingled and talked with the merchants and with even the most pitiful and humble of the native population. Congregated round the door of the barracks almost any day were beggars and children. The desert beggars are like no others; they are veritable derelicts, starving, deformed, consumed with dreadful diseases, with nothing to look forward to but death to release them from their miseries. The children, half-naked, their ribs showing through the skin, are tormented by the flies that hover round them, clinging to their eyelids and lips, drinking the human moisture there. To these unfortunates Saint-Ex gave food and was glad to see their instinctive mistrust disappear and be replaced by smiles and gratitude. For the first time in his life, no doubt, he actually touched human misery.

After the salvage of Riguelle's plane, he wrote to his cousin Yvonne de Lestrange, giving her an account of the dangerous adventure.[10] "I heard bullets whizzing over my head for the first time," he told her. "So now I know how I behave under such conditions; much more calmly than the Moors. But I also came to understand something which had always puzzled me—why Plato [Aristotle?] places courage in the last degree of virtues. It's a concoction of feelings that are not so very admirable. A touch of anger, a spice of vanity, a lot of obstinacy and a tawdry 'sporting' thrill. . . . I shall never again admire a merely brave man."

But his esteem of his comrades of the Line, brave men all, was unbounded and he paid warm tribute to them in his writings. Saint-Ex, who had never made friends easily, now found that he had a lot of friends. He had discovered that "no man can draw a free breath who does not share with other men a common and disinterested ideal," and again in *Wind, Sand and Stars,* "Every pilot who has flown to the rescue of a comrade in distress knows that all joys are vain in comparison with this one."

Guillaumet, Dubourdieu, Lécrivain, Riguelle, Reine, Joly, and others of the same stamp, were the men Saint-Ex sometimes put up for the night at Juby or flew to rescue from the deadly sands or the ruthless Moors. Aside from these occasional meetings with other pilots of the Line, there was the daily life which brought Saint-Ex in close contact with the mechanics stationed at Juby: Marchal, Abgrall, and Toto—to give the third the nickname by which he was always called. In the daily routine they shared the facilities of the barracks.

Toto had worked at Montaudran and was one of the first men employed. During the war he had been a mechanic with an air squadron at the front and had developed a passion for planes and engines. The Armistice suddenly separated him from his beloved magnetos, carburetors, spark plugs, grease guns, all those separate pieces that made the engines throb like hearts. He felt forsaken. And so, when he heard about the airstrip near Toulouse from which planes carrying mailbags rather than bombs were making regular flights to Spain and Morocco, he hurried to Montaudran. Didier Daurat had known him during the war, and immediately hired him.

Toto was a mechanic of incomparable quality, but during the war he had acquired a bad habit. He tippled to such an extent—as much as a bottle of Pernod a day, enough to kill any other man—that Daurat finally got rid of him. Not knowing what to do with himself, wandering desolately for a time, Toto returned to the airstrip and gazed sadly at the planes. Daurat found him one day in the hangar at work with hammer and nails on a crate.

"What are you doing here?" asked M. Daurat.

"I got myself hired by the transport line that handles the Latécoère planes," Toto replied, adding, in a low voice, that he had now "reformed."

Evidently Daurat was touched at seeing this exceptional mechanic, so infatuated with his craft that he had taken an ordinary day-laborer's job to be near the machines he loved, for Toto was hired again. The Line was establishing the airstrips in French West Africa, and Toto was sent to Cape Juby, where, alas, he took to drinking again.

Though Saint-Ex had not known Toto at Montaudran, he had heard about him, and at once recognized the stout little red-nosed fellow who was there to welcome him to Juby—accompanied by a long-tailed monkey—when he first arrived. They would live under the same roof together in the barrack-hut, sharing the same lot, the same hardships of desert life.

The letters Saint-Ex wrote at Juby, particularly during his first months there, give us a detailed and vivid picture of the desert and of the effect this new existence had upon him. "Dearest Mother, you can't imagine what a monkish life I lead," he begins in one of his first letters, which breathes an almost exultant contentment. "A fort on the seashore, our barracks up against it, and then nothing but sand for hundreds of miles. . . ."

And we see again, with him, the desert blazing beneath a sky the blue of hot steel, the air vibrating above the sands, making the horizon waver, dazzling the eyes. As the sun rises higher, a great calm settles heavily upon Juby; men and beasts become immobilized, as though the heat had destroyed all life. The whole world waits for evening to come, taking shelter in the deep shadows, waiting breathlessly for the coolness of night and the sea breeze that will soothe bodies now streaming with sweat.

Night comes at last. The mechanics, Marchal and Abgrall, are already asleep in their bunks. Toto, elbow on table, stares vaguely ahead of him as he gradually empties his bottle of Pernod. Saint-Ex sits down on his bed and begins his letter. On an upturned crate beside him a tame chameleon stares disdainfully at Toto's leering monkey. Only the lapping of the ocean waves against the fortress walls and the regular call of the sentinels in the night disturb the indefinable silence of the desert. From time to time Saint-Ex raises his head to survey Toto or the chameleon or the furnishings of this strange dwelling, itemizing for his mother the contents of his room, which is "like a cell in a monastery," he says. The bed is a plank with a thin mattress on it. A washbasin and a jug of water are on a small table. Besides these necessities there are the usual odds and ends, the typewriter and the Cape Juby documents. "I don't need anything," he adds, and concludes this letter with, "Little mother, you have a very happy son, who has set his feet on the right path. . . ."

We can hardly recognize, in this happy ascetic, the young master of Saint-Maurice, the student at the aristocratic school in Fribourg, the Air Force soldier who had a room in town "in the most fashionable street of Strasbourg." It is hard to believe that this is the same young man who, only a few years before, filled his letters with complaints and demands for money or exulted over having lunch with the Duchesse de Vendôme, "the sister of the King of the Belgians." But the new Saint-Exupéry actually requests his mother not to use his title on the envelopes of her letters.

When the mail plane stopped off at Juby on its way to Dakar, the barracks accommodated two more men. They brought the letters which the isolated men read in silence, sitting on their bunks. Then there was talk, great talk which sometimes lasted far into the night. "It needs the accident of journeyings to bring together here or there the dispersed members of this great professional family," Saint-Exupéry wrote in *Wind, Sand and Stars*. When the two men left Juby at dawn, before the first rays of sunlight cast a rosy glow over the sands, he was there to see them off.

It was good to renew the bonds that united their community, which existed no matter what distance separated them, no matter where they might be on the line from Toulouse to Dakar. While they talked together at Cape Juby, others were gathered round a table at Pepita's in Alicante and others were at Casablanca, at Port-Étienne, at Dakar, and would soon be on the very shores of the Pacific. And they recalled their first meetings at the *Grand Balcon* in Toulouse, where rain sometimes drummed for long hours on the windows. But all these men scattered along three thousand miles of plains, mountains, and desert were less separated than, say, the people sitting at adjacent tables, drinking and talking in a Boulevard Saint-Germain café.

The new form of humanism which Saint-Ex expounded is that of action which, arising from contact with the comrades of the Line, was to grow and amplify and find its full intensity in the struggle for the defense of his country during World War II. Or it might be termed the militant passion which Descartes called generosity.

A great deal has been said of Saint-Exupéry's generosity, and some commentators have regarded it as an innate need to give, to share. It was the hard life he led as a pilot, sharing his existence with all kinds of men in the hangar at Montaudran and at the pension in Toulouse; especially it was the still ruder life at Juby which brought about in him a veritable conversion to life in common with other men.

While at Juby, Saint-Ex became interested in an old slave of the Moors, called Bark, the name bestowed upon all the slaves. When he had been a free man, he was Mohammed ben Lhaoussin, a drover at Marrakech, where his wife and three children still lived. One day, in his former life, he was driving his flocks of sheep to higher pastures, "armed with an olive-wood sceptre," when he was stopped by some Arabs and tricked into following them back to the south. There they sold him into slavery. Saint-Exupéry often saw this old Bark when he went to a certain Moorish chieftain's tent to drink tea. Bark was now getting on in years and would suffer the fate of aged slaves: he would be turned loose to die of starvation when he could no longer work. In some very moving pages of *Wind, Sand and Stars* we are told Bark's story and how Saint-Exupéry eventually procured the slave's freedom.

One night as Bark was serving him tea in the Moorish tent, he implored Saint-Ex, in a low voice, "Hide me in the Marrakech plane!"

Every time Saint-Ex went to that tent, Bark repeated his prayer. But where could a pilot find the sum of money necessary to buy Bark's freedom? For of course, there was no question of smuggling him out.

"We'll see what we can do," was Saint-Ex's usual reply. And he talked about it to friends at home, who made contributions, and to the mechanics, who gave what they could. Adding his own contribution to this, and after much dickering with the masters of Bark, they bought his freedom and had enough money left over to give him an additional thousand francs so that he would not be "flung into the world without a copper." Then they put him on the plane bound for Marrakech.

"We stood about our fifty-year-old, new-born babe, worried a little at having launched him forth on the stream of life," Saint-Ex ends this story whimsically. They called out to him, "Good-by, Bark!" But the freed slave answered proudly: "No. I am Mohammed ben Lhaoussin."

Aside from the weekly arrivals and departures of the mail planes, the solitude of Juby was broken twice a month by the arrival of the supply boat from the Canary Islands, bringing the provisions of food, oil, gasoline, and drinking water. The boat anchored at some distance from the shore, and it was necessary to go out for the supplies in a small launch, negotiating that famous sandbar which makes the approach to the western coast of Africa so difficult. The natives were very skilled in this somewhat acrobatic navigation, but occasionally one of the boats would overturn, when Saint-Ex would have to lend a hand. It was a game, and a welcome distraction.

Indeed, the day the supply boat came was a day of celebration, not only because of the noise and movement it occasioned, but because the supplies usually arrived in the nick of time, when gasoline and water were running low.

With some embroidering of the facts, Saint-Exupéry described one of these incidents, in a letter to his mother:

> *This morning I opened my window and found the horizon had adorned itself with a pretty white sail. . . . It livened the whole desert landscape, making me think of the white linens of houses, the white linens of the most intimate room. . . . And my sail tilted this way and that, gently, like a starched Breton bonnet. But this moment of calm sweetness was brief. . . .*"

There is poetic license in this description since in reality the sailboat was a small white steamer. But, all the same, he conveys in these lines his momentary elation and nostalgia. For surely that reference to white linens is a recollection of the linen room at Saint-Maurice where Mademoiselle burnt her eyes out mending, late into the night. The rude life of the desert, gladly accepted, would have had less worth had it not demanded renunciation.

In several of his letters from Juby, Saint-Ex wrote nostalgically. At Christmas, for example: "Christmas tonight. But it makes no mark in this sand." Or, more frankly: "Sometimes I dream of an existence where there is a tablecloth, fruit, strolls beneath the linden trees, with a woman, perhaps, at my side. . . ." And, with sadness: "I dream of Saint-Maurice with melancholy, and of all the sweetness that is France."

At other times he writes with whimsical irony, particularly to his sister Gabrielle and her husband: "Our life here is jolly. We live outside a Spanish fort on the beach and can go without fear down to the sea—a distance of less than twenty yards. . . . But if we go farther than that, we risk getting shot at. If we go farther than fifty yards, we risk being sent to rejoin our forefathers or being taken captive—it depends on the time of year. In Spring, if one happens to be attractive, one has the chance of being taken and kept as some chieftain's 'favorite,' which is better than being dead. But there's always the risk of becoming the chieftain's head eunuch instead!" Such letters were written to amuse both himself and his readers at home.

The sheets of paper that he covered with his fine handwriting were not only letters addressed to family and friends. In 1926 Adrienne Monnier had already published in the *Navire d'Argent* some pages of a novel Saint-Exupéry had begun but never finished. "I'm accumulating and storing up for the future," he had written to his mother several years before he came to Juby, when he was still leading a rather banal life. Since then his career as pilot and as director of a desert outpost had provided him with a new and virgin field of observation.

He was storing up for the future his experiences as an aviator, and with this supply in hand, what a wealth of beautiful pages he has given us. Saint-Ex flunked his Naval School exams, but his destiny lay elsewhere, in that element which, as the poet Léon-Paul Fargue has said, "has constituted the most fearful, the most mysterious, the most difficult for man to conquer and enter." [11]

Saint-Exupéry thought otherwise. One day, interviewed by the journalist Jacques Baratier, he said: "It's not the plane that led me to write. I believe if I'd been a miner, I'd have tried to extract knowledge from under the ground." That may be true. But what other activity could have been more suited to the writer than that of flying a plane? "My world was the world of flight," he declares in *Wind, Sand and Stars.* "Already I could feel the oncoming of night within which I should be enclosed as in the precincts of a temple—enclosed in the temple of night for the accomplishment of secret rites and absorption in inviolable contemplation." And again, more categorically: "I know nothing, nothing in the world, equal to the wonder of nightfall in the air. Those who have been enthralled by the witchery of flying will know what I mean."

The book on which he was working in the evenings at Juby was *Southern Mail.* The French title, *Courrier Sud,* was taken from the inscription on the Dakar mailbags. He read passages aloud to his friends who stopped off at Juby for the night, insisting that they listen while he read in a rather muffled voice, stressing certain phrases, then he would ask: "Is that it? Does that strike you as being right?" He wanted to be certain that he was accurately rendering what he felt, and he sought reassurance from another flyer. The life, emotions, pride of the pilot were what he wanted to reveal to the earthbound, ignorant of such things. He was eager to portray the reality of a pilot's existence, with all its grandeur. But he did not want to be a witness merely: he had a horror of being a mere onlooker. He wanted to participate.

Southern Mail is, of course, a novel; but Bernis, the hero, is clearly Saint-Exupéry, freed from the life of Paris, freed from the arms of a woman, so that he might accomplish his mission as pilot and man.

"Yes, that's it. That's certainly it," the other flyer would assure him, and Saint-Ex's face would light up in a glowing smile that set two long creases in his cheeks. And his eyes would survey the austere furnishings of his room: the basin, the jug, the bed that was too short; and Toto asleep beside his monkey. And his expression would become more meditative.

"When I think," he said one night within the hearing of one of his comrades, "when I think that had I not become a pilot of the Line I'd still be hanging out in bars in Paris, or playing bridge, or talking about cars!"

The immense silence of the desert hovered soothingly. In the luminous shadow could be heard nothing but the pounding of the surf, and, at intervals, the sinister call of the Spanish sentinels through the night.

Part two

5

For behind all seen things lies something vaster; everything is but a path, a portal, or a window opening on something other than itself.

—The Wisdom of the Sands

While Saint-Exupéry was playing host to the flyers who stopped off at Cape Juby, or flying to the rescue of a crew in distress, or arguing with Moorish chieftains, or playing the diplomat with the Spaniards at the fort, other pilots of the Line were preparing the route which would soon extend the airmail service across the Atlantic from Dakar to South America, and down that coast and across the continent from Montevideo to Santiago on the Pacific, and even southward to Cape Horn.

From its very origin, the Latécoère airline was meant to unite the European and South American continents—an ambitious aim, which had caused the audacious industrialist to be called insane by many people. Yet in May 1924, less than five years after the first mail plane had flown to Spain and thence to Casablanca, Latécoère sent one of his pilots, Captain Roig, ex-army aviation officer, to negotiate a link with Argentina. Roig had already, in May 1923, taken charge of a reconnoitering mission which had traced the Casablanca–Dakar route. Now, aided by compatriots residing in South America, along with aviators of Argentina, particularly Captains Almonacid and Artigau, Roig successfully negotiated with Brazil, Uruguay, and Argentina, and in August 1924 a decree authorized the extension of the Line to Buenos Aires. There remained only to put into operation the Dakar–Natal air route, which happens to be the shortest possible route across the Atlantic. The mail continued to be carried by sea until May 12, 1930, that memorable day when Mermoz, Dabry, and Gimié flew the first mail, a cargo of roughly two hundred eighty-six pounds of letters, in the hydroplane *Comte de la Vaulx* from Dakar to Natal.

But back in 1924, when Latécoère concluded agreements with Argentina and Brazil, the Line faced the task of establishing airfields at strategic points between Natal and Buenos Aires, a distance of about 2850 miles. The planes used were the old Bréguets that were flying the Toulouse–Dakar route. They had overcome the difficulties presented by the mountains of Spain and the desert of North Africa. And the flyers on the Natal–Buenos Aires route were also the same. They had survived the violent windstorms of Spain and the tormenting solitude of the Sahara. Now these men were to conquer the hostile coast of Brazil and the fierce winds that blow all along that coast.

A handful of men disembarked at Rio de Janeiro from the liner *Hoedic*, December 8, 1924. They were the flyers Hamm and Vachet (now director of Air France in South America), and the mechanics Gauthier, Chevalier, and Estival. This little group, with the requisite number of planes and spare parts, established itself on the *Campo de Affonsos*, the Rio airfield. Mme. Vachet accompanied her husband and shared the hard life of the men whose job was to prepare the route, set up landing sites, create airstrips—in other words, forge new links in the chain that the men under Didier Daurat were stretching from Toulouse to the shores of the Pacific.

The sky routes that today are flown at three hundred and more miles an hour and will soon be flown at an infinitely greater speed by aircraft which traverse whole continents without having to land had their origins in such beginnings. At that time no less than twelve landing sites had to be found and laid out between Natal and Buenos Aires. Vachet and his mechanic at once took off in a Bréguet to survey the coast where the surf traced its perpetual silvery hem. He marked the route on his map, indicating the capes, gulfs, beaches, and clearings he discovered in the middle of the forests. He landed on one of these and purchased the field and a part of the adjacent forest. He also hired gangs of natives to cut down trees, level rocks, clear the land. The men of the Line continued to pit themselves against rebellious nature. And within three years the Natal-to-Buenos Aires route was in operation.

One day in November 1927, Jean Mermoz arrived by boat at Rio. Mermoz, the naturally wild and undisciplined flyer who would take orders from only one man, Didier Daurat, arrived in America at Daurat's orders. Before conquering the ocean, Mermoz was to do pioneer flying over the virgin lands, tropical forests, and vast pampas which were now dotted here and there with the new airmail route stations. In his wake came a heroic group of airmen, Guillaumet in the vanguard. Mermoz had asked for him and had reserved for him what seemed to be the finest conquest: the Andes, over which Guillaumet was to fly three hundred forty-three times in a light, single-engine plane. After a crash landing Guillaumet was once stranded in these rocky and snowy wastes for five days and four nights. He lived to tell the story to Saint-Exupéry, who has given us, in *Wind, Sand and Stars,* a moving account of his meeting with "Guillaumet, resuscitated, the author of his own miracle."

One by one the cities of the immense South American continent were united by the airline, as more and more pilots arrived to fly the planes. Among these pioneers were Delaunay, Reine, Deley, Négrin, Depecker, Barbier, Vanier, Guerrero, Etienne, Thomás, Bédrignan, Rozès. The list could be extended with the names of others no less intrepid although they are now forgotten. These men not only flew the mail, they performed feats of daring and courage that became legendary and contributed to the prestige of France in Latin America.

Finally, on October 12, 1929, exactly three years after his arrival in Toulouse, Saint-Exupéry disembarked at Buenos Aires.

He had been recalled to France from Juby almost a year earlier, but his trip home had been delayed by a serious mishap on the Line—Reine and Serre had made a crash landing in hostile territory and had been taken captive by the Moors. But finally he was able to leave and with mixed feelings waited for the arrival of his successor. "I have such a longing to see you again, and such a longing to leave these eternal sands," he wrote to his mother. He wanted to see clouds again, to walk on grass, to hear the song of birds and of fountains. But all the same, his love of the desert remained, and the two loves, as I know from my own experience, are not incompatible.

After spending a month or so resting at Saint-Maurice and at Agay, he went to Brest, where he took a course in navigation at the aviation school established by the French Navy and directed by Lieutenant Chassin (who will figure later on in Saint-Exupéry's life as colonel, then general in the French Air Force in North Africa during World War II). Though not a brilliant pupil, Saint-Ex won his diploma, which he ill merited, according to Chassin, when asked for his opinion many years later. And Dr. Pélissier, writing of this same period at Brest, tells us that Saint-Ex failed to make the grade required for obtaining a certificate to teach navigation, although in that examination there were only three who failed. This course of studies was required of the pilots sent to South America, and apparently Saint-Ex's heart was not in it. At any rate, he had a series of accidents, smashed a Favé quadrant, broke a magnetic compass, and then, one day, almost sank a hydroplane he was flying because he had forgotten to close one of the hatches, flooding the craft and damaging a valuable hydrographic instrument. For one thing, his mind was preoccupied with his first book, *Southern Mail,* which had just been published and was enjoying a success.

He did not conceal his pride. "Tell me what they're saying about my book," he wrote to his mother. "But for goodness' sake, don't show it to S . . . , Y . . . , and some other imbeciles. At least a Giraudoux is needed to understand it." He went on to congratulate his mother: the city of Lyons had recently purchased one of her paintings. "What a family we are!" he exclaimed.

But he was bored; life in Brest was "no joke." It was a life he had known before; outside classes he spent his time in cafés where there was dancing. He did not dance, but sat drinking and smoking and telling anecdotes. Suddenly he needed his mother again. "If I had five or six thousand francs to spend," he told her, "I'd ask you to come to Brest. But all I have for the moment are debts."

This may seem to echo the past, but there is in fact a difference. Before Juby and Toulouse, when he needed money, he had asked his mother to send his "allowance." Now, in 1928 he writes from Brest, "I'd really like to borrow some money, for I'm sure to earn some on my book—but borrow from whom?" This may mean that the source of money he had so often drawn upon had dried up; but it is also possible that, having learned how hard it was to earn a living, he now had some scruples. In any case, a solution to his money troubles was found with his appointment as managing director of Aeroposta-Argentina, a branch of the Compagnie Générale Aéropostale which had recently replaced the Latécoère airline.

When Saint-Exupéry landed at Buenos Aires in October 1929, he did not know in exactly what capacity he was to serve the Aeroposta. Didier Daurat was not one to give explanations to anybody, and never asked a pilot's or mechanic's advice on an appointment to a place where he judged their presence desirable. Saint-Exupéry's uncertainty was great, and it annoyed him. He was glad, however, to meet again his old comrades, among them Henri Guillaumet. But these friends were often absent from Buenos Aires, flying for the company. He had only short talks with them, heard of their exploits, and they were off again.

The most difficult pioneer work of surveying and establishing the new air routes had now been accomplished by Vachet and his companions. Mermoz had already laid down new air routes, flying over the impenetrable tropical forest as far as Asunción in Paraguay or even farther to Corumba in Bolivia. With his faithful mechanic Collenot (who was doomed to perish in the southern reaches of the Atlantic), he had flown over the Andes into Chile. He had also, the previous year, inaugurated night flights, which greatly speeded up the airmail service. Mermoz was at the top of his form: in another six months, he would fly across the Atlantic.

For twelve days Saint-Ex was left more or less to his own devices in Buenos Aires, a town he found "hateful, without charm, without points of interest, without anything"—as usual, exaggerating. This great city where the characterless buildings had shot up like mushrooms in a few years, the long streets intersecting at right angles, the shopwindows devoid of originality, everything about it shocked and bored him, made him wistful for the desert or for the leafy park at Saint-Maurice or the red rocks at Agay or springtime in Paris. Here in Buenos Aires he felt there was a total lack of "that zest for life which comes when the chestnut trees are blooming in the Boulevard Saint-Germain." He wondered how spring would even manage to come to Buenos Aires, for how could any green blade "pierce through these thousands of cubic meters of reinforced concrete."

When his appointment finally came, his melancholy vanished and he wrote home with eager optimism. His salary would be 240,000 francs (about ten million francs today). "Mother, I can't tell you how glad I am about this for you," he wrote. "Everyone reproached you for spending so much money on my education; now, you'll have your revenge, won't you?"

It is doubtful that he really ascribed his success to that early education; probably he merely wanted to cheer his mother, who had given him that education at such sacrifice. What had turned the spoiled youth into a mature man before the age of thirty was the hard life to which he had been subjected in the past few years, the tests of endurance he had met, and the obstacles overcome.

He would have obstacles enough to surmount in South America, but nothing like those of the past three years. For he would again have an easy time, comparable to that of his youth, but without the necessity of asking anyone for money. His salary as managing director of Aeroposta-Argentina was so substantial that he did not know how to get rid of it. "I'm wearing myself out spending money," he wrote, "and am beginning to stifle in a room where I'm piling up a thousand things I'll never use." The minute Saint-Ex was in a city, he had an urge to spend recklessly. No sooner had he arrived in Brest for his navigation studies than he had fallen into his old habit of borrowing money. In Buenos Aires he would not need to borrow, but he spent every penny he earned.

One example out of many will serve to illustrate this aspect of his many-faceted character.

On his way to dine at the home of his chief, Monsieur Pranville—managing director of the Compagnie Générale Aéropostale—he met a flower-seller pushing a cartload of flowers in the street.

"What's the price of your flowers?" he asked the woman.

"Which ones, sir?"

"The whole lot."

"The whole lot?"

"Yes, and with the cart, as well."

We can imagine the stupefaction of the woman and her conviction that she was dealing with a madman. But after some slight bargaining, the mad Frenchman was in possession of the entire load of flowers, with which he gaily arrived at the Pranvilles.

A strange act, but a generous one, for he paid liberally. He was generous and he was spontaneous. Another incident illustrates both these qualities.

One day he met a dockhand, a poor devil of a Frenchman who recognized a compatriot in the aviator. They talked a while, and Saint-Ex learned that the man had come to South America fifteen years before, when he was still young, hoping to make a fortune. He had been cheated in some business deal by dishonest people who had taken all his savings. Now he was in a pitiful plight.

"I'm working here on the docks," he said, "to earn my passage home. But it's hard work, I'm not used to it and I'm not strong enough any more."

He showed his thin arms. Saint-Ex surveyed him as he sat there on a piling and read on his features and in his slightly clouded and wild gaze signs of suffering, sadness, regrets.

"Do you still have a family?"

"Yes, in France. I'd like to see them again. I don't want to drop dead here all alone."

After a moment's reflection, Saint-Ex laid his hand on the man's shoulder and said, "Wait here for me." Then off he went, down the quayside, indifferent to the hurrying travelers and the porters loaded with bags. He went into an office and spoke to the ticket-seller.

"When does the next boat leave for France?" he asked.

"Tomorrow afternoon," the ticket-seller replied, "at four o'clock. The *Mendoza*. Sailing for Marseilles. But she's all booked up, there's no room except in third class."

"That will do," said Saint-Ex. "I'll have a ticket. How much?"

A few minutes later he was standing beside the man sitting on the wharf, and handing him the ticket.

"You're leaving for France tomorrow," he said. And while the surprised man got to his feet, Saint-Ex added some money to the ticket and said, "Tomorrow afternoon, on the *Mendoza*, at four o'clock. *Bon voyage!*"

This is a moving incident. But there is a dark side to it, for, while imitating St. Vincent de Paul, Saint-Ex was neglecting his own family, particularly his mother, who needed to hear from him and no doubt also needed the money he had promised to send her.

At the beginning of 1930, about three months after his arrival in Buenos Aires, he had written his mother that he was sending her seven thousand francs, of which three thousand were for her, the remainder being destined "to repay Marchand." Who Marchand was we do not know; possibly an acquaintance in Brest who had lent him money. In this same letter he advised his mother to spend the winter in Morocco, where she could paint. With the three thousand francs that he intended to send her, he said, she could manage to live. But at the end of the same year, Saint-Ex received, through Pranville, a letter from Didier Daurat in Toulouse, which would indicate that he had not carried out his promise. The letter is dated December 6, 1930, and reads:

The Managing Director [Beppo de Massimi] requests us to inform Monsieur de Saint-Exupéry that he has received a visit from one of his relatives asking for news of him. It appears that M. de Saint-Exupéry has not written to his mother for two months. Although this is a personal matter in which we are not obliged to interfere, we request you to urge M. de Saint-Exupéry to show less negligence.

It was reported that Saint-Ex was leading such a full life in South America that he rather neglected his correspondence. No doubt he was very busy. He had to make flights out of Buenos Aires to inspect the line, but his absences were never prolonged and, when he returned to the city, he found time to see his friends, so surely he could have written a weekly letter to his mother. And he could certainly have spared the promised three thousand francs each month out of his twenty-five thousand francs salary.

No, the "full life" was no excuse for such negligence. The explanation—there could be no excuse—is merely that he was rapidly forgetting his stay at Toulouse and at Juby. He had found comfort and ease again and, from the material point of view at least, he was content. This erased the memory of those who were at a distance. For he needed to see and to participate, in order to feel. When he was having a hard life, he felt close to suffering and misery, close to mankind, conscious of humanity's needs, was at one with the great human community. But the cement had not yet set, and he fell back upon the pleasant and easy ways of a young man about town. A thing to keep in mind is that by the time he arrived in South America he was a celebrity, not only as a flyer and the author of a successful book, but also as a seasoned pilot of the Line.

If we present his life in the form of a graph, we see the ascending line beginning at Montaudran, continuing to Juby, after which a descending line starts during the years in South America and for a while afterward. But the line will rise again in the ensuing difficult years and will continue upward even in the midst of suffering, reaching its peak in the war years when he participated in the struggle for the liberation of France.

This independent man, who loved solitude, also needed group life. And his place was more in the ranks than at the top as leader, although he possessed that essential quality for leadership, the ability to set an example, a quality he never exerted so well as in this milieu of flyers where it developed.

Fortunately, Saint-Exupéry's position as director of Aeroposta-Argentina did not keep him constantly in his office but required him to fly and provided him with the opportunity to travel. The plane he now piloted was not a Bréguet but a swifter and more modern machine which had been adopted for carrying the mail: a Laté 26, equipped with a 450-h.p. engine. It was at the controls of one of these planes that he flew to the airfields of Argentina, Brazil, Bolivia, and Chile.

His first flight over the Andes left an unforgettable impression. Suspended in his plane at more than twenty thousand feet, alone among the giant mountain peaks, he witnessed the beginning of a cyclone. The snow that had accumulated in many winters over a range of mountains more than a hundred miles wide "had brought its peace to all this vastness, as in dead castles the passing centuries spread peace," loosened its hold and "swirled up in the air—a snow volcano."

At that time, the airline already stretched as far south as Comodoro Rivadavia, with two landing fields between, at Bahia Blanca and Rawson. Saint-Exupéry took charge of surveying and organizing the last section of the line south of Comodoro Rivadavia, and flew as far as the Straits of Magellan, coming down at Punta Arenas, the most southerly town in the world.

In *Wind, Sand and Stars* he describes these lands of Patagonia seen from the sky as a "deserted landscape where once a thousand volcanoes boomed to each other in their great subterranean organs and spat forth their fire." Now, between the ancient and fixed dark lava flows gleamed a green turf. Here a little town had grown up "between the timeless lava and the austral ice." It was to this place that Saint-Exupéry paid a visit, arriving from the sky. More than 1500 miles to the north he had left behind him the modern city of Buenos Aires, with its tons of reinforced concrete in which swarmed millions of human beings. He landed at Punta Arenas "in the peace of the evening" and discovered anew the simple and poignant "human mystery."

Fabien, in *Night Flight,* as he flew the mail plane from Patagonia toward Buenos Aires, looked wistfully at those little settlements he was passing over, and as he prepared to land in one, his wings almost grazing the housetops, he caught glimpses of the gardens within the walls and thought about the life that went on there: "friendliness and gentle girls, white napery spread in quiet homes; all that is slowly shaped toward eternity." But Fabien, responsible for the mail, did not linger. Within ten minutes he resumed his flight, continuing toward his destiny, which was to perish in a cyclone.

It was the same cyclone that Saint-Ex had been caught in once, in those very latitudes—a storm of unimaginable violence, the wind attaining at times the fantastic velocity of 145 miles an hour. In his account of his struggle with the unleashed elements he moves us as much by the calm and lucid analysis of his sensations as by the objective descriptions. And he manages to convey all the horror of the interminable battle he waged against that mad wind which was, indeed, indescribable. He succeeds by understatement. "Horror," he writes, in *Wind, Sand and Stars,* "does not manifest itself in the world of reality. And so, in beginning my story of a revolt of the elements which I myself lived through I have no feeling that I shall write something which you will find dramatic." As usual, the experience opened up for him a field of meditation, and he concludes his account of the cyclone by saying that, after all, "There is nothing dramatic in the world, nothing pathetic, except in human relations."

At Buenos Aires, when in the company of his old friends, Saint-Ex could forget everything he disliked in the city. In his letters he described the long evenings he sometimes spent in restaurants where the talk was stimulated by the Gargantuan steaks and heady wines of the country. Occasionally there were dusk-to-dawn carouses in the night clubs, especially at *Armenonville*, noted for its pretty girls. But there were also quiet evenings spent at the homes of the Guillaumets (his old friend had recently married) and the Pranvilles, for Saint-Ex liked to submerge himself from time to time in the calm atmosphere of domesticity.

Julien Pranville, director of Aéropostale in South America, was a young and likable graduate of the École Polytechnique. His learning had left no trace of arrogance, but had trained his mind to think scientifically and methodically, a useful asset for one who sometimes had to hold in check some rather excitable pilots. The flyers were all deeply attached to him, none more so than Saint-Ex who, from his arrival in Buenos Aires, had felt the essential nobility of his character. Pranville had the qualities he most admired and had encountered in his flying comrades at Montaudran and elsewhere. Whenever he could, he liked to spend an evening at 240 Calle Reconquista, where the director lived with his wife and young son. But this new friendship was short-lived, terminating with Pranville's untimely death in the spring of 1930.

Pranville had experienced all the difficulties of creating the airmail lines on the vast South American continent, for he had been there from the outset. He flew with Mermoz to Bolivia and Paraguay and was with him when Mermoz crashed in the middle of the tropical forest. And when Mermoz decided to fly at night, landing on airstrips still without beacons and provided only with torches set down on the strip in triangular formation, Pranville aided and abetted him. Then, on May 13, 1930, when Mermoz, with Dabry and Gimié, had for the first time flown the mail across the Atlantic, Pranville flew from Buenos Aires to Natal to meet him—a trip that ended in tragedy. Pranville's pilot on this doomed flight was Négrin, the mechanic was Pruneta, and they carried with them two passengers who, having been caught plotting against the government, were fleeing their country. Above the Plata River they encountered a blinding fog. Négrin dropped down in search of Montevideo, only to find the fog had enveloped the entire vast estuary. Suddenly the wheels of the plane struck the water, the engine flooded, the machine began to sink. There were only two life belts aboard, and the aviators gave these to the passengers. And three more valuable lives were lost, three more sacrifices added to the numerous ones that had already strewn the air route in South America.

Another friend Saint-Exupéry met in Buenos Aires was Vicente de Almondos de Almonacid, a curious type of Argentinian. Tall, slender, aristocratic, he was a twentieth-century reincarnation of a Conquistador. Loving France as much as his own country, he had fought as pilot in the French Aviation Corps throughout World War I, having enlisted in 1914. When the French airmail project was first suggested in South America, he did everything possible to further the enterprise. Indeed, he even challenged one of his compatriots to a duel and inflicted upon him two saber wounds. His victim was a Major Torres, a notorious pro-German, who had refused to allow the planes of Captain Roig's mission to remain on the Buenos Aires airfield. Saint-Exupéry and Almonacid were often seen together.

But Saint-Ex was never happier than when he was with Guillaumet and his young wife. Guillaumet was his knight *sans peur et sans reproche,* his greatest inspiration, especially after Guillaumet's heroic adventure in the Andes, which occurred at about this time.

The two men met rarely, however, for Guillaumet flew the mail between Buenos Aires and Santiago de Chile, where the young couple made their home. For his part, Saint-Ex was often on the go, visiting airfields, where he had official contacts. His office work, too, consumed much of his time. Often until late at night he remained at the office, drawing up reports. And then there were the nights he spent in his little apartment on the eighth floor—"seven above me, seven below"—hard at work on his second book, a novel: *Vol de Nuit* (*Night Flight*).

While writing, he often meditated upon the character of Didier Daurat, for whom human nature was something as malleable as wax, and upon the courage and self-sacrifice of the air pilot who is dedicated to his work and conscious of the importance of the part he is playing. The resulting book is a mingling of these meditations with actions and scenes drawn from his own experience. The style is pure and rich in poetic imagery. From the very first lines imagination is stirred and interest held:

> *Already, beneath him, through the golden evening, the shadowed hills had dug their furrows and the plains grew luminous with long-enduring light....*

Fabien, the pilot, is bringing the mail plane north from Patagonia at the end of day.

Saint-Exupéry himself had flown above that same landscape "in the peace of the evening" and he, like Fabien, had been "a shepherd of the stars," had watched the tiny villages lighting up and had thought about the peasants gathered round their lamplit tables. Like Fabien, he had felt safe and secure, very "snugly ensconsed" in his plane and had "relaxed his limbs a little, let his neck sink back onto the leather padding" and had fallen into "the deeply meditative mood of flight, mellow with inexplicable hopes." Also, like Fabien, he had wakened out of this reverie to find the sky had darkened, clouding over the ground beneath him, and as a wind made the plane quiver, had begun to search anxiously for those lights of earth, "those vague gleams which, even in the darkest nights, flit here and there."

The wind had risen suddenly and Fabien, close to panic, realized that this might be "a shoreless night, leading to no anchorage... nor toward dawn." In an hour his fuel would run out. Fabien had lost his bearings, and the radio operator could make no contact with ground stations. But Fabien told himself fiercely that "somewhere there were lands of calm, at peace beneath the wide moon-shadows" even though he might never see them. He jerked his plane upward, climbing above the clouds and the threatening peaks they might conceal. "And, at this very moment, there gleamed above his head, across a storm-rift like a fatal lure within a deep abyss, a star or two. Only too well he knew them for a trap." But the relief of seeing light again was great, and though he realized they were lost, he smiled. A strange peace filled him. He had the feeling of being suddenly freed: "those bonds of his were loosed, as of a prisoner whom they let walk a while in liberty among the flowers." The flowers were the constellations glittering above the sea of clouds—beneath which lay eternity. " 'Too beautiful,' he thought. Amid the far-flung treasure of the stars he roved, in a world where no life was, no faintest breath of life, save his and his companion's. Like plunderers of fabled cities they seemed, immured in treasure-vaults whence there is no escape. Amongst these frozen jewels they were wandering, rich beyond all dreams, but doomed."

Daniel Anet, in his biography of Saint-Exupéry, has given us perhaps the best analysis to date of his writings. *Night Flight,* he says, represents a great advance over *Southern Mail,* for it is "more relaxed, more musical, purer." He considers it the most finished in form of any of Saint-Exupéry's books, and the most poetical, for it is "filled with powerful rhythms, with echoes lasting long enough to be heard as song."

Toulouse and the North African desert had made Saint-Exupéry a man among men. South America offered him a wider view, an easier life freed of material cares, and also provided him the occasion for long flights during which he evolved in his meditations *Night Flight* and the book that was to follow, *Wind, Sand and Stars.* Thus we see the various influences exerted upon Saint-Exupéry by his métier, which transformed him and simultaneously created him as man, as writer, as philosopher.

6

How eagerly in my youth I awaited the coming of the beloved who was being brought to me, to be my wife, in a caravan that had set out long since. . . .

—*The Wisdom of the Sands*

One day Saint-Exupéry flew back to Buenos Aires from Patagonia with a vivid recollection of the little town of Punta Arenas. He remembered how he had leaned against a fountain there and watched the girls passing by, girls he did not know and could never know. For, as he reflected, "What can one know of a girl who passes, walking with slow steps homeward, eyes lowered, smiling to herself, filled with adorable inventions and fables?" The thought would be added to others he was collecting for a future book, *Wind, Sand and Stars*.

He had flown over a thousand miles, had stopped off at San Julián and at Bahia Blanca. From the arid, lava-wrinkled lands of the south, he had flown toward the green plains and a noisier, more intense, more civilized existence. But he had returned to the bustling life of Buenos Aires without enthusiasm. And now, in the office, he was reporting to M. Daurat that all was well, that the Line was being strengthened, the airfields organized.

When he had finished this paper work, he may perhaps have wondered how to spend the evening. The Guillaumets were in Chile, other friends were in Rio or Natal or Asunción. He did not want to go to a café or a moving picture. He may have felt sad and rather forsaken, as he sometimes did in the absence of friends. Slowly he went back to his little apartment in the Calle Florida, where he found his table stacked with books and sheets of paper covered with his fine handwriting. Lighting a cigarette and avidly inhaling the smoke, he took up the pages of the manuscript he was working on, reread them, started to rewrite certain passages, gave up. The sounds that rose from the street mingled with a thousand noises in other streets, making a roar like that of the ocean.

No, he was not in the mood to work on the book in progress (*Night Flight*). In order to write, he needed the stimulus provided by conversation and friendly argument. Never did he write better than immediately after such sessions, when he returned to his rooms. But that night he was filled with calm, submerged in solitude.

He took up his notebook, however, reflected a second, carelessly shook off the ashes of his cigarette, then wrote a few lines that continued his memories of Punta Arenas and the pensive girl he had seen: "Out of the thoughts, the voice, the silences of a lover, she can form an empire, and thereafter she sees in all the world but him a people of barbarians. More surely than if she were on another planet, I feel her to be locked up in her language, in her secret, in her habits, in the singing echoes of her memory. Born yesterday of the volcanoes, of greenswards, of brine of the sea, she walks here already half divine." These lines which later appeared in *Wind, Sand and Stars* reflect a state of mind, an awareness of his solitude that sporadically appears in his letters at this time.

"I'm hoping to find a girl who is pretty and intelligent, full of charm, gay and comforting, faithful and. . . . But of course I'll never find her," he had written to his sister Gabrielle six years previously. Indeed, from the age of twenty-three, Saint-Ex had been looking for a wife, if we are to believe what he set down in his letters to his family. In another letter to Gabrielle, he wrote, "I want to get married and have children as delightful as yours."

This yearning to find a wife became ever more urgent and imperious in moments when solitude weighed heavily. Years before, when he was traveling in France for the Saurer truck firm, he returned to Paris late one night and, dreading the solitude of his rooms, he at once began to "take a census of his friends" by telephoning everyone he could think of, but without result. Whereupon he wrote to his mother: "It's midnight, I've just thrown my hat on the bed and feel the whole extent of my loneliness. . . . Mother, what I would ask of a wife would be to relieve this uneasy state of mind." (The word he employed was *inquiètude*, a state of uneasiness and anxiety that he seems to have courted at times.) Paradoxically he wrote in this same letter, "I don't like people who are completely happy and have stopped developing." Then he returns to the subject that is weighing heavily on his heart: "You can't imagine what consolation a woman can and should give a man." And here he was, five years later, free to work on his book *Night Flight*, but disinclined to do so, preferring to unburden his heart in a letter to his mother, repeating, "I would like to get married."

He was to find that long-desired wife, and to find her in Buenos Aires.

How he came to meet Consuelo Suncin has given rise to a number of fantastic stories. According to one version, Saint-Ex was dragged by a friend to hear a lecture on marriage before an audience composed largely of students. The lecturer was against marriage and supported the thesis that "marriage kills love" with a number of original arguments. Saint-Ex was amused, the lecturer was a pretty young woman, he asked to be introduced to her . . . and so they were married.

Then again, their meeting took place in the air over Pacheco, the Buenos Aires airport, where Saint-Ex was taking up passengers for their first flights. On one of these short flights, his engine stalled and he had to make an acrobatic landing that would have frightened the most courageous of men. His passenger happened to be a charming young woman, and throughout the forced landing she maintained a smiling calm, which enchanted him . . . and so they were married.

There is still another version of his first encounter with his future wife, a rather romantic version, yet nearer the truth. According to this story, Saint-Ex was leaving a Buenos Aires restaurant one evening just as a little riot broke out in the streets between the followers of two rival colonels—the beginning of a South American revolution. In the midst of the combatants, unafraid of the flying bullets, the French airman noticed a charming young woman, fell in love with her, and made her Countess de Saint-Exupéry. The anecdote is true, except for certain details. Saint-Exupéry had met the charming young woman before, had been recently introduced to her by Benjamin Crémieux, and instead of confronting the whizzing bullets, she had taken refuge in his arms.

Saint-Ex had known Benjamin Crémieux in Paris. He was one of the brilliant group of writers associated with the Gallimard periodical, *Nouvelle Revue Française,* and Saint-Ex had met him at about the same time that he met the others—André Gide, Ramón Fernandez, Jean Prévost, Jean Paulhan, Marcel Arland, to name a few. During a trip to Argentina, the noted French critic, Benjamin Crémieux, had dropped in to see Saint-Ex, bringing him the news that *Southern Mail* was having a great success. Crémieux was interested in his work in progress, and listened, enraptured, to some passages of *Night Flight* which were read aloud to him, thus giving the critic a foretaste of the book he was to praise in the pages of the *N.R.F.* after publication. (Years later, Saint-Ex read the first pages of *Citadelle* (*The Wisdom of the Sands*) aloud to Crémieux and Drieu La Rochelle, and was very hurt at their obvious lack of enthusiasm.)

In Buenos Aires Crémieux and Saint-Exupéry found much to talk about—Paris, the Gallimard publications, literature generally —and some subjects to avoid. For instance, Crémieux had translated Pirandello into French, and Saint-Exupéry disliked the Italian playwright. "No one has the right to compare a man like Ibsen with a Pirandello," he had said in a letter dated 1925, and he had gone on to compare the Italian with the French playwright Lenormand; according to him, both dramatists made the mistake of trying to put metaphysics on the stage, and Pirandello's metaphysics were, said Saint-Exupéry, written down to the level of a concierge's understanding. In short, Crémieux and Saint-Exupéry talked about

Paris and what was going on there, and about the airman's flights to Patagonia and across the Andes. Then, Crémieux introduced Saint-Ex to some friends in Buenos Aires.

Crémieux's family had lived for a time in Argentina and he still had some acquaintances there. During World War I, when he had been in the Information Service, he had met an Argentine newspaperman, Gomez Carillo, who was a foreign correspondent on the French front. (Some of Carillo's articles were published in book form in French, among them *Au Coeur de la Tragédie*, 1917.) Gomez Carillo had died since then, but his young widow still lived in Buenos Aires, so Crémieux one evening introduced Saint-Exupéry to her.

Consuelo Carillo, née Suncin, was a rather small woman—she appeared particularly so at the side of Saint-Exupéry—and was dark-haired. He had always shown a predilection for tall, blonde women, but he at once fell in love with her and was bewitched by her fine-featured face, lit up by a pair of very expressive eyes, and her character, which was exuberant and full of fantasy. He was even charmed by the way she spoke French, with a Spanish accent. Following this meeting, he dropped a pretty dancer at the *Armenonville* night club, a tall, blonde girl to whom he had been paying assiduous attentions.

A fortuneteller in 1924, laying out the cards for Saint-Ex at the home of his uncle Jacques de Fonscolombe in Paris, had predicted that he would marry "a young widow, soon." The fortuneteller had been mistaken only in the time of the event.

They were married in the spring of 1931, only a few months after their meeting. The marriage took place at Agay in the south of France, where his sister, Madame d'Agay, had her home.

A great many books have been written about Saint-Exupéry, and most of them dispose of his marriage to Consuelo in a few lines. The biography by René Delange, published in 1948, had the advantage of Léon Werth's judicial reflections, added at the end of the book, which is really a condensation of Saint-Exupéry's life.

This work scarcely mentions his marriage. The biography most highly recommended to me, written by Pierre Chevrier, who was a close acquaintance of Saint-Exupéry and his wife, mentions Consuelo in only about a dozen lines which account for their meeting and the wedding. Chevrier, however, drops hints which arouse our curiosity without satisfying it, about the sentimental life of his hero. For instance, he tells us that Saint-Ex "considered the idea of a couple assuming rights over each other revolting" and the atmosphere of marriage "stifling."

Consuelo has suffered from the willful silence that has surrounded her name. And to break this silence she has indulged in certain actions, eccentricities quite natural to her, which have been damaging.

"The people who have written about Saint-Ex," she said to me one day in a voice choked with sadness and regret, "have never mentioned his wife. Yet surely she counted for something in his life!"

Even if this remark were dictated by a kind of pride, one cannot reproach her for it. The woman who has intimately mingled her life with that of a famous man has reason to be proud. Perhaps she was not the only woman in his life, but at any rate she was the only woman to bear his name. Although she did not fit into any conventional category as a wife, it was her originality that probably drew Saint-Ex to her.

Some people who were very close to him have denied that he was ever influenced by anyone. This may be true of Saint-Exupéry the writer: one looks in vain for a literary or philosophical influence in his work. But it is not true of the man, where the outside influences were many. We have seen to what extent his life changed in a few years under the influence of flying comrades such as Guillaumet and the influence of his chief, Didier Daurat, whom he respected and obeyed. Consuelo's influence on her husband seems obvious. It took two different forms, or rather, it sprang from two sources—her esthetic responses and her mercurial temperament.

Consuelo is an esthete with a number of talents. She paints, sculpts, and writes. Her book, *Oppède* (called *Kingdom of the Rocks* in its English version), blends the real with the unreal, and is poetic in tone. It was especially in the realm of literature that she exercised an influence. Sometimes, for instance, in recounting an anecdote or describing an event—which quite often might be based on fact—she would be carried away by her imagination and would let fall some extraordinary words and phrases. Tonio—as she called him—would stop her and say, "Repeat that phrase, Consuelo!" And she would repeat it with still more verve.

Involuntarily, as well, she exercised an inspiring influence over Saint-Ex by her temperamental behavior, to which at times he reacted violently. But these furious domestic scenes, recollected in tranquility, were often transposed into philosophical comments, through which may be glimpsed pangs of regret, as he admits to himself that he was in the wrong.

Consuelo's impulses, good and bad, were like volcanic eruptions —and she was born in a volcanic country, San Salvador. In the old days, when she was erupting, nothing on earth could stop her, neither the gentlest persuasion nor the most obvious arguments; prayers and supplications had no least effect upon the pretty but furious little creature. One day, for instance, there was a fierce argument. Consuelo, typical female, would not admit that she was in the wrong and Saint-Ex would not yield to her viewpoint even for the sake of peace. He soon regretted it, for the argument degenerated into a brawl and Consuelo began to scream like a child in a fit of rage. Her screams threatened to arouse the neighbors; Saint-Ex implored her to be quiet, but her shrieks only redoubled in volume. Finally he pushed her down on the bed and covered her head with the eiderdown quilt. She struggled, scratched, bit, and kept on yelling, but Saint-Ex held her down. Suddenly she struggled less violently, her cries became almost inaudible, and her gesticulations were desperate. Saint-Ex lifted up the quilt, releasing her. Consuelo had bitten through the pillow case, her mouth was full of feathers, she was half-smothered. The sight was funny, and Saint-Ex burst into a laugh. But the scene might well have ended in tragedy.

And that scene is but one out of many, some of which were even more violent. Surely, a married life of this kind could not but have had an influence upon Saint-Exupéry the man and the writer.

In 1925 he had written to his mother on the subject of marriage: "I believe one should always be a little uneasy. . . . And for that reason I fear marriage. But of course it depends upon the wife."

What he feared was a "bourgeois" marriage. He was afraid he might marry a woman who would be contented with her lot and maintain a calm and soothing atmosphere around her. Saint-Ex needed *inquiétude*—that disquieted state of mind was as necessary to him as peace of mind is to others. With Consuelo he had no tranquility, and sometimes he complained about it and left her—only to return eventually. What most men call happiness was to him stagnation. And when domestic life was not sufficiently tumultuous he did his best, unconsciously and instinctively, to stir up trouble. Dr. Pélissier tells us, in his biography of Saint-Exupéry, how he not only exaggerated his afflictions but discovered maladies he did not have. He would become very offended when his doctor refused to treat him for a nonexistent disease.

This *inquiétude,* which Saint-Ex sought and which was provided by his wife, may have stimulated him as a writer, but was certainly a handicap to the flyer. An almost fatal accident in which he was involved in 1935 may partly be traced to a domestic brawl that preceded it. But again, that accident provided us with some of the finest pages in *Wind, Sand and Stars.*

It has been said that Consuelo's spectacular behavior and eccentricities were conscious efforts to attract attention to herself. When in 1944, she outfitted a barge in the Seine as a café-bar and called it *Petit Prince* and welcomed her customers with a sailor's cap on her head bearing the name "Saint-Ex" in gilt lettering, this act was intentional. It was frankly meant to break the conspiracy of silence that had been created around her. But the sacrilege could have been carried out only with the help and encouragement of certain individuals for whom greatness has no meaning.

But that well-known performance was exceptional. What is more important is not spectacular acts but the day-to-day conduct of Saint-Exupéry's wife and its effect upon him. Let us reconstruct a few scenes, beginning with the time she departed for two days and nights without a word. As time passed, Saint-Ex began to be seriously worried and telephoned everywhere, asking if anyone had seen her. Then, in the dining room, he spread out a map of Paris on the table and held above it a pendulum—he had no real belief in such semimystical performances but was ready to try anything in the circumstances. He had not wanted to alert the police, but at length decided to do so and lay the pendulum down on the map. At that very instant the telephone rang and he hurried to answer it. Consuelo's voice sounded in the receiver.

"I implore you," he said, "don't leave me in this state of anxiety. I forgive you. Come back to me."

"No."

"Then at least tell me where you are."

"Near the Saint-Martin canal, and I'm going to throw myself into the water. Farewell, Tonio."

Needless to say, he persuaded her to return—and to torment him some more. This life of conjugal upheaval which, on the surface, would seem to have been so disastrous for him was but one of the stimulants he craved and might be classed with the strong black tea that he drank in such quantities and the cigarettes he smoked continually. Calm and silence did not agree with him; in order to write, he needed to be surrounded with noise and movement. He had a predilection for writing in trains or in cafés. Certainly his wife sometimes went beyond all bounds, and when this occurred, he would unburden himself of his momentary woes, taking someone into his confidence. But then, after a more or less prolonged absence, he would return to the woman who so well knew how to keep him in that uneasy and irritated condition that he required.

Besides, what other kind of wife would have suited him? Consuelo and her Tonio were congenial in many ways—in their bohemianism and disorder and extravagance. They were both spendthrifts. We who knew them in the first year of their marriage have a vivid memory of a certain beautiful old soup tureen which they used as a bank. Saint-Ex cashed his monthly paycheck and deposited the money there. Whenever he or Consuelo—or their Arab servant—needed cash, they simply dipped into the soup tureen. More often than not, it was empty by the middle of the month.

It might be said that a frugal wife would have suited him better, that he needed someone to manage the household so thriftily that he would be spared the money worries which so embittered him in later years. But would he have allowed any woman to prevent him from spending as he liked? It is highly doubtful. Aside from this, he loved children, and Consuelo bore him none. But would he have made his family happy? At times he might have enjoyed family life, but he was no more suited to endure it continually than were Tolstoy and Dickens. He could dream of domestic bliss and praise domestic virtues, but in reality they exasperated him, and there is evidence for this. When he lived in Toulouse, at the beginning of his employment by the Latécoère airline, a very sweet and devoted girl was his mistress. She may not always have understood him, but she adored him. One evening Saint-Exupéry caught her mending his socks . . . and he walked out on her.

Consuelo, excitable and inexhaustible creature that she was, could be charming at times, and as sentimental and cajoling as a child. Saint-Ex was not always convinced of her sincerity, or rather of the quality of the sentiments she expressed, since she went to extremes in everything, as he himself did. However, she knew how to melt his heart.

One evening, a few years after their marriage, when they were living in Paris and were in financial straits, they returned to their apartment to find that electricity, gas, and telephone had been cut off because of unpaid bills. Saint-Ex wondered aloud how he would ever get out of this hole. Whereupon Consuelo, in her sweetest mood, pressed herself against him and said, "Don't you worry, Tonio, I'll go to work."

Saint-Ex smiled skeptically.

"You don't believe me?" she said.

"Oh yes," said Saint-Ex, indulgently. "But what work will you do?"

"I don't know. Oh, anything." Then, pulling away and speaking energetically: "I'll scrub floors!"

He took her small hands in his and shook his head dubiously. "With such slender wrists as these?"

Consuelo withdrew her hands and extended her arms as if crucified. "Christ had slender wrists, too!" she said.

Saint-Ex took his wife in his arms, hugged her, lifted her off the floor, then gently set her on her feet again. "What a child!" he murmured.

"I'm so afraid of acquiring fixed habits," Saint-Exupéry had written in a letter at the age of twenty-six, when he was living in Toulouse. At that epoch, whenever he tired of a café, he emigrated to another; after repeating the same phrase to a newspaper dealer each morning for a month or so, he changed newspaper dealers, obliging himself to "invent a new phrase for the new dealer, a much prettier phrase." In the same letter he declares despairingly, "I'll never achieve anything in life, for I get tired of things too quickly, I get tired even of myself. I have too great a need for freedom."

Of course, freedom is something a man cannot have completely in marriage. The important thing is that Saint-Ex had a measure of freedom, which he craved both as a man and as a writer. For he needed to escape the stormy milieu of home and find elsewhere a serene sky and quiet atmosphere.

He spent these periods of calm with another woman who also occupied an important place in his life. This woman, whom we shall refer to as his Egeria, was a great admirer of the writer and in his first works had comprehended what kind of man he was, had detected the exceptional qualities of this odd-looking person with a round and rather heavy face and a turned-up nose. She was attractive, intelligent and highly cultivated. In her Saint-Exupéry not only found the physical qualities he most admired, but an understanding mind. She was often his refuge from the world. Considerate and sensitive, she forced herself to endure the whims and unreasonable demands of a man who was so often exasperated by the meanness, dullness, or stupidity of mankind. For she escaped no more than others his tyrannical demands, which she indulgently referred to as an admirable quality: he was "so marvelously exigent," he expected so much of life. She was so devoted to him that long separations were hard to bear and during the first year of the war she went to join him in the village where he was quartered and later, during the German occupation, she once managed to join him in New York, and again, still later, in Algiers.

Saint-Exupéry appreciated this woman who seemed to understand every aspect of his complicated character. She always read his manuscripts and was, I believe, the first person to read the entire manuscript of *The Wisdom of the Sands*. And when she had read that book she wrote to him, giving her opinion of the work. This is how Saint-Ex replied:

> *Your letter—it is* exactly, exactly *what I need. I've already read it at least thirty times. You can't imagine how important this is to me. It may set me to working again. I'd like to have another letter of the same kind.*
>
> *You see, it's not the advice and opinions of others that I need at this stage. When the book is finished, then let us have as many criticisms as possible. But at this stage, criticism is stultifying. The only thing that can inspire and help me at this stage is an answer to the question that at present agonizes me: What will the reader think of my book? Your letter has given me exactly that. Exactly.*

This letter shows what a close understanding existed between the two and how subtle was this woman's mind, if she could give an opinion of his book, after a first reading, which would so well satisfy the author.

When one says *Egeria* one thinks "mistress" and one thinks of physical love. Perhaps it is a mistake to associate the two words, for a veritable love, which is the gift of oneself, has little to do with sexual desire, which is a matter of glands. Saint-Exupéry himself clearly marked the distinction. "Confuse not love with the raptures of possession," says the chief in *The Wisdom of the Sands.*

It is only in this last work that he wrote about love and sex. In *Southern Mail* there is one allusion, but very restrained: Bernis spends the night with a girl he has picked up; next day he awakens emptied of desire, and absent-mindedly strokes the side of his companion of a night, finding her "warm, like an animal." And he thought of that ecstasy which had fluttered its wings within him for a few seconds, that insane bird which flutters its wings and dies. In *Night Flight,* Fabien's wife makes but one appearance, to confront Rivière with her distress. In *Wind, Sand and Stars,* love is only mentioned as a part of the dream world of young, virginal girls, who have known nothing of physical love. Saint-Exupéry, I believe, was very appreciative of that kind of purity—the purity of children, of fruit still on the tree, still unspoiled, untouched.

The writer, as pilot and man of action, had something else to tell us in those books. But his intention, from the very beginning, in *The Wisdom of the Sands,* was to speak of passionate love. He does so in a biblical style (which on the surface removes it from contemporary life). But to those who knew his private life it is easy to identify him with the desert chief, who becomes his spokesman. Thus we learn his opinion on women and their sexual role. To the man, she is a need, a physiological necessity; she is also a relaxation. And his protagonist discusses the place of women in the three roles of wife, courtesan, mistress. "What may you hope to get of the courtesan? Only a tranquilizing of the flesh after your battles in the oases." "Stay," says the mistress, "stay with me always.... When desire comes you need but stretch forth your arms and I will bend under your embrace like a young orange tree laden with its fruit." And as to the wife, the chief says, "I did not lay up my stores to house them in a woman and gloat over them." Saint-Ex liked change in all things, women not excepted, for he rejected the dominion of one woman. However, he did not demand exclusive "ownership" either, readily accepting the idea of sharing, and scorning jealousy, "for notwithstanding the general opinion," he has his desert chief say, "love does not cause suffering; what causes it is the sense of ownership, which is love's opposite."

It would also seem that a single life can experience but one great love—and those who have never experienced it deny its existence. Such a feeling is like the exceptional abundance of some trees which, in a year, bear so much fruit that they will never yield more.

Saint-Exupéry knew such a love, at the age of twenty-three, for the girl to whom he was then betrothed. She was slender, pretty, full of grace. Their engagement was abruptly broken off. The young girl's parents had demanded that he renounce his flying career. It is easy to see why the Geneviève of *Southern Mail* has been identified with Saint-Exupéry's fiancée. True, Geneviève is married, but Bernis behaves toward her more as though she were a very young girl. While she remains attached to everything that so well fills her material life—the life of a child of fortune surrounded by beautiful heirloom furniture, tapestries, paintings, the leafy park where the linden trees each spring renew their green domes, deep and moving as water—Bernis goes off toward his destiny, that of a pilot on the line between Toulouse and Dakar, and to live as best he can.

Thirty years after the event, a magazine article recounted the story of this betrothal to Saint-Exupéry "just for the fun of it." Perhaps she had no idea of the wound she had left in his heart, or that seven years after their engagement was broken Saint-Exupéry almost fainted when he caught a glimpse of her across a ballroom floor. Apparently she never realized, in reading *Wind, Sand and Stars,* that the author may have been thinking of her when he wrote: "Men who have lived for years with a great love, and have lived on in noble solitude when it was taken from them, are likely now and then to be worn out by their exultation. Such men return meekly to a humdrum life, ready to accept contentment in a more commonplace love."

Certainly, Saint-Exupéry could never be identified with a man ready to accept a commonplace love. However, another book, *The Wisdom of the Sands,* abounds in passages that show how he had once been torn by love for a young girl, "with her young breasts, soft and warm as doves, and her smooth belly apt for giving sons to the empire." This love is always pictured in the past, as something ended and doomed to end. By the time this book came to be written, he had experienced love on various levels and had come to terms with himself. Henceforth he would make no distinction between love for a woman, whether wife, mistress, or a companion for the night and the love for a comrade. By that time he knew that "there is but one way of loving, and that is loving not so much the woman herself as what lies beyond. Not the poem, but what lies beyond the poem."

Many hasty judgments have been made on Saint-Exupéry's affairs with women. Hasty, because the judgments were based upon a rapid reading of his works and of published letters (often without interest, but the label "Saint-Exupéry" has been of commercial value) or documents available to the writers. Definite opinions have been advanced which are patently absurd. A magazine—fortunately with a small circulation—once published comments on some merely friendly letters Saint-Ex had sent to a young woman who claimed that she had "rejected" him and that, though he abstained from mentioning love in the letters, they all had the stamp of love letters. Yet all but one are obviously written by a lonely man who turns to a friend in order to maintain contact with the outside world and to escape a rude life by reviving memories. All except one, the last, written in the spring of 1931, perhaps a few days after his marriage. It is rather enigmatic; while it is hard to decipher, the conditions in which the letter was written are known.

It begins: "*Et voilà . . .*" Which might mean, "So, this is it" or "So, it's done." He is perhaps only setting a period to a stage in his life. He is alone, in the house of his sister Didi at Agay. The time is midnight, all the family have gone to bed, even his young wife. He gazes through the window at the sea, sparkling in the moonlight, and is reminded of the metallic glint of street lamps on the foliage in a leafy market place, empty after a festival, a wide market place enlivened in the daytime by the white wings of gulls. Punta Arenas! And he recalls the day in this most southerly town when, leaning against the fountain, he had looked at the young girls. It was not long afterward that, returned from Tierra del Fuego to Buenos Aires, he had made the acquaintance of a woman. . . . In the street as they walked together, a riot had broken out, rifle shots had cracked. And that young woman had clung to him and said, "Hold me in your arms!" She was pretty, very small and frail against his big body. Now she was his wife.

We can imagine how Saint-Ex left the window, turning back toward the fireplace where some eucalyptus branches and pine-cones were burning, shedding an aromatic perfume in the room; we can imagine how he was seized with the need to talk to someone, unburden a secret. He would confide in that young friend, the girl to whom he had often written, although she had not always replied. And so he took a sheet of paper and sat down beside the fire and wrote: "*Et voilà . . .*"

The letter that followed is, as we have said, enigmatic. To Saint-Exupéry it represented a stirring of ashes, from which at times some bright sparks escaped.

"*Et voilà . . .*" The irremediable has been accomplished. No more would there be in his life a virgin with "breasts, soft and warm as doves"—but there would be tranquilizing love, and real affection, the yielding up of self, in which his wife would have her share.

For those who claim that he did not care for his wife are mistaken. Simply because he remarked once or twice "She's the cross I have to bear" is no indication of a lack of love, for as he writes in *The Wisdom of the Sands*, "Not love alone, but suffering, too, goes to the making of man's plenitude." When he spoke of a cross he had to bear, he was of course exaggerating, as usual; and he may have made the remark at a moment of annoyance. Quite often, and justifiably, he was irritated with her. But he readily forgave her and was full of indulgence for that poor "little bird of the islands" who had been brought far from her familiar skies. He felt responsible for her, and in general he had a great sense of responsibility. When, for instance, he crashed in the Libyan desert and believed he and Prévot were doomed to die of thirst, his thoughts flew homeward, toward his mother and his wife. Afterward, writing to his mother, he said, "It was terrible to think I was leaving behind me someone as in need of protection as Consuelo is. And I felt a great urge to return so that I might shield and protect her again." Repeatedly in his letters, he associates Consuelo with his mother in his thoughts. During that same ordeal in the Libyan desert, he imagined "the wail of desolation," that "cry that would be sent up at home" if he and Prévot were not rescued. "I was haunted by a vision of my wife's eyes," he wrote in *Wind, Sand and Stars;* "I could see only the eyes, questioning me, looking at me yearningly." All the same, she caused him suffering. She is now aware of it, and does not try to defend herself, but she does resent being maligned. Whenever anyone asks to see it, she unhesitatingly shows a page he wrote especially for her, a "Prayer that Consuelo should say every Evening," and which runs as follows:

> *Lord, I do not ask a great deal of You, for there is no need. I merely pray that You will keep me as I am. In small things I seem vain, but in big things I am humble. In small things I seem to be an egoist, but in big things I am capable of giving everything, even my life . . .*
>
> *Lord, grant that I may always be the woman my husband knows I am.*
>
> *Lord, Lord, safeguard my husband, because he truly loves me and because without him I would be too orphaned, but grant, O Lord, that he may be the first of us two to die, because, though he appears strong, he suffers too much when he does not hear me moving about the home. Lord, above all things, spare him that anguish. Grant that I may always be making a sound in the house, even if I must at times be noisy and break things.*

Help me to be faithful, help me to remain apart from those he despises or those who hate him. Such behavior wrongs him, for he has centered his life in me.

Lord, protect our house.

And to this prayer, I, Your Consuelo, say Amen!

One cannot help but compare this letter with certain lines in *The Wisdom of the Sands*, a few among the many lines clearly referring to or addressed to her:

> *God sent to me that woman who lied so daintily, so simply, with a cruelty redeemed by the sweetness of her voice. I bent toward her as toward a cool sea-wind.*
>
> *"Why do you lie?" I asked.*
>
> *She fell to weeping, and her face was hidden by a veil of tears. And I pondered on her tears.*

Pondering her tears, he realized that her tragedy was that she had "so great a yearning to be that other woman, the woman of her dream." And realizing this, he neither spoke nor listened to her explanation, "for in the silence of my love I heeded not the vain sound of the words, but only the struggle going on within her." Surely, this is a proof of his love.

Separated from Consuelo, often voluntarily, he wrote to her with great tenderness. It is impossible to doubt the sincerity of those letters. The generation that comes after us will be able to judge between them and the letters he wrote to his good friend, his Egeria—a hundred years after Saint-Exupéry's death is the delay presumably fixed by her for their publication—and it is possible that more love letters were written to Consuelo than to the other lady.

In 1940, before the launching of the German offensive, Saint-Exupéry managed to obtain an appointment as a junior pilot in an air reconnaissance unit known as Group 2–33, which was stationed at Orcante, a small town in the Champagne region. He foresaw more clearly than most people at that time the frightfulness of the war about to begin; to him, it represented "a threat to the future of man." His sweet Egeria had visited him at the farm where he was billeted. But she had barely left him when he wrote to his mother, mentioning Consuelo with great solicitude: "As time goes on, I am more and more anxious about those for whom I feel responsible. I am filled with an infinite pity for poor little Consuelo, so forsaken."

It is true that he had forsaken Consuelo. He was bitterly to regret it later. But in 1942 she was to rejoin him in the United States, when once more, for a time, she would alternately enchant him and drive him wild. The book he was then working on, *The Little Prince,* contains in the parable of the rose the story of his marriage, and all the love and poignant regrets that overwhelmed him when he thought of Consuelo. "The fact is," says the little prince, who had forsaken the rose, irritated by her lies and vanity, "that I did not know how to understand anything! I ought to have judged by deeds and not by words. She cast her fragrance and her radiance over me. I ought never to have run away from her.... I ought to have guessed all the affection that lay behind her poor little stratagems. Flowers are so inconsistent! But I was too young to know how to love her...."

In the letter he had written to his mother in 1940, Saint-Exupéry had expressed his pity and compassion for Consuelo. Already, at that time, he had begun work on *The Wisdom of the Sands,* which devotes so many pages to extolling acts of pity and compassion. With Saint-Exupéry these sentiments could not remain sterile and futile, as with so many men; they could only become merged with the sentiment of love.

7

Now, a watchman from the heart of night, he learnt how night betrays man's presence, his voices, lights, and his unrest.

—Night Flight

In 1931 Saint-Exupéry returned to France from South America, bringing Consuelo with him, and bringing also the finished manuscript of his new novel, *Night Flight.* He stopped off in Paris only to leave the manuscript with the publisher, then went to Agay with his bride-to-be. After the wedding, and after a three months' honeymoon, the young couple did not return to South America but instead went to Casablanca. Saint-Exupéry was once more a simple pilot of the Line, flying the mails on the Casablanca–Dakar stretch.

Why did he leave his post as director of Aeroposta-Argentina, which he had held from October 1929 to January 1931? According to one rumor, he had been found to lack some of the qualities needed in a director of the Line. He preferred flying to office work, and often took up a plane that could and should have been flown by another pilot. According to another account, he disliked Buenos Aires and wanted to return to France. But he may merely have been impelled to leave South America because of his natural restlessness and his inability, as he himself realized, to settle down anywhere. J.-G. Fleury, who was traveling in South America at this time gathering material for his book about the Line (*La Ligne*), tells us that Saint-Ex was recalled to France simply because Aeroposta-Argentina was reducing its activities, the need to retrench arising from the financial problems of its European affiliate, the Compagnie Générale Aéropostale.

The position Saint-Ex had occupied in Buenos Aires was extremely well paid and in many ways was enviable. But he had accepted the job mainly because it would enable him to keep on flying. He seized every opportunity to fly, especially at night, when the darkness hid the earth or when there were only occasional glimpses of sleeping towns. Sometimes a single light glimmered in a humble home, and in thought he would drop down toward it, speculating about what that lamp shone upon, whether a scene of distress or love. Navigating among the stars, he gave himself over to meditation in the vast temple of night. And, suspended in the sky on calm nights, he meditated upon the human condition, its grandeur and flaws. Poet, he discovered a new form of poetry in the night sky, forged in rare metal, enriched with the power and energy that go into a life of action, and he discovered a world till then unknown. "The airplane has unveiled for us the true face of the earth," he wrote. His books are filled with these new revelations.

Once more stationed in Morocco—at Port-Étienne, this time—his night flights would not now be made alone, but with a new comrade of the air, the radio operator. Sitting behind the pilot, crowded in between the bags of mail, earphones on, this newcomer would henceforth link the plane with the ground stations scattered along thousands of miles of coast, where operators were constantly on the alert. Saint-Exupéry's radio operator was usually Jacques Néri. Both men being artists of sorts, they often communicated with each other by sketching little pictures on scraps of paper they passed back and forth. They were good comrades, and when Saint-Ex came to write *Wind, Sand and Stars*, he was careful to mention Néri by name when recounting an adventure they shared.

Néri was destined to be Guillaumet's radio operator over the South Atlantic for many years, thus holding the record for Atlantic crossings at a time when such flights were hailed as exploits. Deported by the Germans during the occupation of France, he managed to escape the extermination camps. Liberated in 1945, he recuperated from his privations for several months in his native Corsica, then resumed work with the Air France line (as it was by that time called), first flying over the South Atlantic, and then on the Far East extension. Quiet, self-effacing, conscientious, he had a real vocation for flying and dreaded the time when he would be retired. But one day, when he had totted up 16,000 hours of flying, the Line's physician ended his career. Mme. Néri recalls the day when she awaited the results of the physical examination, pacing the floor in their small apartment in the Rue de Poissy in Paris. The walls were covered with Jacques' paintings, the room was filled with souvenirs of his adventurous life, and she remembered the countless times she had waited anxiously here for his return from some long flight. Her pet parakeet, infected by her present anxiety, was flying about the room excitedly, settling now on the chandelier, now on the top of the wardrobe, now on Mme. Néri's shoulder. At last the door opened softly, and Néri appeared, very downcast. "It's all over," he said, "they've rejected me. My flying days are over." His wife flung her plump arms around his neck. "Oh," she exclaimed, "if that's the truth, I'll send flowers to the doctor!"

Casablanca . . . Agadir . . . Cape Juby . . . Villa Cisneros . . . Port-Étienne . . . St.-Louis-du-Sénégal . . . Dakar. How many memories were awakened in Saint-Exupéry as he saw once more these desert stations of the Line in Africa. For again, three months after his marriage, he was plunged in the desert life of hardships and solitude, of dangers and comradeship. Juby, and the memory of old Bark, the slave he had liberated. Port-Étienne, where Lucas, chief of the airport, wound his squeaky old graphophone, playing it almost night and day, flinging up a music which "would speak to us in a half-lost language, provoking an aimless melancholy which curiously resembled thirst." Then, Nouatchott was beneath his wings, almost invisible in the night, and he recalled his first taste of the desert when, with Riguelle and Guillaumet, he had crash-landed nearby and had spent the night.

He was carrying the mail, as in his first years with the Line. At Dakar the mail would be handed over to comrades who would take it to South America. And at Casablanca it was passed on to men who, next day, would set it down in France.

But then, one day in December 1931, as a flyer stationed at Toulouse has recounted,[12] Saint-Ex himself flew the mail plane into Toulouse, having come on a special and private mission. The coveted *Prix Fémina* had just been awarded his novel *Night Flight*, and he had obtained a leave of absence to receive the prize in Paris. When he got out of the plane he looked more like a tramp than a writer whose fame would soon be worldwide. "A three days' growth of beard covered his face," said Dubourdieu, "and the beard was spattered with oil from the engines not wiped off during the twenty hours of flight; on his feet were a pair of old canvas espadrilles; his trousers were as stained as they were ragged; he was wearing no shirt, and his old navy blue raincoat was tied round his waist by a string." He stayed at Toulouse only long enough to fish out of a suitcase he had left there "a soiled shirt and a wrinkled suit."

The fine qualities of *Night Flight*, Saint-Exupéry's second published work, which he wrote in South America, have already been noted. The man who inspired the book, his chief to whom it is dedicated, with two other airmen, Guillaumet and Hochedé, represented to Saint-Exupéry the best in man. But it is not merely the dedication of *Vol de Nuit*—"To Monsieur Didier Daurat"—that has led readers to identify the Managing Director of the Aéropostale with the hero, Revière, although Daurat himself has always denied it.

I paid Daurat a visit at Le Bourget Airport when I was gathering material for my biography of Henri Guillaumet and the present work which was to follow. The time was shortly after World War II, and M. Daurat was in his office at the airport, which was gradually rising again from its ruins. There he was, that indomitable man with the piercing eyes and impassive face, sitting at his desk, smoking his eternal cigarette. And still, as twenty-seven years earlier in Toulouse after another war, he was constructing, forging, struggling with the same determination and tenacity which pulverizes obstacles. The war had disrupted the French airmail service which he had organized; now, with insufficient means and with what men could be found, he was putting this service on its feet again. He talked about the difficulties encountered by the crews who were flying decrepit planes in all weather over territory where ground stations and landing strips were almost nonexistent. At the moment he was evolving, with his pilots, the techniques of landing in zero visibility. I compared his present problems with those of the past, and spoke of the men he had had under his orders, especially Guillaumet and Saint-Exupéry. Then I embarked on the subject of *Night Flight* and the protagonist, Rivière, and repeated what others had told me—that Saint-Exupéry had been thinking of M. Daurat when describing this character.

"It's sheer legend," Daurat commented in his grave, precise way.

"Perhaps," I replied, "but some legends are based on fact, derive from history."

M. Daurat's gaze wandered toward the airfield where some dark "Junkers" were being readied for flight. Then, as if talking to himself, he murmured, "I didn't need to be that severe. With the men I had, men who asked nothing better than to serve, it wasn't necessary."

Had he forgotten? Of course not. But he did not like to think that he had any of the inhuman traits of Rivière. As time went on, he refused more and more to admit that he had served as model for that character. But all the same, in the film *Au Grand Balcon,* which Kessel made from the book, there is a character who strikingly resembles Didier Daurat—or Rivière. In the film, the director is called Carbot, and Pierre Fresnay played the part well. In September 1949, the movie was shown at Toulouse during a gala evening celebrating the anniversary of the departure of the first mail plane from the Montaudran airfield. Didier Daurat was present, and a few days afterward I asked for his opinion of the film.

"It's cinema," he said, adding what he had said before, "it's sheer legend."

"Yes, of course, but there's good and bad cinema, and I thought this was good. I thought Fresnay . . ."

"Fresnay is a talented actor," M. Daurat cut in. "But he needn't have exaggerated."

To prove that the character of Rivière was not based on himself, Daurat cites the story line of the book, and points out that he did not launch the first night plane, which in the story is lost, and that he did not, despite this misfortune, launch another plane with another crew immediately after. It was Mermoz, probably, who first had the idea of flying the mail by night. Be that as it may, Saint-Exupéry used Daurat as his model for Rivière. The ruthlessness of Rivière is the ruthlessness that was absolutely necessary in a man who attempted, and obstinately succeeded in accomplishing, one of the most extraordinary ventures of the century. A hazardous venture, for it involved the unknown, and a grandiose venture of incalculable scope. Had Daurat not been what he was, and what he refuses to admit he was, the Line would not have endured and commercial aviation would have been greatly retarded, not only in France, but in the world. For the prodigious success of this project led to efforts of the same kind in other countries after World War I.

Daurat knew better than anyone how perilous the venture was, and for that reason when he was put in charge of the crews—he had piloted but a short time when he emerged as leader from the dozen or so military airmen who first came to Montaudran—he realized how much flawless will power would be required to shape the pioneer pilots of Toulouse. He realized that they must be made to feel that they were an integral part of the venture; and the ones who failed in some small way must be rejected ruthlessly. They were of inferior clay, incapable of being molded. And so this commander of men concealed his feelings beneath an apparent indifference and callousness, became taciturn, speaking only to issue orders or make comments which were never complimentary.

Rivière, in *Night Flight,* abruptly dismisses an old mechanic who has made one mistake, and only one, after years of painstaking work. M. Daurat, in real life, was capable of similar harshness. A story often told to illustrate this bears repeating.

One of the pilots of the Line had two accidents in quick succession.

"Have you forgotten how to fly?" asked M. Daurat.

The pilot, who had enjoyed a good reputation up to this time, stammered out a bewildered explanation. "You . . . you see, M. Daurat, I've been unlucky."

"Report to the office, where you will be paid off. I don't want unlucky pilots in this organization."

In Daurat's view, there was no reason to compliment a flyer for bringing his plane through safely, no matter what the dangers encountered; in succeeding, the pilot was merely doing his duty. If he failed, then he must go elsewhere.

Rivière, in the book, hears a pilot recount the events of a perilous flight in a squall which might have ended in catastrophe. "You've too much imagination," he says curtly. But when the pilot withdraws, Rivière reflects, "I've stopped him from being afraid." By seemingly making light of their courage, he saved his airmen from fear and therefore perhaps from death.

When Daurat denies having been the model for Rivière, he is less in opposition to that character than to all the tales told by the men he dismissed and who became his enemies. Naturally he made enemies. But the very accusations of these men against their former chief show their spitefulness and lack of dependability, thus justifying Daurat's original judgment of them and adding to his stature as a leader. M. Daurat had many qualities, but perhaps the greatest was his ability to distinguish quickly the men of worth from those who were merely lucky, the men of courage from those who were merely daredevils, and promptly to eliminate the undesirables.

Whether or no Rivière is a fictional Daurat, *Night Flight* made of the living man a legendary character. That is a heavy responsibility. M. Daurat is a modest and retiring man, but he has not escaped a sort of permeation with the character of the fictional person which is usual in such cases.

One evening at Mme. Guillaumet's, Daurat recounted to us some of his memories and in doing so quoted unconsciously but textually phrases that occur in *Night Flight*. He talked like Rivière—but, of course, Rivière talked like Daurat. Curiously enough, the phrases he used were Rivière's at his most humane, and not Rivière at his most ruthless. But then, "His harshness evolved in a steadily descending curve," to quote a remark made by one of the finest pilots on the Line.

Thus, between Saint-Ex and Daurat there was a kind of exchange, although they saw each other almost never except professionally. Indeed, none of the flyers was ever able to set up friendly relations with Daurat. The young pilots were always greatly impressed by him, from their very first contact, but his impassive face, steely gaze, aloof manner, and authoritarian way of speaking did not make him very likable. Saint-Ex had immediately found him interesting and worthy of respect. As time went on, he saw no reason to revise his first judgment, although he was often disappointed in a mentality he later discovered to be "a mechanism that could easily be taken apart." Daurat's utter subjection to an ideal, his concealment of feelings beneath a harsh exterior set him apart from other men. Saint-Ex not only respected him but was drawn to him. He wanted to observe and analyze his behavior and reactions: a difficult task, for Daurat was as if hermetically sealed. However, Saint-Ex gradually discovered clues to the real nature of Daurat, and was able, in the character of Rivière, to reveal Daurat to himself as a harder man and a greater man than he had ever believed he was.

Twenty-five years after the publication of *Night Flight*, Daurat published his own memoirs. In his book, *Dans le Vent des Hélices* (*In the Wind of the Propellers*), he flatly refuses to see a reflection of himself in Rivière. He exclaims, in the words of Racine's Junie in *Britannicus:* "*Je ne crois mériter ni cet excès d'honneur ni cette* *indignité.*" * In sum, Daurat is unable to estimate himself in comparison with Rivière, nor can we, because his attitude and actions, like the organization he established and shaped, exceed the usual standards.

The Line has often been written about as though it were a religion, with its own mystique. An explanation, or rather a definition, of mystique has been offered by a monk—a monk who left the monastery to become a worker-priest. He states that mystique implies a clear vision of a goal to be attained, knowledge of the means, and the strength to attain it. We can therefore logically speak of Daurat's mystique—and of Rivière's. It is the attitude of the man of action, and explains everything in his character. This presupposes withdrawal from or disdain of anything that interferes with, or is not a means of, attaining the end. When we realize this, we can accept without demur the idea that justice had little meaning for Rivière. "It was no concern to Rivière whether he seemed just or unjust. Perhaps the words were meaningless to him. . . . For him, a man was a mere lump of wax to be kneaded into shape. It was his task to furnish this dead matter with a soul, to inject will power into it. Not that he wished to make slaves of his men; his aim was to raise them above themselves. In punishing them for each delay he acted, no doubt, unjustly, but he bent the will of every crew to punctual departure; or, rather, he bred in them the will to keep to time." It is therefore irrelevant to judge as a right or wrong action the dismissal of an unlucky pilot or blundering old mechanic, or the withdrawal of Guillaumet's no-cash bonus. Such acts entered into the mystique of Didier Daurat.

When Daurat commented, "I didn't have to be so severe with the men I had," he should rather have said, "Those men accepted even injustice, because they knew they were involved in something that went beyond the bounds of justice."

As it happened, some of those men did not at all appreciate

* "I do not think I deserve either that extreme honor or that infamy."

Night Flight. And oddly enough, what aroused their ire was exactly what Daurat protested against.

"Even though human life may be the most precious thing on earth," Rivière reflects, "we always behave as if there were something of higher value than human life." Such reflections cannot mean the same thing to the armchair reader as to a pilot about to climb into his plane and take off in far from favorable weather, a pilot who has seen fifty or so of his comrades vanish from the earth—for one hundred and twenty men lost their lives for the Line. The pilot may be gladly risking his life, but he does not enjoy such analytical thinking.

Some readers saw in *Night Flight* an effort to justify a man and his principles; these readers did not comprehend that the author was glorifying them at the same time.

Another factor conspired to separate his comrades from Saint-Ex, something not entirely unrelated to these objections. In fact, he disclosed this in the letter to Guillaumet, already quoted in part. The rest of the letter is worth noting here: "Because I wrote that wretched book I have been made to suffer. My comrades have ostracized me," he says, with his usual exaggeration. "Mermoz will tell you what things have been said about me by those whom I have not seen for ages but whom I was once fond of. They will tell you that I am pretentious! And there's not a soul from Toulouse to Dakar who doesn't believe it."

Naturally, he was not called or thought pretentious by any except a few men of the Line, and none of his close friends was among them. For though he had, as he said, a fraternal feeling for all the pilots of the Line, he had made intimate friends of only a few. The flyers came to Latécoère from every class and rank of society. Some, of quite humble extraction, evolved and became polished by their contacts. Others, on the contrary, were incapable of development. And these men had always considered Saint-Ex as aloof, an aristocrat—to their minds the word had a disparaging meaning. "He's a snob," some of them said. And it must be admitted that Saint-Ex did bear the imprint of his upbringing and schooling, which had been aristocratic. But those who blamed him for this found it hard to see one of themselves promoted, and resented it when Saint-Ex, who had cleaned spark plugs at Montaudran before flying the Toulouse–Casablanca route, was sent to Buenos Aires as director of the Aeroposta-Argentina. Worse still, this ex-comrade, while holding down that enviable job, had written a book in which he had put the managing director of Aéropostale, quite obviously, for the fictional Rivière was a silent man who spoke only to give orders or to criticize. No, this was too much!

They felt too that Saint-Ex had changed, had become proud and vain over the success of his book. They interpreted as vanity the justifiable pride of an author who has done a good job of creative writing and has seen it awarded a literary prize. These comrades who were so united in their work, so fraternal, even great when confronting danger, were not entirely free of ordinary human defects. They were jealous, and they "ostracized" him. One can imagine the remarks repeated perhaps to Saint-Ex, that sensitive plant. He was filled with a great bitterness—the first time in his life that he had known such bitterness. But also, he had never known the pleasures of comradeship until he became a pilot of the Line. And now this comradeship was denied him. They called him pretentious! He felt utterly abandoned.

The one friend who could and would have consoled him was Guillaumet, and he was in the depths of South America. And Saint-Ex had not dared to write to him, fearing that he, too, believed he had changed. Then, hearing of Guillaumet's imminent return to France, he had eagerly dashed off that letter: "Guillaumet, I hear you are coming back, and my heart throbs at the news. . . ." A memory must have surged up as he held out his arms to this friend —"Don't go to a hotel, come here to my apartment, it's yours. . . . But perhaps you'll refuse and then I shall have lost my best friend!"—the memory of the night he had gone to Guillaumet's in Buenos Aires with the manuscript of *Night Flight,* which he had wanted Guillaumet and his wife to be the first to read. He wanted the opinion of that man of real "substance." Saint-Exupéry was once heard to say of Guillaumet, "There's a man presumably devoid of culture. But ask his opinion on a book and you'll see; he never makes a mistake."

That evening, while Saint-Ex impatiently walked up and down the room, Guillaumet and his wife, sitting side by side, read the manuscript in silence. Saint-Ex poured himself a drink, sat down, lit a cigarette, then got up again and looked distractedly out of the window. Now and then he glanced at the two heads bent over the manuscript, or leaned over them to see how far they had got. But his friends, enthralled with what they were reading, were unaware of his presence.

Finally they put the manuscript aside.

"Well, what do you think of it?" asked Saint-Exupéry.

"Look at my wife," said Guillaumet.

Mme. Guillaumet was quietly weeping.

The year 1931 was certainly a crucial year for Saint-Exupéry. It was the date of his return to France from South America; of his marriage; and the publication of *Vol de Nuit*, which was issued in its English version (*Night Flight*) very soon afterward in New York. A practically unknown writer before this, he was now established and famous. And thereupon he asked for a few months leave of absence from the Line. Just what his intentions were is not known. No doubt he wanted to write and to travel a little, perhaps in his own plane. The young couple found an apartment at 5 Rue de Chanaleilles, where they lived rather sketchily, since Saint-Ex often went to visit his sister at Agay or his mother at Saint-Maurice.

The *Prix Fémina* assured the book important sales and a far from negligible income in royalties. But Saint-Ex now had a young wife to help him spend money, and it melted like wax. After a few months of high living, they were without a penny. He asked to be re-employed on the Line and was assigned as junior pilot on the seaplane route now operating between Marseilles and Algiers. But after only six months on the job, he again asked for a leave. It would seem that he was hesitating between the careers of flying and writing, that he wanted to have both simultaneously. His publisher had contracted with him for five novels; this held out hope for the future. But in the meantime, he had his career as airman, which he loved, and it enabled him to pay expenses. His money ran out again, and again he asked for a job. But this time his application was rejected.

A great deal had happened to the Line in 1931–1932, all of it bad and calculated to upset completely the men connected with the enterprise. For Aéropostale had gone into liquidation.

This organization, which had developed and expanded so prodigiously, had always seemed to us above financial questions. We knew the men, their courage, devotion, abilities; and it seemed to us that what counted in the organization was not money but ideals and *esprit de corps*. There had to be a financial side, but this was secondary—or so we thought. Alas, this heroic enterprise met the unenviable fate of ordinary business firms when inefficiently managed. Beside Daurat and his pilots, radio operators, mechanics, and secretaries, there were eventually the financiers. This need not have been harmful, but could on the contrary have been useful had not the financiers been involved in politics. But finance and politics go hand in hand, and if they are not accomplices then they are apt to be enemies.

When, in 1927, the Lignes Latécoère had become the Aéropostale, greater changes than the mere title were involved. Pierre Latécoère, in the course of these transactions, ceded eighty-three per cent of the shares of his air-transport company to a wealthy Frenchman, Marcel Bouilloux-Lafont, who had lived in South America for twenty-five years and, thanks to his energy and intelligence, had brilliantly established himself there in a variety of enterprises. This industrialist enjoyed great prestige in South America, and when Captain Roig went there to lay down the bases for the Line, Bouilloux-Lafont placed all his resources at the service of his compatriot. Then, infected by the faith of the air pioneers, charmed by their enthusiasm, and glimpsing the great future that lay ahead, he invested money in the company and gradually brought more and more financial aid to it. The buying up of airfields, the installation of airports scattered across a vast territory, demanded the expenditure of huge sums. Even Marcel Bouilloux-Lafont's fortune was swallowed up.

The French government had promised subsidies to the industrialist, but suddenly these were not forthcoming. Bouilloux-Lafont was ruined, and the Aéropostale was sunk. Dirty politics was involved, and the epic enterprise was spattered with filth. The men of the Line were as shaken up as if they had run into a cyclone. Everything they had suffered thus far was nothing beside this wretched collapse.

But the Line could not disappear. The mail could not, next day, be carried by the planes of another nation which was preparing to spread its wings as ours folded. Mermoz, at the time in South America, used all his energies, revived the faith and tenacity of his comrades, reminded them of the sacrifices of those who had died in the service, raised new crews. And after a bad period of disorganization, the new company, Air France, was organized—but not until 1934—to continue flying the mail. There was a time when the men received no salaries, but they continued to fly the mail and risk their lives for an enterprise that would have otherwise disintegrated without leaving a trace. And the radio stations continued to function, under the same conditions.

At the lamentable trial of Bouilloux-Lafont, who was accused of misappropriation of funds and of bribing government officials, Didier Daurat was interrogated.

"And you mean to say," he was asked, "that you did not know of the financial situation of the company?"

Didier Daurat, that indomitable man of quiet energy, who had assumed the most terrible responsibilities, who was noted for his harsh discipline, but also for his probity and utter disregard for the material comforts that money can buy, replied in his usual grave way: "I always knew what was in the hearts of my pilots, but always ignored what was in the coffers of Monsieur Bouilloux-Lafont."

But Daurat did not get off with a mere questioning. Worse was to come. He was soon to find himself hemmed in on every side by enemies. The ringleader was the pilot Serre, who was devoured by political ambitions. This pilot of the Line who had once crashed in the desert and, with Marcel Reine, was taken captive by the Moors while Saint-Exupéry was at Juby, was an odd mixture. An ardent syndicalist, he believed in state-owned enterprise; he was also an intellectual snob—a graduate of the École Polytechnique—and had always chafed at accepting orders from a man less educated than he was himself. He had long held a grudge against Daurat and, embittered and ambitious, had gradually drawn followers to him, discontented men who liked to hear him spout his ideas. According to Serre the time of pioneer heroes was past, the time of technicians had come; the era of a mystique, of great-hearted impulses and enthusiasms, was over and must give way to reasoning and calculation. Daurat exemplified everything Serre detested, and Daurat seemed invulnerable, that is, until the trial.

The basest kinds of machinations were set on foot against Daurat, who was even accused of pillaging the mail. Witnesses were found —a dismissed pilot, a telephone operator—who were ready to testify that they had seen him burn mail in his office at night.

Daurat had no difficulty in defending himself. True, he may have been seen burning envelopes. When the Moors pillaged the mail bags of a wrecked plane, they opened the envelopes in the hope of finding banknotes, then left them scattered on the ground. The envelopes were salvaged and sent to the Postal administration, if the address were still legible. If not, they were thrown away. Besides, in an effort to preserve the mail as much as possible from both water and fire, Daurat had carried out numerous experiments. One of these was testing the low degree of inflammability of tightly compressed bundles of envelopes.

His arguments were of no avail, however, nor was the vehement testimony offered in his behalf by Mermoz, Guillaumet, Dubourdieu, and Saint-Exupéry. For the moment, calumny triumphed, and Daurat was relieved of his duties.

At this point Saint-Ex intervened personally by writing a long letter in favor of Daurat, addressing it to Raoul Dautry, who had been appointed by the government as director pro tem of the bankrupt company. In this letter he not only refuted the accusations leveled at Daurat, but criticized the decision taken against him by the Aéropostale board of directors.

"Pilot of the Aéropostale since 1926," the letter begins, "my esteem for Monsieur Daurat has constantly increased with the passing years. I do not know what the real motives are that have relieved him of his office as General Manager, but can only consider the ones furnished as mere pretexts."

He goes on to list the "grave acts" which Daurat had been accused of committing, but which had not been proved against him "because the accusations were too clearly spurious." With his well-known logic, he quashes the false witnesses, and ends by declaring: "No matter what reasonings led the Aéropostale Board of Directors to prefer another manager to Monsieur Daurat, there is surely no comparison possible between his twelve-year record and the unproved accusations of a telephone operator and a pilot, yet these accusations alone motivated the dismissal of Monsieur Daurat. Every directive board has the right to dismiss a manager at will, even without a pretext, but it does not have the right to use such pretexts as these. Still less does it have the right to use such pretexts to refuse just damages to the man to whom Aéropostale owes everything."

This letter was to weigh heavily against Saint-Exupéry when, in 1934, he applied for a pilot's job with Air France. Even without it, his book *Night Flight* weighed heavily enough against him. He was reproached not only by pilots, radio operators, and mechanics who identified Rivière with Monsieur Daurat, but by others, for having too passionately defended his chief. But this was not the sole reason why Air France turned him down.

His faults as pilot were well known to the directors of Aéropostale, particularly to Daurat, who could see and put to use the great qualities of the man. But now these defects were being spitefully described to the new directors; Daurat's enemies and Saint-Exupéry's detractors did not seem to differentiate him from Daurat in their malicious campaign. It was easy to exaggerate his absent-mindedness while flying—and a pilot could have no more serious defect. Then, was he not first of all a writer and poet, that is to say, the opposite of an attentive and reasoning man? On the Marseilles–Algiers line, to which he was assigned for a few months, he was never allowed to pilot a hydroplane alone, but made all trips as co-pilot. In trying out a seaplane at Saint-Raphaël, Saint-Ex had an accident which might have been fatal not only to himself but to his companions on the plane as well.

Aside from this, his attitude was calculated to support another ill-natured piece of gossip circulated by his enemies, who represented him as a devil-may-care fellow, impervious to discipline. For, at the end of his leave, Saint-Ex had not reported for work. The management had to remind him of this in a letter, which clearly indicates dissatisfaction with his behavior: "We are very surprised.... We are very astonished...."

But Saint-Ex believed that Air France refused to take him back chiefly because of his book, *Night Flight,* and particularly because of the place he had given Daurat in that work. There were other reasons too; one of the proofs is that Daurat was reinstated in August 1933, while Saint-Ex was not taken back by the Company until April 1934. Three months before that, Saint-Ex wrote to the manager of Air France, mentioning the Rivière–Daurat case.

"Having taken a regulation leave of absence from Aéropostale," he wrote, "I did not return to work at the expiration of my leave. I felt it would be painful to face the thousand and one difficulties, moral and material, in the course of my work, these difficulties stemming solely from the fact of my having written *Night Flight.* It had seemed to me that a book translated into every European language, adapted for the stage and screen abroad, comprised publicity for Aéropostale which no expensive newspaper campaign could have equaled, and that it was of little importance whether or no my Monsieur Rivière resembled Monsieur Daurat. The fact that I am being so bitterly reproached for this resemblance seems all the meaner to me since my book was entirely written in Argentina, long before the dissensions sprang up within the company, so that quite obviously it was not written with the set purpose of taking sides in those dissensions." [13]

In this long letter he attempts to justify himself for having requested a leave of absence, enumerating the reasons why he should be reinstated—not forgetting those of a sentimental category—and he concludes by repeating that he would not return to Air France except as a pilot. The letter had no more success than the previous steps he and Mermoz had taken.

His situation was now precarious, and as time went on it became ever more so. Somehow he had to find a way of earning a living. His money worries were such that he was unable to write. He was obsessed by the need for a steady job, and he could only see a job with Air France. As a last resort he took a surprising step which shows how desperate he was. He let it be casually known, with the help of a friend who rather frequently met M. Allègre, a director of Air France, that he intended to publish, in an important newspaper, an article on "The Rise and Fall of the French Air-Lines." M. Allègre pricked up his ears; Saint-Exupéry was a famous writer, such an article would stir up a commotion. The nasty Aéropostale affair had been forgotten—in France, shady affairs are quickly forgotten, the French people having too great a taste for the splendid and the grandiose. Air France was developing rapidly, the directors foresaw a brilliant future. It was not the moment to revive old controversies and grudges, or to discover the toadstool quietly rotting away under the moss.

And so, one day in April 1934, Saint-Exupéry received a letter informing him that, although there was no need at the moment for pilots, the flying crews being complete, the company was considering the idea of employing him in their publicity department, entrusting him with missions at home and abroad.

Saint-Exupéry accepted the job offered, in spite of what he had said in his February 2 letter. But even though he might believe that the missions entrusted to him would not be of secondary importance, he had no illusions on one score: clearly, they did not want him again as a pilot.

8

Once we know the hates and fears and loves that rule their lives, we can foretell men's acts.

—The Wisdom of the Sands

The publicity job with Air France represented a welcome break in a period of misery that had lasted two years and was destined to last five more. The seven darkest years of Saint-Exupéry's life had at least this one bright interval. For seven long years he was to attempt time and again to raise himself toward a more clement atmosphere, toward the sky, where he belonged, but all his efforts were to end in frustration. He who had said he needed to be in a state of restless anxiety if he were to do creative writing was now overwhelmed with anxieties of every kind. The publicity job would at least relieve him of some of his worries, but he accepted it without enthusiasm.

His first mission was to Indochina "to carry out some studies," and it consumed one month including the flight out and back. We do not know what he was expected to accomplish there; of this mission we know very little. However, we have one anecdote, and it is typical.

The day after his arrival in Saigon, he expressed the wish to visit Angkor, and asked the managing director of the Saigon airbase permission to use an old hydroplane, the *Lioré*, which had been standing idle for months in a hangar. The permission was granted and he was assigned an Indochinese mechanic and a French co-pilot. The pilot happened to be a former classmate at the navigation school in Brest, Pierre Gaudillère.

Saint-Ex was at the controls. Gaudillère, well acquainted with the country and not having much confidence in the plane's engine, had traced their route so that it would follow the waterways of the Cochin China delta, the Mekong and Tonlesap rivers, and the lake of Angkor.

Following the waterways turned out to be a wise precaution, for after only twenty minutes in the air, the engine abruptly stalled. Saint-Ex managed to bring the hydroplane safely down on a muddy river, the Soirap.

Gaudillère has described the warm and luminous night they spent on the hydroplane, which was anchored to the root of a mangrove tree, with mosquitoes dancing over the water and the frogs trilling, and Saint-Exupéry in an elated and talkative mood.[14] Sitting on top of the plane, his legs dangling over the dark water, he talked and talked to Pierre Gaudillère beside him, reviving old memories, mingling observations of the moment with his eternal meditations. Then, as he was fond of doing, he sang an old song of his childhood, after which he withdrew into a long silence, as he sometimes did, even in the presence of a friend. Gazing at the constellations sparkling above the dark forest, lulled by the gentle lapping of the water against the wooden sides of the *Lioré,* he was recalling, no doubt, his nights in the desert or in Argentina when, alone in his plane, "shepherd of the stars," he traversed the sky.

The voyage to Indochina provided a welcome escape from the life he had been leading in Paris, a life that had become more and more futile as he felt himself a spectator of a world of people solely preoccupied with material satisfactions. No doubt, too, the voyage enriched and broadened his mind, for he was perpetually on the alert and nothing that could instruct ever passed unnoticed.

He was sent on no other such missions but instead made a lecture tour in the principal towns of the Mediterranean: Casablanca, Algiers, Tunis, Bengasi, Cairo, Alexandria, Damascus, Beirut, Istanbul, Athens, and Rome. A *Simoun* plane was put at his disposal, along with a mechanic, Prévot, who was from then on to be his flight companion. They were accompanied by Jean-Marie Conty, the organizer of the trip, who always introduced Saint-Ex on the lecture platform. Conty's speech was confined to factual matters relating to Air France, while Saint-Exupéry usually spoke of the pioneer years and the heroes of postal aviation, a subject which permitted him to expatiate on his favorite philosophical themes. He was a good lecturer when allowed to talk on these subjects, for his enthusiasm soon effaced his habitual shyness.

The lecture halls in every city were packed, but Conty, in charge of the finances of the trip, never had enough money. However, the three men were often invited to dine; at least they needed to spend very little on food. At one stage of the tour Conty had to turn himself into a nurse, when Saint-Ex woke up one morning with a very sore throat—the consequences of a sudden chill, no doubt, but also of an overindulgence in cigarettes, for he smoked to excess. At any rate he had a bad cough and almost entirely lost his voice—a serious illness for a lecturer.

They had other troubles. In Turkey, Saint-Ex landed the *Simoun* just over the border in a deserted field, but they were soon pounced upon by the local people, who mistook them for Bolsheviks—the plane was painted red. Unable to make themselves understood, and fearing imprisonment, Saint-Ex and Conty climbed into a peasant's cart and went off in search of the authorities. They finally had their permit to continue on their way, but only after some argument and loss of time. The lecture in Rome had to be canceled, at the request of the French ambassador, because of tensions between France and Italy: belligerent Fascism was rampant, Mussolini was claiming Nice and Corsica, and in the Italian Parliament insults were being hurled at France. Therefore, after a final lecture in Athens, Saint-Exupéry and his two companions returned to Paris by way of Brindisi and Marseilles.

This lecture tour was not triumphal, but it could only have benefited French aviation and spread its fame. For Saint-Exupéry, it had been a pleasant evasion; he had enjoyed visiting cities he had not seen before. He had encountered new people, made new observations, heard new things, and had had some good conversations. But all this was not enough to satisfy him; it had merely provided distractions. He needed something else. But what?

This was the period, throughout the world, of spectacular feats in aviation, attempts at long distance and speed records. In only a few years, aviation had made extraordinary advances. The engines were more powerful without being heavier. The shape of the planes had changed, had become more "streamlined." And the pilots, more often than not flying solo, were out to break all records—chiefly in distance—from 1918 to 1932. A French pilot, André Japy, in a flight to Tokyo, had flown from Paris to Saigon in eighty-seven hours. A prize of 150,000 francs (the equivalent today of five million) was offered to the owner–flyer who would break that record before January 1, 1936. Saint-Exupéry thought he could do it with a plane similar to the one he had been flying. The *Simoun* was a Caudron machine, equipped with a 240-h.p. Renault engine; a fast plane with a variable-pitch propeller, it represented at the time a great improvement in aeronautical techniques.

Saint-Exupéry therefore had to find a plane of this type. He thought at once of Didier Daurat, who had recently founded, in collaboration with Beppo de Massimi, the Air-Bleu company, whose mail planes were then streaking across the skies of France, and those planes were *Simouns*. At first Daurat was not very enthusiastic about his former pilot's plan. He knew Saint-Exupéry's situation and thought that it "forbade his having the calm necessary to succeed in such an attempt." But on the other hand, he realized that "the adventure he was going to attempt would save him from a threatening mental and physical breakdown." Besides, Daurat was interested in any performance in a plane of the type Air Bleu was using. He also must have felt in the depths of his soul that he owed a debt to the author of *Night Flight*. Aiding him now offered the opportunity to pay that debt, at least in part. He therefore helped Saint-Ex to acquire a *Simoun* on the most reasonable terms, and had it outfitted by his own mechanics, one of whom happened to be Prévot, who was to accompany Saint-Ex on the long-distance attempt.

Jean Mermoz and General Davet of the French Air Corps had

also done "everything required" to implement this record-breaking attempt. But the time limit was approaching; already it was Christmas, and in order to break Japy's record Saint-Ex must reach Saigon by January 1. The money offered as prize was important to him, for he had pressing debts and his financial worries made it impossible to do any writing.

The circumstances in which he prepared for this air race are typical of him and very different from the calm, methodical, even finical preparations of a Codos, a Bossoutrot, a Costes, or a Maryse Bastié. Saint-Ex took rooms at the Pont-Royal hotel, at the corner of the Rue du Bac and the Boulevard Saint-Germain. And there he was, for the three days preceding the flight, with his wife and a few friends, living in a noisy and quarrelsome atmosphere, not at all conducive to preparing him for an important event in which so much was at stake, including his and Prévot's lives. For three days it was a combination tea party and comic-opera regimental headquarters, melodrama mingling with comedy. Consuelo, very excited, chattered and gesticulated, made scenes, badgered her husband. Only Jean Lucas (the comrade from Port-Étienne) went on calmly working; he was an earnest fellow, knew the problems of navigation, and deemed the moment serious and important. There he sat, bent over the maps, estimating the distances between stops, looking like a studious schoolboy and acting like a big brother aware of his responsibilities. Meanwhile Saint-Ex wanted to lie down for a short rest. His wife was lying on one of the beds, smoking cigarettes, and kept right on talking. She sat up occasionally, waved her hands, moved about, then went back to bed.

At last, losing patience, Lucas scolded her roundly for the way she was behaving. With a bound, Consuelo pounced upon him and slapped his face. She sometimes did that to Saint-Ex. But Lucas, usually so calm, was furious. Grabbing Consuelo under one arm, he turned her over his knee and gave her a sound spanking.

When it was over and Consuelo was set on her feet, she exclaimed, "You, at least, are a *man!*" But when Lucas turned to Saint-Ex and remarked that this was the way to treat an obstreperous woman, Saint-Ex merely shook his head and sighed. "Yes," he said resignedly, "but I'm her husband."

For two whole days she did not stop tormenting him. Nothing and no one could restrain her, not even the rebukes and threats of their friends. When he needed rest and relaxation so badly, she gave him no peace. But perhaps she herself was nervous about the flight and took it out on him.

In Saint-Exupéry's own account of the flight in *Wind, Sand and Stars,* he does not mention that when the day came for the start, December 28, he had scarcely had a wink of sleep for forty-eight hours. Apparently he had just dozed off when "At four in the morning Lucas shook me into consciousness. 'Wake up!' And before I could so much as rub my eyes he was saying, 'Look here, at this report. Look at the moon. You won't see much of her to-night. She's new, not very bright, and she'll set at ten o'clock. And here's something else for you: sunrise in Greenwich Meridian Time and in local time as well. And here are your maps with your course all marked out.' "

As they drove out to Le Bourget, Saint-Ex noticed that he had forgotten to take thermos bottles, so he had the car stop at a pharmacist's, bought two, and had them filled at a nearby café, one thermos with white wine, the other with coffee.

It was cold, misty, and dark at the airport, but soon, with Prévot, in the heavily laden *Simoun,* Saint-Ex had taken off and was making toward Marseilles, having his last glimpse of France through showers.

He was flying over the Mediterranean when he noticed "a little stream of vapor rising from the fuel gauge" on the port wing. That meant a leak, and there was nothing for it but to turn back toward Marseilles and land on the Marignane airstrip for hasty repairs. Then once more they were airborne and flying toward Tunisia.

While refueling there, he witnessed a head-on collision of two high-powered cars. "It was as sudden," he wrote in *Wind, Sand and Stars* "as a raid in the desert" when marauding tribesmen crept up on silent feet in the night, and then suddenly there is the "clashing tumult of a razzia," after which "everything has sunk back into golden silence. The same peace, the same stillness, followed this crash. Nearby, someone spoke of a fractured skull. I had no mind to be told about that crushed and bloody cranium. Turning my back to the road, I went across to my ship, in my heart a foreboding of danger. I was to recognize that sound when I heard it again very soon. When the *Simoun* scraped the black plateau at a speed of one hundred and seventy miles an hour, I should recognize that hoarse grunt, that same snarl of destiny keeping its appointment with us."

In the darkness of the night, lost between Bengasi and Cairo, flying well out to sea while believing he was in line with the coast, Saint-Ex began a slow descent through the clouds, under the impression that he was flying toward a lighthouse and believing he was near Cairo. Suddenly he crashed, at a hundred and seventy miles an hour, upon a plateau in the midst of the Libyan desert. The two men, unhurt, survived the accident which destroyed the plane. Had the plane been flying only a few feet lower, it would have exploded in flames. The two flyers were unhurt; but they were going to have to live in the desert for three days without food and drink.

The chapter entitled "Prisoners of the Sand" in *Wind, Sand and Stars* describes this ordeal in "a mineral world" beneath a merciless sky. Other men have been lost in the desert; their ordeal has lasted longer, they have exhausted themselves like mechanisms without oil in their long march toward food and drink, they have suffered, hoped, experienced anguish and despair as Saint-Exupéry and Prévot did. But none of them ever left us an account of their sufferings in any way comparable to these pages. For, beside the factual account, there is the illumination of Saint-Exupéry's thoughts and imagination. Even his comments on the life of the little sand fox he encountered are brilliant—and the description of the fox, with its long, pointed ears, strangely resembles the fox he drew to illustrate *The Little Prince,* published many years later.

Whether his thoughts were spontaneous at the time or meditations after the event, they are logical and original, and they move us. Thus, the desert which shaped him as much as flying did provided him, as a "prisoner of the sand," with the opportunity to learn still more about it and about himself and mankind.

At the end of three days, the two men, dying of thirst and at the end of their strength, were rescued by some nomads and taken to their encampment. Not long afterward an automobile of the "Salt and Soda" factories bore them to Cairo.

Meanwhile, at the Pont-Royal hotel in Paris, the friends who had seen him off, along with others who had come there, hoping to have news, waited in great anxiety. At last the report of the rescue came through, and there was great rejoicing. A few days later, when Saint-Exupéry had returned to Paris, his rescue was celebrated at a dinner, with much singing and drinking, the celebration lasting till dawn.

This flight which might have ended far more tragically, was a costly one, for which Saint-Exupéry cannot be blamed entirely. He had chosen to take a mechanic rather than a radio operator with him, and because of the absence of a radio operator, he became lost over the desert. But, limited by weight and foreseeing engine trouble, he cannot be blamed for having chosen a mechanic. Flying on a moonless night above the desert between Bengasi and Cairo, with no landmarks, he had to depend entirely on his watch to follow his course. The meterologists in Paris, Tunis, and Bengasi had informed him that he would have a tailwind of nineteen to twenty-five miles an hour. As the distance between Bengasi and Cairo was a little more than six hundred miles, he calculated that after flying three and a half to three and three-quarter hours he should reach Cairo. Instead of a tailwind there was a stiff headwind, so that after slightly more than four hours of flight, when he believed he had gone beyond the Nile and decided to drop down, he was still 125 miles from Cairo—about three quarters of an hour to fly—but still on his course.

The festive night after his return to Paris was only a brief, happy interlude, for next day he found himself in his usual financial troubles which seemed far harder to bear than the painful and dangerous hours he had survived in the desert. Not only had he lost the important prize money he had hoped to win, he was deeply in debt for the costs. He managed for the next year to eke out a living by writing occasional magazine articles. But to take care of his immediate emergency he needed a job. He searched and found one; and a period of nomadic wandering began.

In February 1937, exactly a year after the ill-fated flight to Saigon, he was given an assignment by Air France, approved by the Ministry of Aviation, to prospect an air route between Casablanca and Timbuctu, which would link up with Gao–Bamako–Dakar. He made this flight without mishap, in a new *Simoun* he had bought with the insurance money he collected on the plane wrecked in the Lybian desert. The more than twelve hundred miles of desert between Casablanca and Timbuctu was first flown over by Saint-Exupéry in this prospecting flight. He was elated. "I've an old grudge to settle with the desert," he said. Prévot went along on this flight, and apparently set out with less apprehension than Saint-Exupéry, for his confidence in his pilot was flawless, as was his faith in his engine, upon which he lavished exaggerated care, listening to its throbbing as though it were the heartbeat of a loved one. But Saint-Ex, with his lively imagination and propensity for self-analysis, realized they were setting out, that morning in February, with "the uncontested right" to risk their lives and that the dawn light toward which they flew might be the last dawn they would ever see.

At Dakar someone presented Saint-Ex with a young lion cub which they embarked quite readily, for the frightened animal was quiet. But soon it began moving about so dangerously that Prévot had a hard time mastering it and they set the cub down at the next refueling station.

The lion incident supplied Saint-Ex with one more extraordinary story which he liked to tell. In several pieces of writing he describes himself sharing his plane with a furious lion cub and performing "all kinds of acrobatics" as he tried to dominate it. On the face of it, this is incredible. What kind of acrobatics? Did he perform loop-the-loops, rolls, and nosedives? But these would have rolled the animal about dangerously as far as both pilot and mechanic were concerned. What really happened was that Prévot had a hard struggle with the furious beast but at last succeeded in quieting it. "I saw traces of the struggle on his arms and hands," we are told by Georges Pélissier, who welcomed the flyers at Algiers.

On the return flight, at Oran, Saint-Ex wrote to his Egeria: "I'm pleased with my flight. I followed no route previously traced but flew straight across the sands, searching for the settlements as if searching for islands in mid-ocean. . . . I loved this part of the gamble. . . . I felt sure of myself and I risked everything gaily, trusting to my eyes and my reckonings."

However, next day, from Algiers, where he had "tried to write some articles which will pay a part of the costs of the trip," Saint-Ex wrote to his friend Guillaumet somewhat differently, for Guillaumet well knew that flying over the desert was no joke. "I did some good flying with my de luxe compass and my driftmeter, latest model, painted white, looks cheap but isn't," he wrote. "I found and landed at Atar without the least difficulty. I spent the night there, with high hopes of orgies I'd heard about. Unfortunately the Colonel is virtuous, and we had something more like hymn-singing. Then, next day, still flying by compass and disdaining the routes, I made straight for Fort-Gouraud, then Tindouf, bisecting the Río de Oro. I hoped to see someone I knew, but recognized no one. When you see Prévot, he'll verify this for you. I missed Tindouf by about three kilometers. When some philanthropist gives me a compass the size of a soup-plate, I'll not miss my goal by an inch."

This coasting flight over the Sahara cheered him, for his greatest joy was to fly above the desert. Alas, such flights were now rare, and the occasional trips he made subsequently in his *Simoun* scarcely satisfied his need to pilot a plane and satisfied not at all his need

Antoine and his mother,
ıntess Jean-Marie de Saint-Exupéry.

'he Château de La Môle,
'here Saint-Exupéry
pent his childhood.

Air France

Henri Guillaumet and Saint-Exupéry beside a *Laté* 26 plane when they both flew for Latécoère Airline.

Pioneer airmen Saint-Exupéry, Dumesnil, Guillaumet, Antoine, Reine (left to right) with Moorish tribesmen at Cape Juby in 1926.

Air France

Saint-Exupéry beside wreckage of his *Simoun* plane after crash in Libyan desert.

Photo by M. Racaud

Didier Daurat, manager of Latécoère Airline, who inspired Saint-Exupéry's *Night Flight*.

Saint-Exupéry and his wife Consuelo at Chamonix in 1934

With Henri Guillaumet and his wife, Saint-Exupéry flies over Luna Park in Buenos Aires in 1930.

Photo by John Phillips

aint-Exupéry works on manuscript in his cell at
ardinian air base between flights during World War II.

Saint-Exupéry at controls of *Lightning* plane
before take-off on final reconnaissance miss
Photo by John Phi

Captain Gavoille helps Saint-Exupéry into flight gear. Guatemala crash left airman with stiff shoulder that made dressing torturous operation.

Photos by John Ph

Photo by John Ph

One of the last photos of Saint-Exupéry before fatal flight over Mediterranean.

for evasion. In *Flight to Arras* he was to write, "There is a cheap literature that speaks to us of the need of escape. It is true that when we travel we are in search of distance. But distance is not to be found. It melts away. And escape has never led anywhere."

His desire to set out for distant places was not prompted merely by the taste for research and discovery, but also the urge to leave behind him an existence which had become almost intolerable. As the great traveler Paul Morand once wrote, "Traveling no longer represents for me the discovery of something but rather the losing of myself." Apparently Saint-Exupéry's desire at this time was to forget his troubles, to lose himself.

One day in January 1938, Saint-Ex and Prévot disembarked from the *Ile de France* in New York. Next day a landing crane deposited on the docks an enormous crate containing the *Simoun*. Saint-Ex was going to attempt another long flight, this time from New York to Tierra del Fuego.

What purpose this long-distance venture could serve is not apparent. Pan American Airways had already connected the big cities of the western hemisphere, except perhaps the farthest point south where, in fact, Saint-Exupéry himself, when managing the Aeroposta-Argentina, had established airfields in Patagonia—airfields that had subsequently been abandoned by the American lines. Clearly, he wanted to lose himself again and also do something spectacular to prove his abilities, refute his detractors, and, who knows, perhaps enable him to find some kind of steady job again.

On February 15, accompanied by Prévot, he took off in the direction of Brownsville, Texas, where, after refueling, he flew to Veracruz and then to Guatemala. The airport in Guatemala City is about 5000 feet above sea level, and the air at that altitude has very little density, thus providing less lift for a plane and making it almost impossible for a heavily loaded plane to become airborne. Because of the structure of the *Simoun*, a very long runway was needed, even in normal conditions, before she could have sufficient lift for a take-off. Apparently neither Prévot nor Saint-Ex was aware of the unusual conditions which would require special care in refueling, and therefore did not check the amount of fuel the mechanic at the airfield put in the tanks. The mechanic apparently filled them to capacity. One can imagine the confusing exchange between the Frenchmen who spoke almost no Spanish and the Guatemalan who knew no French.

At any rate, as the *Simoun* sped down the runway it was obvious that she was heavily overloaded. Both men listened anxiously to the throbbing engine as it raced at over sixty miles an hour and the plane showed no sign of being airborne as the far end approached, with a rough and rocky field ahead. Saint-Ex jerked the stick back at the last split second. The plane rose a few feet limply, the engine stalled, and there was a crash.

From the shapeless mass of wreckage they hauled out an unconscious Prévot with a broken leg, and a bloody-faced Saint-Exupéry, suffering from a fractured jaw and other wounds, among them a deep one in the right wrist and left clavicle. The latter wound caused a stiffening of the shoulder which continued to trouble him for years. He was also left with a scar that raised an eyebrow in a perpetually quizzical look. For many days he was in a state of shock from the head wounds and from the wrist wound that had become infected, but he was finally pronounced out of danger.

Undoubtedly, he was careless in preparing for this important long-distance flight. Not only did he fail to check the amount of fuel put in the tanks at Guatemala City, but he waited till the last minute to question the mechanic about the most favorable direction for the take-off. Moreover, what questions he asked had to be largely dependent upon gestures because of the language barrier.

Miraculously the two men survived this accident which, as airmen put it, "grants a pardon" only once in a hundred times. It was the last flight the two men made together, and it was also Saint-Exupéry's last chance to pilot a plane in peaceful skies.

Between these two attempts at long-distance flights, Saint-Ex had done some occasional flying which had no relation to professional aviation but concerned a form of activity which he did not much like—journalism. Obliged at times to earn some money, he wrote now and then for magazines and newspapers, and his plane merely took him to places he intended to write about.

At the age of twenty-three he had already done some journalistic writing for *Le Matin*. That was during the period when he was trying his hand at everything—bookkeeping at a tile factory, aerial photography, selling trucks. His efforts were printed as simple news items, however, and this did not at all suit him, for he was unwilling to start at the bottom in anything except aviation, where he had known how to submit to the strictest discipline and go through all the stages of apprenticeship, working at the back of the hangar as assistant mechanic, learning how to use a spanner and an oil-rag, learning not to mind getting himself smeared with oil. But it is hard to imagine this independent young man writing articles to order on a subject of no interest to him. If he agreed to do this at a later period, it was only to earn money so that he could travel and experience again the human drama which was so important to him.

After the lecture tour in the Mediterranean cities, Saint-Ex had spent a short time in Morocco, where Paul Billon was shooting the film adaptation of *Southern Mail,* starring Pierre-Richard Wilm and Jany Holt. He watched the shooting of the scenes, and also made the take-offs and the landings for Wilm in the role of Bernis. He was afterward to complain that the movie had little relation to the book, that film producers, either because of something inherent in the medium or for purely commercial reasons, deformed or misinterpreted an author's ideas. For one thing, he felt that a film was the result of a collective effort, which meant it was shaped through concessions and compromises. "I can't prevent cinema producers from playing with a signature for which they've paid," he wrote to his mother, "but I cannot join my efforts to theirs." [15] He went to great lengths in condemning the cinema, calling the producers "idiots," complaining that they "didn't know how to use their eyes," that they "didn't understand even their own enthusiasms," that they were "incapable of giving meaning" to human expressions and movements but did "nothing except take pictures."

The adaptation made from *Night Flight* by an American company pleased him not a whit more. But on the other hand, he highly appreciated the musical work by the Italian composer Luigi Dellapicola inspired by the same book, pronouncing it original, powerful, and evocative.

For all his diatribes against the cinema, Saint-Exupéry wrote two scenarios, *Anne-Marie* and *Igor,* both of which were rejected.

After his short stay in Morocco he went by train to Moscow, where he was to write some reports for the evening paper, *Paris-Soir,* arriving there on the eve of the 1935 May Day celebrations. "The town has been transformed into a construction-yard," he wrote. "Gangs of workmen are ornamenting the monuments with lights, flags, and scarlet banners. . . . The night was animated by that special fervor of nocturnal work which resembles a game or a muffled, almost silent dance around bonfires. And the red draperies on the houses, clothing them from top to bottom, were so generously displayed that they bellied in the wind like sails. . . ."

Generally a writer, when he turns to journalism, changes his style because of the limitations of time and space, but not Saint-Exupéry. Reading these newspaper articles is like reading again *Wind, Sand and Stars,* less corrected and polished, but with the same density, wealth of description, and communicative emotion. His description of the May Day parade is magnificent; we see, to begin with, deserted streets, and then an entire population moving toward Red Square, where Stalin is waiting in the reviewing stand. Raising his eyes, Saint-Exupéry watches "the steel wedge of the flying squadrons" passing in the sky. "The rigid formation of the groups of planes gives to each formation the coherence of a tool. The slow progression of those dark masses, the full, solemn, endless roar of a thousand planes, all form a spectacle so oppressive that no one could help but have an impression of power. And as it kept on passing, I leaned against a wall and, staring upward, I discovered that, although a squadron flies, a thousand airplanes pass like a rolling-mill."

He then describes a lively street, full of a crowd moving along slowly and "inexorably, like a flow of black lava." That human flood, disciplined and subjected, which flowed between the houses was indeed impressive. "The passage of an entire population, like that passage of a thousand planes, had something inexorable about it, like the unanimity of a jury." Then there was a pause in the parade, and suddenly he felt as though he were witnessing a miracle, "the return to humanity . . . the breaking up of that unity into pieces, into living individuals." As if suddenly liberated, people began to dance to the music of a brass band that accompanied the parade. Then the frozen faces relaxed into genial smiles. A stranger in the crowd offered Saint-Ex a cigarette and another lit it for him. "The crowd rejoiced."

Then there was "an eddy in the crowd, the band put away their instruments, flags were unfurled, the marchers were lined up—I saw a leader of one group tap a woman marcher with his stick to get her back into ranks—and then there were no more familiar gestures, the demonstrators recovered their self-possession, for they were going to appear before Stalin."

In August 1936, Saint-Exupéry flew to Spain to report on the Civil War for *L'Intransigeant* from the Lerida front. The following year, June 1937, he flew to Spain again to report on the Carabancel and Madrid front, this time for *Paris-Soir*. Since he went to Spain alone he was accused, later on, of having convoyed aircraft destined for the Spanish Republicans.

This accusation was unwarranted, for he was not the kind of man to be attracted to an essentially political idea or to adhere to a political formula. Yet at this period he was said to be dabbling in communism. For one thing, Gide's patronage of the young writer led to this rumor, as did his "left-wing intellectual" looks and behavior, the remarks he dropped, and the articles he wrote when with the Loyalists in Spain. Also, there were his strictures against Mermoz who, at that time, was vice-president of the French fascist group known as the *Croix de Feu* and headed by Colonel La Roque. Whatever the cause, the legend grew. But Saint-Exupéry never belonged to any political party. Nor was he a Marxist—there is a wide difference between communism and Marxism—and those who have accused him of being one, through misinterpreting some of his remarks or writings, are mistaken. Léon Werth, a close friend of his, has quoted a phrase from Saint-Exupéry's *Lettre à un hôtage* [*Letter to a Hostage*] which should definitely refute this legend: "And so, to confine myself within the circle of some partisan passion would make me risk forgetting that a political tenet has no meaning except when placed at the service of a spiritual evidence." To him, "spiritual evidence" took precedence over all else.

When he went to Spain on assignments from two different newspapers, it was doubtless not he who chose to go among the Loyalists, although his tastes and preferences would make him find their company more congenial than that of the followers of Franco. He mentioned this in a letter written to his Egeria from Valencia—with her, he liked to exchange philosophical views. "As it happens," he wrote, "there are certain instances where spiritual concepts enter into conflict with sentiment. Otherwise, I would have been an anarchist. I have found among the anarchists of Barcelona, during the Civil War in Spain, the same comradeship that prevailed among the Aéropostale crews. There was the same cooperation, the same willingness to take risks, and the men were of the same type. They might have said to me, 'You think as we do.' But instead they asked me, 'Why aren't you with us?' And there was nothing I could reply that they would have understood. For they lived on the level of sentiment, and on that score I have no objections to make, either to the Communists or to Mermoz or to anyone in the world who is willing to risk his life for what he believes and places the sharing of bread with comrades above all pleasures and possessions." [16]

This, then, was his state of mind when he went to report on a fratricidal war in which "men are cut down like trees." And he was going to mingle with these men for whom life—their own as well as others'—no longer counted. "I had to spend an entire day here," he wrote from Valencia, "to get my papers in order to obtain the introductions that will allow me, in Madrid, really to live on the front. I am not at all interested in visiting a city, even a bombarded city, or in dining at a hotel and sleeping in a bed. Nor am I at all interested in interviewing generals. I want to live with the men who are risking their lives, men who have immediate problems to solve. I want to get as deeply as possible into this land in upheaval, I want to plunge as far as possible into the human adventure. . . ." [16]

He hated being a mere witness; what he always wanted was to participate. In Spain he would be an onlooker, but so much a part of the drama that his testimony would have the force and merit of a combatant's. For the first time, in addition to sharp observation and subtle thinking, his writing demonstrated a deep love for mankind, a quality that was soon to appear in greater amplitude in *Wind, Sand and Stars.*

His description of a Madrid shattered by bombers, along with his other accounts of the Civil War, are unforgettable. And since they were included, with some polishing and cutting, in that book, we will quote from those portions. Madrid under bombardment: "Suddenly in the place of Madrid I felt that I was staring at a face with closed eyes. The hard face of an obstinate virgin taking blow after blow without a moan." At the crash of each bomb "meant for Madrid," he thought of the thousands of "men, women, children, all that humble population crouching in the sheltering cloak of stone of a motionless virgin." And he visualized those people, as they tried to carry on their normal existence. Perhaps, just as the bomb crashed, the servant maid was taking out the white tablecloth for the evening meal, or a mother had just placed her cool hand on the feverish cheeks and burning forehead of her sick child, and the father, at that moment, had been thinking of some new device he intended to make next day. And he thought of all those people who had the illusion that their lives were eternal but who were scooped up, as if by a dump truck, and poured out at the frontier.

Among these newspaper articles are two on the subject of war and peace, written after the Munich compromise of October 1938 for *Paris-Soir*. Léon Werth has called these meditations "a beautiful edifice of thought," beautiful, but not constructed with "hard metal, capable of resisting variable temperatures."

Saint-Exupéry, on his first assignment to report on the Spanish Civil War, in 1936, showed in his writings that he then believed man to be closer to perfection than later events proved: "Mankind was being brought to bed of something here in Spain; something perhaps was to be born of this chaos, this disruption." Eventually, he realized how mistaken his optimism had been. However, the "beautiful edifice" remains, and one would like to quote the newspaper articles almost in their entirety.

"If we had only descriptions of horror, that would give us no reason with which to oppose war," he writes, "but also, if we restricted ourselves to exalting the delight of living and the cruelty of useless deaths, we would still have no reason. For thousands of years we have been told about the tears shed by mothers; but talking about those tears has in no way prevented the death of those mothers' sons. We will not find a way to save ourselves from war by reasonings, or in deploring the slaughter. Such and such a number of dead. . . . But up to what number are they acceptable? With such miserable arithmetic we cannot lay the foundations of peace. Either we must say 'Necessary sacrifice . . . Grandeur and tragedy of war . . . ,' " he concludes, "or we can say nothing," because "all beliefs are demonstrably true, as all men are demonstrably in the right," which is why we mistrust reasonings. . . . "A truth is not demonstrable; but a truth is what simplifies the world."

In Barcelona, looking down from a window, he saw a devastated cloister beneath him, the roof and walls shattered, revealing the convent's "most humble secrets." And suddenly, he tells us, "I thought of the great anthills of Paraguay which I had once ripped open with a spade, in order to penetrate the mystery. And no doubt this little temple represented to its besiegers no more than an anthill. No doubt those humble nuns ran hither and thither like ants when the soldiers kicked down the last stones of the walls, and the onlookers did not realize what tragedy was being enacted. But we are not ants and human drama does not show itself on the surface of life. The laws of numbers and space do not count for us."

Look what happens, he says, when a single miner is buried in a mine that has caved in: "Then other miners may be killed in the attempted rescue," and some people will comment, "What inept cost accounting!" An individual life has its value but no man lives his life alone: "One man in misery can disrupt the peace of a city . . . a victim of cancer walled up behind his hospital window goes round and round in a circle striving helplessly to escape the pain. . . . There is no pain or passion that does not radiate to the ends of the earth." He had heard people exclaim, "Terror in Barcelona? Nonsense. That great city in ashes? A mere twenty houses wrecked. . . . A few hundred killed out of a population of a million." Such arithmetic, says Saint-Exupéry, is meaningless when applied to human tragedies, for "man's domain cannot be measured. Within reach of me, apparently, are men cloistered in a monastery or in a laboratory or in a love affair, but in reality they are as beyond reach as if they were in the most remote parts of Tibet, no, farther still, for no journey I could ever take would bring me close to them. And when I break down these walls, I know not what civilization has, by my act, sunk out of sight forever, like Atlantis beneath the seas." [17]

In the outskirts of Madrid, stopping at the top of a hill, they "looked down upon a clump of trees out of which, a quarter of a mile away, stuck two tall chimneys." Suddenly "a volley of rifle-shot crackled in the still country air." It came from the factory. The sound had been no more ominous than that of a partridge shoot. But presently they were told that "a girl had been killed at the factory, together with her brothers." Death itself was not horrible, for "death is sweet when it comes in its time and in its place, when it is part of the order of things." He imagined that a natural death in a cloister might be celebrated like a festival day. What rendered death monstrous in the Civil War was "all these algebraic justifications, and the sudden disregard of the meaning of human life. . . . Men no longer respect each other. Hard-hearted sheriff's officers, they throw on the rubbish heap furnishings, without realizing that they are abolishing a domain. You have committees which assume the right to purge, in the name of criteria which, if they change two or three times, leave behind them nothing but corpses. And you have a general leading an army of Moroccans, who condemns whole populations to death with a clear conscience, like a prophet putting down a schism. In Spain there are crowds of people moving, but the individual, that universe, imprisoned in the depths of the mine, calls in vain for help."

In the years 1934 to 1939, Saint-Exupéry traveled a great deal. There were his special missions, the lecture tours, the long-distance flights that misfired, his work as foreign correspondent, a short trip to Germany, two stays in New York, and numerous visits to Agay. But despite all this moving about, he was never away from Paris for long, and Paris was mainly his headquarters at this period. He was often to be seen at a Left Bank café, particularly Lipp's or the Deux Magots. And customers who saw that tall, husky fellow, carelessly dressed, puffy-faced, half-bald, were surprised to learn that he was no other than the famous airman and writer Saint-Exupéry, author of *Southern Mail* and *Night Flight*.

Sometimes with friends, he might be in a talkative and gay mood, capturing their attention, but at other times he would sit silently withdrawn, listening to the others. He was often alone, however, when sadness could be read on his face. A few years earlier, in this same Paris, the young Saint-Exupéry had frequented these same cafés, often alone and sad. But he had then been at the beginning of his life, had still been searching for a career, haunted by a secret ambition, not yet clearly visualized but which destined him to an uncommon life. He had been like a butterfly beginning to stir in its chrysalis, wings still folded beneath the thin, imprisoning envelope. The chrysalis had been broken, his wings had spread, the sky had opened up to him, he had had the life he was destined for, a hard but noble life which employed all his great powers.

Then everything had again become bleak and aimless. The sky had clouded over, as if before a storm, and there were no openings. The pioneer flights that had so delighted him had been replaced by frustrated attempts at long-distance records, the comrades of the Line had been replaced by casual café acquaintances, the books he had written and in which he had unburdened himself of all the thoughts that crowded his mind had been replaced by articles for newspapers and magazines.

He was restless, even distraught, and was beginning to lose faith in himself, to believe he was a has-been, a failure. A bitter state for one who had so often declared that man must fulfill himself. And an aimless existence was all the harder for one who had written so much in praise of action as the panacea for all ills, fear, weaknesses, death. He longed for that salutary activity, but searched in vain for it. Besides, without a steady job, he was oppressed by financial worries.

When he first worked for the Latécoère airline, he had hoped eventually to land a position that would pay him a big salary. Indeed, this had been his dream always, as may be seen from his youthful letters to his mother. His spending was not always for personal gratification. He was generous, and sometimes disbursed sums in a grand way to help out others. His experience of life had taught him how much suffering can result from poverty. His mother's resources had now diminished considerably, and he was doing what he could to help her. It was during this hard period that the greatest demands were made upon him by his family.

Only a few years earlier he had written from Buenos Aires to a friend about his promotion as manager of the Aeroposta-Argentina line, saying he didn't know what to do with his salary, that he was exhausting himself spending money—and spending it foolishly. And we cannot help but recall that soup tureen at Casablanca. He could have put something aside, as Guillaumet had done while earning less. For in addition to his salary, Saint-Exupéry had royalties on books. Guillaumet and his wife, while living well, had managed to save in a few years the sum of 600,000 francs (equal to more than twenty million today). Ironically, however, the Guillaumets lost a portion of their savings in unfortunate investments; Guillaumet knew how to save, but he was on dangerous ground when he entered the realm of stocks and bonds. When Mme. Guillaumet told Saint-Ex of their loss, he exclaimed, "If Henri had spent money as I do, you'd not be where you are now!"

Even during this "blue epoch"—as he called these years when he was harassed by summonses to pay overdue bills, the notices being printed on blue paper—whenever he had money it ran through his fingers like water. On the day he received a check—payment for a newspaper article, or royalties on his books—he would at once invite his friends to dine out, the kind of restaurant depending upon the size of the check. However, as Pierre Chevrier tells us, "No matter what the restaurant, it had to meet certain requirements, must not be either pompous or stuffily middle-class." Saint-Ex enjoyed good food, was particularly fond of chocolates and pastries; he was eclectic in his tastes, appreciating the humble sausage as much as smoked duck, garlic soup, caviar, and beefsteak *tartare*. He could often be seen at the restaurant Androuet, which specialized in cheeses, and had a predilection for Roquefort served with gooseberry jelly. He had strong prejudices in foods, detesting Brussels sprouts, spinach, and string beans. He was extremely fond of highly seasoned foods and indulged this taste to such an extent that at one time he believed he had a stomach ulcer. On his travels, he never hesitated, when dining in a strange restaurant, to go into the kitchen to ask the chef, "What's cooking?" His boyish gaiety and charm disarmed the most ill-tempered chefs, who would let him raise the lids of the saucepans and sniff with pleasure the inviting odors of, say, a *civet de lapin* cooked to perfection. When he first married, he had bought all kinds of kitchen utensils so that his wife might prepare his favorite dishes. But whenever possible he ate in a restaurant, paying the gas, electric, and telephone bills with what remained of his money.

Some of his friends have blamed Consuelo for the chaotic life he led. She did keep her husband constantly upset, but aside from this it is unjust to blame her for all their ills. What woman could have held him in check, and conquered his bohemian and spendthrift habits? The order and equilibrium of his Egeria's life, the economies practiced by the Guillaumets, had no effect upon him. Could another woman have kept him tied to the home when he wanted to leave? It is very unlikely. For Saint-Exupéry, his apartment was merely a stopping-off place, and he even changed flats quite frequently, moving five times in Paris during seven years.

Their first apartment was a tiny one in the Rue de Chanaleilles, "where the trees in a garden outside seemed to thrust their branches into the rooms, furnishing the place," Léon Werth tells us.[18] From there they moved to the Rue Michel-Ange; then there were several other addresses until they landed in the vast duplex apartment on the Place Vauban, overlooking the Invalides. The enormous rooms were full of light which entered by bay windows. The large drawing room with its wall-to-wall carpeting looked almost empty, and indeed was very sparsely furnished. And the furniture was of every kind—he never attached much importance to such things. There was a grand piano in the same room with garden chairs painted green and a plain deal table. Saint-Ex's room had the disorder of every bedroom he ever occupied, with a jumble of shirts, ties, electric razors—he had several of every brand—cigarettes by the wholesale, papers, socks, shoes, books, medicine bottles littering the floor, the bed, the table, the chairs. The picture is not complete without the cigarette ashes that fell everywhere, burning the sheets, and usually a forgotten stub burning away all by itself on the bedside table.

For a short time there was a Russian servant at the Place Vauban, Boris by name. And Boris' salary made heavy inroads upon the budget already burdened by the rent which, as might be expected, was very high—25,000 francs, at the 1936 value.

The view was of course wonderful, and the windows were full of the boundless sky, which often made Saint-Ex recall his past, although he never let such memories weigh heavily upon him. But sometimes he would remember those days when he had been an airline pilot, and in these nostalgic moments he would sit down at the piano, lay aside his cigarette, and would carelessly play tag-ends of his favorite music. Sometimes too, when he came home late at night, he would go to a window and stand looking out at the lights of the city, at the stars in the sky, those stars which had once been like presences to him, and then he would draw up one of the garden chairs to the deal table and would write: "Tell me what I am seeking and why, leaning against my window, leaning against the city which holds my friends, my desires, my memories, for I am full of despair."

The composer Honegger has told of how he was welcomed one day at Place Vauban. Saint-Exupéry himself opened the door—Boris was no longer there—his face half covered with shaving cream. Presumably his electric razors no longer functioned.

I believe that Honegger was one of the guests who dined with Saint-Ex at Place Vauban the night, December 7, 1936, when everyone was tensely waiting for news of Mermoz and his crew. Every few minutes Saint-Ex excused himself to telephone for information. That morning, Mermoz's plane, *Croix-du-Sud* ("Southern Cross"), had taken off from Dakar for Natal in South America, and there had been no news since he had radioed back in midocean "Am cutting off rear right-hand engine." After that, there had been only silence. Recounting in later years this last fatal flight of Mermoz, Saint-Exupéry wrote, in *Wind, Sand and Stars,* "We waited. We hoped. Like all men at some time in their lives we lived through that inordinate expectancy which like a fatal malady grows from minute to minute harder to bear. . . . We were haunted for hours by this vision of a plane in distress. . . . Slowly the truth was borne in upon us that our comrades would never return, that they were sleeping in that South Atlantic whose skies they had so often ploughed."

The dinner party broke up early, and Saint-Ex was alone with his memories, the haunting faces of his lost friends. "Mermoz had done his job," he realized, very late in the night, "and slipped away to rest, like a gleaner who, having carefully bound his sheaf, lies down in the field to sleep." However, once relieved of the tension of waiting, he was resigned to the death of his comrades, for "when a pilot dies in the harness his death seems something that inheres in the craft itself. . . . Bit by bit, nevertheless, it comes over us that we shall never again hear the laughter of our friend . . . , and at that moment begins our true mourning, which, though it may not be rending, is yet a little bitter."

Indeed, he had felt the loss of his comrades for several years now. There were his friends—or rather, acquaintances to whom he was attracted and who could be seen almost daily. But those comrades of the Line, though scattered to the ends of the earth from Paris to Santiago de Chile, had met at times to carry on "conversations interrupted by years of silence." Even when separated they were close in spirit because they had the same ideal, the same goal, and were made of the same substance.

With his friends, he did not seek to console himself for the absence of his flying comrades, but found other things to talk about. To begin with, his friends were men of quality. As in all things, Saint-Ex had a horror of mediocrity. He liked to enter into long discussions on a variety of subjects—there were few subjects on which he was not sufficiently informed to discuss them even with a specialist. His universality of interests and knowledge smacked of genius. He was a writer, poet, philosopher, and aviator, but he could talk interestingly on biology, genetics, physics—even the quantum theory or the theory of relativity—astronomy, sociology, painting, music. He impressed even the learned. General Chassin, his professor at the navigation school in Brest, whom he met again in Algiers in 1943, tells us that at this epoch Saint-Exupéry, "when he had nothing else to do, solved difficult mathematical problems." When Chassin showed Saint-Exupéry's solutions to a professor at the University of Algiers, he was told, "Your friend is a mathematical genius. You must get him to demonstrate the theories of Fermat for you, something no one has been able to do since the seventeenth century. He's capable of doing it." According to General Chassin, Saint-Exupéry, starting from zero, had rapidly accomplished all the stages reached by mathematicians through the centuries. The eminent Professor A. R. Métral of the Conservatoire des Arts et Métiers wrote a tribute in which he said: "I shall long remember our conversations on the gyroscope, on the utilization of sound and light waves, and on other scientific subjects." [19] Léon Werth recalls that he accompanied Saint-Ex one day to the laboratory of Professor Holveck (the great Hungarian biologist who was assassinated by the Nazis), imagining that the scientist would greet Saint-Exupéry with benevolent condescension. But, says Léon Werth, "the two of them were soon well beyond the threshold of the subject under discussion, the photoelectric cell, and Holveck showed no sign of condescension, but on the contrary displayed lively interest. As for me, I might as well have been a deaf-mute, for all the attention they gave me." Later, the names of Holveck and Saint-Exupéry were mentioned together in a preface which M. R. Barthélémy of the Academy of Sciences wrote for a work by M. D. Strelkopf, engineer-in-chief of the television laboratory of the Compagnie des Compteurs.

During his stay in New York, Saint-Exupéry met Professor Theodore Von Karman, the aerodynamics expert. They met at the home of Dr. Lapeyre and saw each other only that one time. Professor Von Karman was "fascinated by Saint-Exupéry's personality" and they "talked about many things," chiefly about a new starting system for airplanes and a purely aerodynamic stabilizer. For Saint-Exupéry was also an inventor.

Indeed, had he not been drawn to other interests which were all-absorbing, he might have won recognition as an inventor. He took out patents on several gadgets calculated to improve aviation, but soon lost interest in them and never put them into practical use. But it is certain that his ideas inspired or helped other inventors. In the same way, one cannot say that Leonardo da Vinci created the airplane; but it can be surmised that his design for a helicopter inspired, three hundred years later, George Cayley, who is usually called the "inventor of the airplane"; and Leonardo's design for an artificial wing does not differ from that of the "Eole" of Clement Ader, "father of aviation." To quote A. R. Métral again, since his opinion is valuable: "As concerns the patents on instruments using electromagnetic waves, and so forth, it is possible that the inventions that issued from the necessities of war surpassed the designs and projects of Saint-Exupéry. But even so, it was unquestionably remarkable that their author . . . was able to work on difficult problems, without the help of laboratories, and to find solutions and suggest concrete methods for applying them at a time when eminent technicians and even some experts were still in the preliminary stages of the same studies."

Naturally, his researches were particularly aimed at improving flying methods, and several of the devices he patented were navigational aids: a blind-landing device, an angle gauge, a starting device that used the principles of jet propulsion. Professor Métral has said that the texts Saint-Exupéry prepared for this latter patent not only show that the inventor was amazingly intuitive but that he had obviously not realized the full potentiality of the device. It was this intuition, so typical of his intelligence, that often enabled him—as in this case—to leap to a conclusion that researchers would arrive at in their laboratories only after long and careful experiments.

Other devices patented by Saint-Exupéry were also for perfecting air navigation. The dates of the patents show that he worked out these inventions during the "blue epoch," when he was more or less stranded in Paris, without wings, without his old comrades, and when writing had come to a standstill; but also when he was meeting and exchanging ideas with a number of distinguished men. Besides Honnegger, Métral, Holveck, there was a politician and writer, Anatole de Monzie, and a religious of note, the Dominican Father Théry, whom the skeptic Anatole de Monzie introduced to Saint-Exupéry at a dinner in 1936, mentioning in a note, "You'll have at table a guest you'll immediately like." Besides Father Théry there was Léon Werth, an avowed atheist. Yet the four men had so much to say to each other that after the dinner party at Anatole de Monzie's, they moved on to Léon Werth's apartment and talked till dawn. "In fact," Father Théry tells us, "none of us liked labels or deceptive appearances. That night we were four men, simply men, brought together and united in our deepest and highest thoughts, our fundamentally identical aspirations." [20]

At this same epoch, he was often seen with the poet Léon-Paul Fargue. The author of *Piéton de Paris* could not but please Saint-Exupéry, and his virtues as well as defects were bound to attract him, for Fargue combined the subtle mind of the good conversationalist with the refinement and fantasy of the poet and the paradoxical qualities of a man equally at home in the most refined Parisian salons and the most bohemian night clubs.

Saint-Ex often sought out Fargue, sometimes taking him to visit an aviation factory or an aeronautics exhibition, but they usually wound up by calling upon a mutual friend or going to some favorite restaurant—Androuet's, Souty's, Lipp's, or the Lutetia. They were most often seen at Lipp's, talking, smoking, drinking—the saucers stacked up in a leaning tower of Pisa which often toppled. They talked for hours on a fantastic variety of subjects, and it was a pleasure to listen in on their conversations. Saint-Ex would become excited, and not only did he use his hands to express a range of feelings, but his mobile features were very expressive: even the tip of his nose moved "like a rabbit's, or like the blinking of eyelids," as Werth has noted.

One after another, people would leave the brasserie until only Fargue and Saint-Ex remained, Fargue leaning back on his banquette, Saint-Ex usually straddling a chair on the other side of the table, and as the lights went out and the last waiter wearily stacked the chairs, the two continued to talk in their center of light while shadows filled the room and Saint-Ex cast anxious glances at the waiter. Then, there was nothing for it—the two had to leave. And there they were on the deserted sidewalk, "arms and minds linked together." After walking a while, they would hail a taxi on the Boulevard Saint-Germain. "Take us wherever you like!" Saint-Ex would say. And in the taxi their dialogue went on and on, until at some distance in nocturnal Paris, say, the Faubourg Saint-Martin, Fargue would spot a bistro with its lights still burning and would tap his stick against the glass panel behind the driver, signaling him to stop. Then, in the midst of the somewhat wine-soaked habitués of this all-night bistro, the conversation continued. Sometimes they had picked up companions in the course of the evening, and these hung on, listening. At Lipp's the manager sometimes had to use all his patience and diplomacy to get rid of his distinguished but too talkative customers. Fargue was in the habit of going to bed at dawn, but the others, though not ordinarily night owls, listened avidly as the hours passed, and without complaint. Saint-Exupéry was a wonderful talker; no one ever wearied of his conversation, his anecdotes, his brilliant descriptions, his subtle arguments. And so people gathered round to listen to him, whether in a drawing room or a café, and no matter what the subject under discussion.

Léon Werth recounts amusingly an instance when Saint-Ex cast a spell. The two had paid a visit to a great industrialist, the very type of magnate that both men held in contempt, and whom Werth describes in outrageous terms, as "a prognathous and apocalyptic beast . . . with an enormous chin . . . eyes that glared in a truly horrible way . . . His face was that of a strangler of little girls. . . ." This portrait strangely resembles the portrait of a businessman which Saint-Ex drew in *The Little Prince*. Werth frankly says that he was afraid of the beast. But, he goes on, "when Saint-Ex approached him, I witnessed a strange spectacle: the man was put out of countenance, not abashed by the prestige of the writer–aviator, since such values were not respected by him, but obviously uneasy, like an animal under some spell. The man was completely overcome; overcome by a presence, by a mystery against which both his shrewdness and his money were powerless. . . . I saw the Orpheus myth enacted before my very eyes."

Of course, Léon Werth has dressed up this incident in his own way, but he did not invent it. And he has another story of the same sort to tell. One Sunday afternoon in summer, Saint-Ex was looking out of the window, and seeing two West Indian mulattos walking down the street, he waved at them and invited them up, sure that their manners would be simple and perfect—as they turned out to be. Without any hesitation, when requested to sing some of their native songs, they began singing, completely at ease. "Saint-Ex, in the wink of an eye, and from a second floor window, had charmed and adopted them, had guessed their background and foreseen the tact of their behavior." [21]

Among his many other gifts, he possessed unusual psychological insight. His famous card tricks, which baffled and even at times upset those who witnessed them, depended more upon psychological acumen than any real dexterity or the usual sleight of hand. Whether in a drawing room or a café or the squadron canteen, Saint-Ex would first of all isolate his "subject," and while shuffling the cards and chatting, would draw him out, observe him, and learn what kind of man he was dealing with. But also, he was actually an expert in hypnosis—as a boy he had practiced it on his sisters' governess—and knew instinctively how to choose his medium.

His card tricks were inimitable, and even close friends who witnessed his demonstrations many times, and those men who had some knowledge of card tricks such as General Chassin or Father Théry (who declared that Saint-Exupéry's performance was terrifying), were never able to guess the secret. To those who were determined to find out and put too many questions, Saint-Ex replied: "I am master of my own ceremonial." Some of his friends, very intrigued, tried vainly to penetrate the secret. Among them were Polytechnicians who called upon mathematical calculations to solve the mystery. "I know the secret of one of his card tricks," Léon Werth tells us. "It is the simplest, and requires merely a great deal of practice. I could divulge it. But few people would be able to use it if I did." They would lack that special intuition which sometimes bordered on divination.

Saint-Ex claimed that he rarely was mistaken in his judgment of people. In making this claim, he was neither vain nor presumptuous, for it was the simple truth. He did size up people almost instantaneously; and he knew how to handle them accordingly. Once, he made a landing on a Saharan airfield where he was greeted rather curtly by a grouchy colonel. There happened to be a pack of cards on the table, and Saint-Ex, while continuing to argue some point or other with the officer, picked up the cards, as if absent-mindedly, spread them out, and began to perform one of his tricks. A few minutes later, the colonel, completely captivated, was all smiles. Now, Saint-Ex was neither being bold nor audacious; he was by nature shy. But in a few seconds he had sized up the man, and had the pack of cards not been within reach, he would have exerted his charm, smiled engagingly, and found the right word.

His powers of divination were best displayed in his ability to read character in handwriting. Although he did not seem to follow the rules of graphology, handwriting was to him more than a reflection of the writer's character; in itself it was a source of vibrations. He not only could tell you the character of a writer, but could give you a physical description, a detailed portrait. Hélène Froment and Georges Pélissier have both described this gift, which they both found disturbing as well as edifying. Hélène Froment relates that in 1939 an Aéropostale pilot he had not seen for many years handed him a letter and asked him to try his powers on it. Saint-Ex glanced through the letter and declared, "The fellow who wrote this is a sick man, probably a consumptive. . . . He's in Spain, held captive. . . . He doesn't know how to get away." It was the exact truth. Hélène Froment also witnessed another one of these feats, which she describes. "The last time I saw him," she relates, "I submitted a page of writing to him. He studied it for a few minutes, then took out his pen and wrote down a striking analysis of the person whose writing it was. It ended with these words: 'He must be in need of a monastery or a physician.' As it happened, the person in question, affected by a serious nervous disease, had spent a year in a monastery." [22]

Georges Pélissier tells how a rapid reading of a letter permitted

Saint-Ex to draw "an absolutely amazing physical and mental portrait" of the lady who had written it. She was, he said, "a blonde, fat woman, muddle-headed and extravagant. When she goes into town, she returns home laden with parcels." The description was so accurate that Pélissier accused Saint-Ex of knowing the lady so unflatteringly described. Saint-Ex denied it and said, "Very well, give me another letter to analyze." Dr. Pélissier then selected "a short note from a young girl who had been a bedridden invalid for months, displaying a resignation to her fate that approached saintliness. I first glanced through the letter again," Dr. Pélissier goes on, "to make sure that it contained no information of this sort. Saint-Ex then read it and once again drew a faithful portrait of the correspondent: even to the illness from which she suffered, and her state of mind. I was simply flabbergasted." [23]

Just as his intuitive sense made him judge people quickly, his exigence sometimes caused his relations with others to be difficult. He attached less importance to education or culture than to native intelligence, and liked to see an educated man occasionally forget his bookish learning and relax and jest. "People who believe that culture consists in the capacity to remember formulae," he writes in *Wind, Sand and Stars,* "have a paltry notion of what it is. Of course any science student can tell us more about Nature and her laws than can Descartes or Newton—but what can he tell us about the human spirit?" He liked men with strength of character, and Pierre Chevrier quotes him as saying in regard to the rather blunt-minded proprietor of a newspaper, "That fellow, a man? No, a mere geometrical *locus!*"

He was an extremist in all things. As a boy, he had beaten his sisters when they refused to listen to one of his poems or to admire a design for one of his inventions. In later life, he intensely disliked contradiction. He wanted to have sympathetic listeners, and once he had assembled them and the atmosphere was favorable he could talk in a steady stream. But, as he once said in a letter, "if the conversation falls by chance on a subject dear to me, I can become intolerant." Intolerant and, it must be confessed, disagreeable. For at such moments his usually muffled voice which was so moving when he told a story was apt to rise, become shrill, as his words came tumbling out and he made his points with violence. Or else he would shut himself off in a dour silence from which nothing could entice him, neither the entreaties of his friends nor even his natural and much-vaunted courtesy. And sometimes, embarrassed at one of these prolonged silences, his friends took their leave, one by one, at the end of a hot argument. Whereupon, he would react with compunction and would telephone his excuses or, more often than not, write a letter of remorse. One day he had a violent argument with Georges Pélissier about isotopes. "Next morning," Pélissier relates, "I found a note of apology under my door. The note read: 'My dear friend! I'm terribly sorry, I behaved abominably yesterday, I know I'm frightfully unpleasant in arguments, I get very irritated when contradicted, yet I myself contradict others when the occasion offers. I will try to change.—A." And below the note, Saint-Ex had made a pen drawing of a little prince with open arms, and a bubble of words coming out of his mouth: "Forgive me." [24]

Pélissier was deeply moved. The letter bore the imprint of Saint-Exupéry's sincerity and charm; even his smile was there, that smile which creased his cheeks with long dimples, boyish, inexpressibly radiant. No one could resist it, not even the militant Spaniards who held him prisoner for a time in a cave, during the Civil War, when he was acting as a foreign correspondent. A militiaman stood guard, but with a smile Saint-Ex caused the man to unbend, and won his liberty.

Writing in the 1947 memorial issue of *Confluences,* Guillain de Bénouville recalls particularly Saint-Exupéry's "fraternal smile, holding an indescribable light." De Bénouville had but recently arrived in Algiers from France, in 1944. The other Frenchmen who were gathered round a luncheon table that day were all self-exiles, and they listened with tense interest to his account of the sufferings still being endured by French people after four years of the German occupation. As Bénouville talked, sadness weighed heavily on everyone, and soon all eyes were brimming with tears. Then, says Bénouville, Saint-Exupéry's face lit up with a strange and compassionate smile which "brought comfort to our distress and encouraged our hopes."

Léon Werth, in the same periodical, also mentions this smile, which could be "boyish and tender or the smile of a comedian, but at any rate would melt any heart"—even the heart of a friend wakened at midnight to help solve a mathematical problem or hum a tune he was trying to recall. Saint-Ex was often wakeful, habitually went to bed very late, particularly when traveling, and he had no least compunction over waking up his friends with importunate telephone calls.

On the boat that was bringing him back to France from Buenos Aires with his mother, who had visited him there, he woke her up one night suddenly by turning on the light in her cabin. Antoine was standing at the foot of the bed, a sheet of paper in his hand. He wanted to read aloud to her a page he had just written!

"But dear," said Mme. de Saint-Exupéry in gentle reproach, "couldn't you wait till morning?"

"No," replied Saint-Ex. "I want you to hear it now, for when one is wakened up suddenly, one's mind is clearer."

"Which is not true," the old lady added, when she told me this story twenty-five years later.

Georges Pélissier recounts how he was wakened after midnight once, when stopping off in Paris. It was Saint-Ex, calling: "I must see you immediately." And when he demurred, Saint-Ex persisted. "What? You're in bed? Be a good fellow, put on your clothes and meet me at the Regence Hotel." Saint-Ex had his way, and they spent the night rambling in Paris, first walking through the nocturnal streets, then taking a taxi to a café where they talked till daylight.

The whimsical demands that Saint-Ex made upon his friends verged on tyranny. Like many writers, he liked to have his manuscripts read by others and to have their opinions. But he was only interested in favorable opinions, really, and if someone dared to give him advice or suggest the modification of a piece of writing, he turned a deaf ear—and quite rightly. He did not, for instance, follow Léon Werth's advice to suppress the last sentence in *Wind, Sand and Stars:* "Only the Spirit, if it breathe upon the clay, can create Man."

In 1944, Madame X flew from England to be with him in Algiers. Immediately upon her arrival he asked her to read the manuscript of *The Wisdom of the Sands,* upon which he had been working during his years of self-exile in New York. He forced her to read at one sitting the more than five hundred pages of a work which is at times somewhat wordy. After reading a hundred pages, she pleaded fatigue from the trip and the intense heat, and laid the manuscript aside. He implored her to go on. She gently refused, and suggested a swim in the sea to provide some relaxation. Saint-Ex still insisted that she must read the entire book. She was again the willing victim of his "marvelous exigence" as she called it, for she was fundamentally glad to render him this service. By force and by guile he made her swallow two tablets of benzedrine, which kept her awake for the next forty-eight hours, when she read the entire manuscript, even rereading certain portions. Saint-Ex demanded a great deal of his friends; the greater his love, the greater were his demands.

Much has been said about his courtesy and tolerance, for which his education and innate nobility are credited. He himself often mentioned his "respect for man," and some commentators feel that this consideration of his fellow men was the mainspring of his behavior. Thus, some have concluded that Saint-Ex loved all men, and had no feeling of enmity for anyone. This is a gross error. We need only remember the inspector Robineau in *Night Flight;* his slackness and inertia are incessantly contrasted with Fabien's courage, his futility with the useful activity of the mechanics and radio operators. In this character Saint-Ex was satisfying an old grudge—a charge of no great importance. Certainly he had no love for this man. In *Night Flight,* Rivière says of Robineau, "He is far from intelligent, but very useful to us, such as he is."

Saint-Exupéry had little patience for military career men. During his military service he had much to say, in his letters, about a "rampant sergeant" who was his *bête noire*. In later life he referred to "the crass stupidity of generals." Nor did he have a higher regard for politicians, whom he handled without gloves. I well remember the sarcastic epithets he used in talking of Colonel de La Roque: he was "that invertebrate," a "poor creature," whose "sloppy language indicates a sloppy conscience." But Saint-Ex never published these remarks, confining them to private conversation or letters, since he detested polemical writing.

Of course, he had some enemies, as who has not? But those who disliked him rarely acted openly against him, for he was almost invulnerable. The only instance of an open attack I can recall was when *Le Voltaire* attacked him with a spitefulness that to this day, twenty years after, fills his friends with rage and disgust. Describing his misfired effort to fly to Saigon, this periodical said that the aviator had "deliberately made a forced landing in the Sahara, conveniently close to Cairo, so near, indeed, that no one thought of looking for him there, and that while an imbecile press was giving his disappearance the wished-for publicity, he was calmly waiting until his provisions should run out. . . . He recounted afterwards how he had suffered from hunger and thirst, but he didn't breathe a word of how he had strewn sand on the wings of his plane to hide the tricolor insignia from the searchers!" [25]

The truth is, the *Simoun* Saint-Ex used on that unfortunate flight was a civil airplane and bore no tricolor insignia. Of course, he sued the magazine, claiming damages for libel. All his life—and particularly in the last years—he suffered greatly over anything that could blemish his honor. He was as sensitive to injury, injustice, and ingratitude as he was to friendship.

Saint-Exupéry said, "Few can claim to be my friends." He also said, "There isn't a corner of the world where I do not have a friend." The contradiction is merely superficial, for there is a distinction between pleasant human relations and true friendship, of which he said, "By true friendship I mean a friendship that cannot be shaken." And in *The Wisdom of the Sands* he states: "A friend is, above all, one who judges not." With this in mind one may say that Saint-Exupéry bestowed his friendship—"which was like air breathed on the hilltops," wrote Werth—upon two men only: Henri Guillaumet and Léon Werth.

At first view one could not imagine two men more unlike than Saint-Exupéry and Léon Werth, distinguished novelist, journalist, art critic, and inveterate "outsider" who belonged to no clique. But Werth's sincerity, his "indomitable fidelity to everything that elevates a man," [26] his horror not only of meanness and compromise, would of course attract Saint-Exupéry, although Werth's personality was crabbed and he alienated rather than attracted most people.

A mutual friend introduced them, much against the inclination of Léon Werth, who was then getting on in years. "You ought to know Antoine de Saint-Exupéry," said the friend. "What could I have in common with an aviator?" replied Werth. But from their first meeting their friendship was signed and sealed, and with the passing years it became ever more firmly established. Shared feelings and identical points of view on certain problems drew them together and made them often seek one another out. Werth has reported one of their later meetings, and it may have been typical of others.

Saint-Ex had telephoned. "I'd very much like to see you, but my means of locomotion are limited," he said, meaning that he could not afford the taxi fare. But since Werth's means were no better, one of them had to go on foot to the other's apartment—Saint-Ex lived at the time in the Rue de Chanaleilles and Werth in the Rue d'Assas. Apparently Saint-Ex did the walking, for Werth describes him seated in the Rue d'Assas flat talking endlessly, smoking quantities of American cigarettes, while Werth puffed on his pipe. Between them on the table was a decanter of brandy and two glasses. "And the doctor forbade you to drink any alcohol," Saint-Ex wrote in his *Letter to a Hostage,* recalling another such evening, "but you cheated on important occasions."

What did these two men talk about for hours on end? "In ten years I don't remember our having discussed literature except for a few minutes, now and then, by chance, and it was never a subject for prolonged conversation," wrote Saint-Ex. Although they did not discuss literature in general or the works of any particular author, they certainly talked about his own writing, and Werth at least read *Wind, Sand and Stars* in manuscript, for, as we have noted, he wanted Saint-Exupéry to delete the last sentence. Their serious conversations were more apt to turn on philosophical subjects. "We both had the same adoration for Pascal," Werth tells. And they were both seekers after the facts and principles of human nature and conduct.

It is well known that Saint-Exupéry's *Letter to a Hostage* was directed to Léon Werth. It was published by Gallimard during the war, in 1944; Saint-Ex had written it while in America and hungering for friendship. His other close friend, Guillaumet, had been shot down in an air battle. And Léon Werth. . . . "The friend who haunts my memory tonight," he begins, "is fifty years old. He is ill. And he is a Jew." It is to this old friend that he addresses himself across the closed frontiers, gathering together a sheaf of memories, picking up their conversation where they had left off. The conversation continues in *The Little Prince,* that other work written in exile, and dedicated "To Léon Werth when he was a little boy."

No matter where their conversation took place—in streets or cafés or at their respective homes or in a humble inn on the banks of the Saône—its tone was always measured, intimate, and confidential. They never raised their voices in argument, although both men were positive by nature and held opposite views on some essentials—Saint-Exupéry being a seeker after God all his life, while Werth, an atheist, stopped short before the abyss of nothingness. "Traveling our roads in opposite directions," Werth writes, "we were always encountering each other, whereas each step should have taken us far apart. With my other friends, I walked a short way in the same direction; but we never reached the same point, for halfway there we separated. . . ." [27]

Sometimes the two men took a taxi to go to one or another of their favorite restaurants. There was one in the tiny Rue Gît-le-Coeur which they preferred; the owners were natives of Marseilles, Werth tells us, "and they served a garlic soup that overcame you with drowsiness for two days afterwards." At times, Saint-Ex took Werth for a long drive or even for a flight in his plane, when he would skim low over the countryside, literally hopping the hills, "of course, to impress his passenger a little," Werth writes, and the passenger, with slightly sinking heart, "affirmed his confidence in his pilot." Once, caught in a fog, they had to land at Romilly and spend the night in that melancholy little town. Sometimes, too, Saint-Ex dragged him away from his apartment to take long walks in the deserted streets. Werth was his senior by twenty-three years, but allowed this without demur, just as Saint-Ex, who hated to be contradicted, permitted Werth, and only Werth, to contradict him.

Through long and difficult years, Saint-Exupéry found in Léon Werth a safe refuge, a mind and friendship worthy of his own.

9

And in the phrase, too, you are building something up; and it is, above all, this building up that counts.

—*The Wisdom of the Sands*

On May 25, 1939, the Académie Française awarded the *Grand Prix du Roman* to Saint-Exupéry for *Wind, Sand and Stars,* which had been published three months earlier. This distinguished award once more drew attention to the writer and airman who, seven years earlier, had enjoyed celebrity when his *Night Flight* had been awarded the *Prix Fémina.* During the interval, although he had not been forgotten, his star, which had glowed for a moment in the firmament of letters, had become dimmed.

Literary fame needs to be firmly established in order to endure. How many writers awarded the *Prix Goncourt* or the *Prix Fémina* have had the ephemeral destiny of fireworks. In order to maintain one's reputation, book after book must be produced in rapid succession. Saint-Exupéry's published work in the interval had not sufficed, though he had been writing quite steadily. In 1933 he had contributed a preface to Maurice Bourdet's book on aviation, *Grandeur et Servitude de l'Aviation;* for two Paris evening papers, *Paris-Soir* and *L'Intransigeant,* he had written reports on the 1935 May Day celebrations in Moscow, on the Civil War in Spain in 1936 and 1937, and had done several articles for the magazine *Marianne.* But Luc Estang, who made his start in journalism in 1939, confesses in his book on Saint-Exupéry that, up to the time of the Academy award that year, he knew practically nothing about him as a writer. He remembered the tragic crash in the Libyan desert, for the newspapers had been filled with accounts of this episode. To him, as to many others, the name of Saint-Exupéry called to mind, at that period, merely an aviator, a comrade of Mermoz and Guillaumet.

Eventually it was rumored that Henry Bordeaux's efforts had persuaded the Academy to acclaim his *Terre des Hommes* as the "greatest novel of the year"—although it is as far as possible removed from the fictional form. Saint-Ex had first met the famous writer and Academician in the course of a trip to Germany in March 1939, soon after the publication of his book. Quite understandably, Henry Bordeaux succumbed, as had others, to the charm of the younger writer; probably he discovered in Saint-Exupéry's work the new wealth brought to French literature by a man of action who was also a humanist. He may well have mentioned his "find" to his fellow Immortals. But it is less certain that such an intervention was enough to bring the majority of Academicians to award the first prize for fiction to what is really a collection of essays. Some more discreet steps must have been taken in favor of a writer of real talent who had been for some time silent, no doubt because of personal and domestic troubles and as a result had sunk into obscurity. In any case, this book was bound to affect its readers and to achieve recognition even had there been no such intervention.

Certainly Saint-Exupéry owed a great deal to his cousin, Yvonne de Lestrange, his confidante and "best pal," as he called her. It was at her home that he had met, while still a novice writer, a great number of noted writers and publishers.

One of the first things Saint-Ex had done when he came to Paris from Fribourg to continue his studies was to call upon this cousin, who was then twenty-four and endowed with gifts rarely found assembled in one person: intelligence, distinction, beauty, and wealth. She was delighted with her young cousin Antoine, six years her junior, whom she had not seen since he was a little boy, wearing a black suit, in mourning for his dead father. That little boy had had the same strange eyes that she found again in a tall young man, a little too tall, shy and diffident, hesitating how to address his cousin, whether or not to use her first name. She had at once put him at his ease, and he often called upon her afterward. Indeed, he became something of a burden at times for a young woman leading a busy social life and often entertaining friends. Those friends were a little amazed at Yvonne's cousin, that young fellow who was so carelessly dressed and had black fingernails. But she would not allow him to be criticized and defended him valiantly.

Sometimes she had taken Antoine on long walks in Paris—at that period of his life he detested walking, but he accompanied her without protest. One day, on a long promenade, he timidly asked her if he might recite for her some poems of Baudelaire. "Why, of course," she said. And Antoine repeated some poems—he recited rather badly, but she was amazed at the emotion he showed, for it not only revealed poetic feeling, but also a communion with Baudelaire, the kind of communion that can only be established between poets.

Later on, she was to read some of his letters to the famous critic, Ramon Fernandez, who exclaimed: "You know, that young fellow has talent!"

When Yvonne de Lestrange decided to ask Gide to write a preface for *Night Flight,* she used all her persistence and subtlety, for she knew what weight such a preface would have. And she made her request in a favorable stage setting: at Agay, where André Gide and Saint-Exupéry were her guests at her country place, Baumette, its vast white façade overlooking the blue sea. For a day or so she had almost not let Gide out of her sight for fear he might leave suddenly, as he was apt to do, going off to nearby Italy, for instance.

A true talent rarely goes unrecognized, but perhaps there are a few: those who lack perseverence and tenacity, qualities that take the place of serious and astute backing. At any rate, there is no doubt that in 1930 Saint-Exupéry was fortunate to have a publisher such as Gallimard, a preface by André Gide, a favorable criticism by the influential Edmond Jaloux— "Have you read Edmond Jaloux's article on Saint-Exupéry?" he triumphantly wrote to his mother after the publication of *Southern Mail,* "Just think, he's the most celebrated of all critics!"—or puffs by Benjamin Crémieux, Marcel Prévost, Schlumberger, and others of their stamp. Such formidable backing was certain to reveal a talent very rapidly. He had met all these distinguished people in Yvonne de Lestrange's salon.

Yvonne not only introduced her cousin Antoine to her friends, but gave him every possible encouragement in his writing. And he needed encouragement. He strove for perfection and was unsure of himself. When he was working on *Southern Mail,* he wrote to his mother from Juby: "I've already done a hundred or so pages and I'm in rather a mixup as to what structure to give the book." Shortly afterward he wrote to his sister Gabrielle: "I've finished writing a novel of 170 pages, and I'm not sure what to think about it." But as soon as the book was published, Yvonne kept a close check on the reactions of her friends, and religiously passed on their comments to Antoine. On the eve of his departure for Buenos Aires—when the book was soon to appear—he mentioned her in his last letter written to his mother before sailing, again referring to his "little book": "Yvonne came here to see me off; she says everyone in the literary world is talking about it." Could a young man on the threshold of a writer's career have had better encouragement?

Before this, Jean Prévost had also rendered the young writer invaluable aid by having his first efforts, a short story, *"L'Aviateur,"* published in the periodical *Navire d'Argent,* introducing it with a note which said in substance: "This direct art and this gift for depicting the truth appear to me surprising in a beginner," adding, "I understand that Saint-Exupéry is engaged in writing other stories."

Years afterward, in New York, where Saint-Ex was sojourning while convalescing from his accident in Guatemala, he met Jean Prévost and was introduced by him to Curtis Hitchcock of Reynal & Hitchcock, who became his American publishers beginning with *Wind, Sand and Stars,* which appeared almost simultaneously with the original French *Terre des Hommes* and became a best-seller. This book was partly written in New York. At least, it was while staying at the home of General Donovan there and while still not recovered from the severe accident that he gathered together the articles which comprise the book.

For *Wind, Sand and Stars* is in a way an anthology of the articles written and published during the "blue epoch," augmented by his memoirs of the Line and of voyages he had made, enriched by some profound thoughts, the fruit of long meditations. The pages on Guillaumet in the chapter devoted to his comrades of the Line, entitled "The Men," had first appeared in *L'Intransigeant,* April 2, 1937, under the title, "The pathetic adventure of Guillamuet, pioneer flier of the South Atlantic and the Andes." Even when it first appeared, the accident in the Andes was already a thing of the past, having occurred seven years previously. The day it was published in the newspaper, Guillaumet received the following letter:

> *Dear old friend,*
>
> *I hope you will forgive me for having written an article for you in* "L'Intran." *The only way I could think of to take your part in the Farman affair, and to get it printed in J.-G. Fleury's section in* Paris-Soir. *I then sent the article to Cot [Air Minister], telling him what I thought of the whole business.*
>
> *Don't hold a grudge against me.*
>
> *Affectionately,*
> *Saint-Ex*

The Farman affair was a reference to arguments over the four-engine *Centaure* in which Guillaumet had flown several times across the South Atlantic. The military who had flown it were dead set against it, claiming that the plane was dangerous and incapable of flying over 1800 miles of ocean without accident—only two pilots among those who had test-flown it were sure of its good qualities, Guillaumet being one of them, Coupet the other.

The chapter entitled "Oasis" in *Wind, Sand and Stars* had been published in a weekly magazine under the title "Argentine Princess." The chapter recounting the crash in the Libyan desert and entitled "Prisoner of the Sand" had also been published in the same magazine, *Marianne*. The chapter "Barcelona and Madrid" had been composed of his reports for *Paris-Soir* on the Civil War in Spain, and the concluding short chapter, though not previously published, recounts what he saw and thought on the train that was taking him to Moscow to report on the 1935 May Day celebrations for the same evening newspaper.

In this chapter, he tells us that one night on the long railway journey he decided to leave the almost empty first-class coaches and see what was happening in the third-class coaches, crowded to suffocation with refugee Polish miners and their wives and children.

> *I sat down face to face with one couple. Between the man and the woman a child had hollowed himself out a place and fallen asleep. He turned in his slumber, and in the dim lamplight I saw his face. What an adorable face! A golden fruit had been born of these two peasants. Forth from this sluggish scum had sprung this miracle of delight and grace.*
>
> *I bent over the smooth brow, over those mildly pouting lips, and I said to myself: This is a musician's face. This is the child Mozart. This is a life of beautiful promise. Little princes in legends are not different from this. Protected, sheltered, cultivated, what could not this child become?*

Scattered, the chapters which constitute *Wind, Sand and Stars* would have lost their force, the thought which unfolds might have escaped those for whom it was destined. But it is impossible to believe that the materials of such a masterpiece could have remained forever scattered or that its message could have failed to reach an audience. Saint-Exupéry had long wished to gather the dispersed articles together. The Guatemalan accident provided a stimulus, reminding him that he might suddenly disappear, and it also provided him, in the period of his convalescence, with the calm and idleness favorable to creative work.

Upon his return to France, he continued shaping up the material for the book. But he went about it in his own way. He did not, as one would expect, settle himself tranquilly in his apartment. Instead, nomad that he was and eternally restless and unsatisfied, he wandered from place to place, carrying with him his notes, the published articles, the manuscript in rough draft. Sometimes he worked at his sister Gabrielle's house in Agay, sometimes at an inn in Switzerland, or even on a Lake Leman boat, and sometimes at the Deux Magots café in Paris. But no matter what the setting, writing was, for him, a painful process. A work of such density and richness could only be the result of sustained effort and severe application. But, unlike many writers, he did not follow a plan. Indeed, he rejected the very idea, as we find by leafing through *The Wisdom of the Sands,* where the subject is referred to many times. The logicians, says his desert chief, discover a plan "in that which has been created" and "assume that it originated the creative act; whereas it is by means of the plan that the creation reveals itself." And again, the chief, speaking more symbolically, says: ". . . all that is strongly built tends to shape itself into a plan. And if that which chiefly I see in the city is a plan, this means that my city has expressed itself and is complete. But it was not the plan that founded the city." Pierre Chevrier quotes Saint-Exupéry as saying that literary works may be compared to symphonies "for which there are no previous plans yet which, when finished, display a perfect coordination." A debatable comparison. And he went still further, saying "The expression 'order is necessary in a discourse' is absurd. A discourse becomes order once it is delivered. Like a great destiny, or like a tree." No doubt many authors would disagree. A writer's method depends more upon his temperament than on a school of thought. Saint-Exupéry's method was a good one for him, since it produced some admirable books, but it may have added to the already heavy labor of writing.

Saint-Ex had a taste for work well done—*bien faite,* as he said, after Péguy. He had almost an obsession for the finished, polished, matured and perfected work, and for the right word—even though his use of words differs from established usage. Here, again, his style was personal and original, for he was essentially a poet. What could be more daring, and more poetical, than his description, in *Wind, Sand and Stars,* of a plane speeding through the evening air, like a drill boring through crystal? "... the impalpable eddies of evening air drum softly on the wings and the plane seems to be drilling its way into a quivering crystal so delicate that the wake of a passing swallow would jar it to bits." He has been reproached for his repetitious use of certain words, for instance, "knot," "bind," "gold." True, these terms are often encountered in his pages, and sometimes in close sequence.

But let us see what he does with the word "gold" in the chapter "Prisoner of the Sand" in *Wind, Sand and Stars,* describing his landing at Bengasi by the beacon light of the airdrome. On a single page we find: "... the rays of a floodlight rose into the sky like a jet from a fire-hose. It pivoted and traced a golden lane over the landing-field." Two paragraphs down, he writes: "I rolled down the golden lane toward an unimpeded opening." And a few lines farther: "... the searchlight caught me between the eyes again; but scarcely had it touched me when it fled and sent elsewhere its long golden flute."

He could not but be conscious of this repetition and retained it willfully. The bright vein of poetic imagery that flashes in his powerful and substantial prose is one more reason for classing him among the great.

Daniel Anet calls his style "Homeric" because, like Homer's, it has "a robust nudity, that of a stout, plain, marble column, porous but indestructible, absorbing sunlight, glowing ..." [28] And indeed, there is some relationship, some mysterious affinity—completely involuntary and therefore authentic—between Homer's descriptions of certain aspects of the sea, the cliffs of Ithaca, and Saint-Exupéry's descriptions of seas and mountains.

Already, with the publication of *Night Flight,* Edmond Jaloux listed Saint-Exupéry's works as among the classics of the twentieth century, and with the publication of *Wind, Sand and Stars* his place there became secure. To achieve such a place something more than talent is required; hard, strenuous work must round it out. Saint-Exupéry put himself wholly into his work; his labor was physical as well as intellectual. He suffered, sweated, toiled. Apparently he made more than thirty false starts before he finally found the right one for the chapter "The Plane and the Planet" in *Wind, Sand and Stars.* He did not hesitate to delete a sentence, no matter what effort it had cost him, if it seemed to make a passage heavy or to weaken its thought. By such laborious cutting he managed sometimes to reduce the initial size of a manuscript considerably. In fact, all his books except *The Wisdom of the Sands* are short. But how compact! *Night Flight,* when he first finished it, was twice the size of the manuscript that he finally gave to the publisher.

Pierre Chevrier, who saw the writer at work and was in his confidence, has some interesting things to say about his methods and style. "Saint-Exupéry discovered how to take the reader from action to meditation without a break," he tells us. "We read his pages without experiencing that sinking feeling that accompanies the usual abrupt ascensions from one level to another. But he accomplished this not without some trouble." Saint-Exupéry, in his own life, made no distinction between action and meditation. He meditated while flying. In *Night Flight* he depicts Fabien at the controls of his plane: ". . . the engine was running smoothly; so now he relaxed his limbs a little, let his neck sink back into the leather padding and fell into the deeply meditative mood of flight, mellow with inexplicable hopes." That is exactly Saint-Exupéry himself with wings spread.

Ideas came to him in abundance, intermingled with odd associations. He jotted them down; and the little notebooks which he always carried with him were filled; the text is sometimes illegible —and was often illegible for him, as well. In those notebooks are found especially the subjects that preoccupied him most, those of a spiritual order. Many of these thoughts, in a more crystalized form, were set down in *The Wisdom of the Sands,* including many pages on language, on words. But the notes themselves are exciting enough—for instance, "I cannot make people realize how convenient it would be if they possessed a language. It is as though one were to try to make people who lived before Descartes (or even Marx, perhaps?) realize how clear everything would be if only they were to adopt certain concepts. But no Descartes has explained that there is a much greater and more general truth and that it is possible for Man to communicate with Man." Or this note on education: "Modern man does not represent a biological advance in comparison to the cave man; the advance is conceptual. Education takes precedence over instruction: it creates man . . . The sole aim of education should be the acquiring of a style." And, farther on: "Instruction merely provides so much impedimenta; what counts is knowing how to put it to use—that is education. . . . To teach is to teach how to define, how to see. . . . There has been added to normal pedagogy a constant pedagogy of amazing efficacy; it is called publicity. Industry based on the profit motive tends to create, by education, men who will consume chewing gum or men who will consume automobiles. Thus in 1926 we have such a consumer in the little gigolo. And thus the cinema has produced, out of most admirable human clay, that silliest of all products, the film star." [29]

The work in which action and meditation are most closely mingled is *Wind, Sand and Stars.* This book does not mark—as doubtless would be the case with many writers after seven years of silence—a turning point or a new orientation. Instead, it merely shows more explicitly the steadily upward trend of both the man and the writer. But then, Saint-Exupéry's life and work are one, for the work is completely imbued with the life of the airman, the man of action. Thus, the main themes of this book issue from the airman's craft; the human relations are those of the men of the Line; courage and heroism of the noblest kind are described in aviators such as Guillaumet, a hero much closer to the Greek hero than to the flamboyant hero of the Romantics; love is depicted in its purest form, the love for an ideal which imposes the sacrifice of self. His subject is man, and how to deliver him from his base life and enable him to find his true destiny, his sovereign vocation.

"My world was the world of flight," he wrote in *Wind, Sand and Stars*. "Already I could feel the oncoming night within which I should be enclosed as in the precincts of a temple—enclosed in the temple of night for the accomplishment of secret rites and absorption in inviolable contemplation." Lines such as these, written in his maturity, indicate that no other career than that of a flyer would have produced them. The works of Saint-Exupéry are as if borne aloft by the airplane. It served him as "a tool"—and in how many passages does he celebrate this tool of man, which he likens to the plow and the ship, for, "contrary to the vulgar illusion . . . the machine does not isolate man from the great problems of nature but plunges him more deeply into them." Seated in the tiny cockpit of his plane, before "the magical instruments set like jewels in their panel," hands on the controls, feet pressed on the rudder-bar, alone in the sky, high above the world of men, the pilot sees "the true face of the earth" and is "able to judge man in cosmic terms," scrutinizing him through "portholes as through instruments of the laboratory." Thus writes the airman–poet, while fashioning a whole new literature of action and lyricism, as original in kind as he was original in personality.

Yet some critics have called his work derivative, and have pointed out the literary influences that shaped it. While he was an assiduous reader of Jeans, Eddington, Broglie, and Lemaître, they left only slight traces in his writings, and these could be detected only by people who had discussed scientific questions with him. Saint-Exupéry was not a bookish man, nor was he easily influenced. As a writer he was self-taught and learned through experience.

Gide has been named among those who presumably influenced him, despite the vast difference between the two writers. The critic André Gascht comes to this conclusion because he "senses" that Saint-Exupéry's hero in *Southern Mail*, Bernis, had enjoyed reading

André Gide." [30] One looks in vain for any sign or trace of Gide in Saint-Exupéry's work. No doubt Gide offered advice, and from the literary point of view such advice could not but benefit a young writer. Gide himself pays admiring tribute to this new kind of writing in his preface to *Night Flight*. "The quality which I think delights one most of all in this stirring narrative is its nobility," he says. "Too well we know man's failings, his cowardice and lapses, and our writers of today are only too proficient in exposing these; but we stood in need of one to tell us how a man may be lifted far above himself by his sheer force of will."

Some critics have called Saint-Exupéry "the Conrad of the air," and there is no doubt that he admired the great writer of the sea. He begins his description in *Wind, Sand and Stars* of the terrible cyclone he ran into in the skies of Patagonia by evoking Conrad's *Typhoon* and commenting in a few lines on Conrad's aims and methods: "When Joseph Conrad described a typhoon he said very little about towering waves" and so on; but instead "took his reader down into the hold of the vessel, packed with emigrant coolies" and it was "this human drama" that was described. Saint-Exupéry then proceeds to describe the cyclone as a human drama. Between the two writers it is possible to see a relationship, but no traces of influence.

Saint-Exupéry has also been found to resemble Giraudoux, but the very difference between these two spiritual kinsmen is almost enough to prove that Saint-Exupéry did not succumb to influences. Daniel Anet compares passages of *Night Flight* with passages in Giraudoux's work and draws this conclusion: "The profound ingenuity and the crystal-clearness of the images, the presence of a destiny of living creatures and of things no less living, existing side by side with the destiny of man, the reality of the world apart from man, in which things and creatures have an infancy, a future, an urge to live, and experience the sadness of decline—this, and the very style, are they not secrets of the spritely wisdom of a Giraudoux?" [31]

Others have compared Saint-Exupéry and Malraux, because they were both "committed" to the improvement of man's estate. The French word *engagé,* applied to such writers, seems to have lost some of its original meaning since Pascal. There is no doubt that both André Malraux and Saint-Exupéry committed their lives to their work, really lived their work. But the political ideal of Malraux—which has varied, moreover—played a more restrained and less elevated role than did that of Saint-Exupéry. It is also a strange fact that Malraux, although he flew, seems not to have been greatly impressed by his experiences in the air, unlike most men of a passionate nature. Like Saint-Exupéry, Malraux was concerned with "the human condition" and dwelt upon the weaknesses as well as the grandeur of that condition. For Malraux, destiny weighs heavily upon mankind, whose whole effort is to throw off this weight; there is hope only in man himself, and it disappears with him tragically into the void. With Saint-Exupéry hope also resides in man, but is perpetuated with the virtues of one who can see the distant gleaming of a divine light.

Not only are Saint-Exupéry and Malraux both "committed" but, as R.-M. Albérès has more acutely pointed out, both are moralists. One could add Camus, and name them as the three writers who have had the most influence upon the generation immediately succeeding them—and, let us hope, on the generations to come.

The literary work of Saint-Exupéry is deeply rooted in the life of action, a rich sap of experience vitalizes it, and it develops in a fertile soil. The power it exerts over us is due to the fact that it is so very rich, personal, original. Hermann Korth, the German aviator who has written on Pascal and translated some of Saint-Exupéry's works, has said: "Saint-Exupéry is a literary gem; he is the only one in the world who succeeded in synthesizing the aviator, the mechanical universe, and the poet in one great talent." And Aldington, so coldly exigent in literary matters, states: "Saint-Exupéry seems to be a brilliant and unique personality. . . . And this is the real importance of Saint-Exupéry: he represents the merging in one person of an authentic man of action, a thinker, a moralist, an artist."

But more than all this, he is a humanist. In our century the word has come to have another meaning, or rather, its meaning has been broadened. Today we have the new humanism, scientific humanism, even cosmic humanism. Emile Bréhier, reminding us that humanism is a way of life, writes: "It is a question of education.... Humanist education is a cry for liberty, for reflection, for spontaneity. The aim of humanism is to bring about a world in which man will be master of himself and find within himself his own discipline; social discipline should be only the reflection of this inner discipline..." [32] It would therefore seem that the best form of humanist education is through example, and we can do no better than to take Saint-Exupéry as an example. Where others taught, he acted; while tracing new routes in the sky, he opened the way to a new humanism.

In moments of great despondency, he missed the horse and carriage of the past, but this nostalgia was the product of his weaker moments, as he confesses. He believed in the machine, believed in progress as a gradual liberation of mankind. "It seems to me," he writes in *Wind, Sand and Stars,* "that those who complain of man's progress confuse ends with means...."

He had found fulfillment by overcoming obstacles, by bartering himself for something greater than himself. In a life of action he had transcended himself; action, he thought, carried man toward the highest goal. To him, stagnation was a form of death, "for all life is a building-up, a line of force." When he began his career as a pilot of the Line, he had looked at the humble clerks and little bureaucrats who traveled in the same bus that took him to the airfield outside Toulouse, and was saddened to think of "the dismal prison in which these men had locked themselves up." Their murmured talk was "about illness, money, shabby domestic cares." And mentally he addressed the dull clod of a man sitting beside him: "You, like a termite, built your peace by blocking up with cement every chink and cranny through which the light might pierce. You rolled yourself up into a ball in your genteel security, in routine.... You have chosen not to be perturbed by great problems, having trouble enough to forget your own fate as a man." And he thought, with pity, "No one ever helped you to escape." The freeing of

Bark, the slave at Juby, which he recounts later on in *Wind, Sand and Stars,* appears to be symbolical. He bought Bark's freedom not so much to provide him with a better life, materially, but to make him a free man. And when he heard how Bark squandered his money at Agadir, buying golden slippers for the beggar children that swarmed round him, he was aware that Bark, liberated, "would go back next day to the poverty of his family, to responsibility for more lives than perhaps his old arms would be able to sustain; but already, among these children, he felt the pull of his true weight."

Wind, Sand and Stars is couched in lyrical language; throughout all its pages there is a song of praise for men in action, but also of meditation as the fruit of action. There is no doubt that after seven long years of silence and inactivity he found new strength in writing this book. It was like slaking his thirst at a spring he had perhaps feared was dried up.

With the work on this book finished, his main hope was to be at the controls of a plane again. But war was imminent, and when he next flew a plane it would not be in the skies of peace. Never again would he fly a mail plane and feel that he was carrying in those mail bags letters that were binding men together in bonds of friendship. Opposing ideologies had produced hate, hate had produced war. Quite appropriately, in this book which was published in 1939, the final pages are devoted to a meditation upon the causes of war. "Why should we hate one another?" he asked. "We all live in the same cause, are borne through life on the same planet, form the crew of the same ship. . . ." But how make the voice of reason heard, while clamorous voices were being raised, soon to merge with the roaring of tanks and the thunder of bombing planes? Surely, he said, "There are other ways than war to bring us the warmth of a race, shoulder to shoulder, toward an identical goal." If there was to be fighting, however, he foresaw that he would join his comrades in the fight. For he could not remain an onlooker; even if the game were a cruel one, he could not refrain from participating or stand aside from the ranks that were to struggle for the defense of liberty.

Part three

10

"The war," I said to myself, "is that thing in which clocks are no longer wound up. In which beets are no longer gathered in. In which farm carts are no longer greased...."

—*Flight to Arras*

Following the publication of *Wind, Sand and Stars,* and the fame attendant upon the Academy award, Saint-Exupéry enjoyed some needed tranquility. The bohemian life that had been his during the seven years of discouragement and silence was now a thing of the past. Thanks to the sales of the book, his financial worries were temporarily over, he could afford to relax and come out of his shell, forget his frustrations both as writer and airman.

"Saint-Exupéry cared not at all for fame," Pierre Chevrier has said in his biography; "he was amused, however, to note how much importance others attached to it." This statement runs counter to what we are told by Luc Estang, who interviewed him on the day he was awarded the Academy's *Prix du Roman.* Estang quotes Saint-Exupéry as saying, "I fully appreciate the widening of my audience which a distinction like this signifies. It proves to a writer that his words have been heard beyond the circle of friends, in whose praises kindness naturally plays a part." Indeed, no matter how modest a writer is, there can surely be none who remains indifferent to anything that might make known a work into which he has put himself almost entirely, and which represents a message addressed to mankind, as this book does.

In July 1939, two months after receiving the award, Saint-Ex embarked for the United States, where *Wind, Sand and Stars* was enjoying a huge success. The American edition differed considerably from the French text of *Terre des Hommes.* After compiling the book the previous year while convalescing in New York from his Guatemalan crash, Saint-Ex had given the manuscript to Lewis Galantière, whom he had first met in Paris. Galantière was so enthusiastic about it that he agreed to translate it, and proceeded with the task at the house of Sherwood Anderson in the mountains of Virginia. Then Galantière began to receive "an absolute rain of letters transmitting changes that he was then engaged in making in the French text." [33] Saint-Ex had discarded the title *Du vent, des sables des étoiles* in favor of *Terre des Hommes.* He had become dissatisfied with what he regarded as the too-literary, falsely poetic passages, and was rewriting entire chapters, substituting meditation for action and description. He did not want the book to be considered an adventure story, but was eager to show "how the airplane, that tool of the airlines, brings man face to face with the eternal problems." Altogether he cut two thirds of the text he had left with Galantière, who protested that Saint-Ex was discarding a good deal of beautiful and moving prose, and that "he knew how to write but not how to read." Finally, he allowed Galantière to transmit his version to the American publisher, while Saint-Ex sent his own amended draft to the French printer.

In February 1939, Saint-Ex unexpectedly turned up in New York, explaining that he was staying only four days and would return on the same boat. He had come for the sole purpose of telling Galantière how sorry he was for the trouble he had caused him with the manuscript. Duly touched, Galantière reminded him that he had promised to furnish his publisher with two additional chapters. Saint-Ex said he thought he could write at least one chapter in a couple of days. Though always a slow, painstaking writer, he had already given the chapter some thought and was able to complete it, while staying at the Ritz Hotel, with the aid of a French secretary. This chapter, called "The Elements," proved to be one of the most exciting portions of the American edition, but it was written too late to be included in the French version.

Wind, Sand and Stars became a best-seller, acclaimed by American critics and public alike; in addition to the Reynal & Hitchcock edition, it was distributed by the largest American book club, the Book-of-the-Month Club, and was later issued in a paperback edition by Bantam Books.

In New York in the summer of 1939 Saint-Ex was regarded as a literary celebrity; invitations were showered upon him; he had to autograph copies of the book, give interviews to newspapers and magazines, make radio broadcasts. But then, suddenly, he vanished from the literary cocktail parties and was seen no more by his friends in the publishing world. The interruption was caused by the arrival of Henri Guillaumet in the seaplane *Lieutenant-de-Vaisseau-Paris* on his seventh flight across the North Atlantic. Saint-Ex scarcely left the side of his friend for the rest of his stay in New York.

After his epic flights over the Andes, Guillaumet had been occupied for almost a year in testing planes suitable for the new France–North American airline. They had seen each other briefly several times in recent years. Only a few months before, in Paris, Saint-Ex had given Guillaumet a copy of *Terre des Hommes,* which was dedicated to him. Then, as recently as the month of May, at Parentis, they had celebrated two anniversaries together: Guillaumet's thirty-seventh birthday and Saint-Exupéry's award of the Legion of Honor rosette. That dinner party had been a memorable and moving event. The two friends were each supposed to make an after-dinner speech, but when the time came, neither could utter a word, so great was their emotion.

But this meeting in New York was different from the others, for it was also a reunion with the crew, a select crew, many of them old comrades of the Line with whom Saint-Exupéry had once flown. The men Guillaumet had assembled for the North Atlantic flights included Néri, who had been Saint-Ex's radio operator on the Casablanca–Dakar route. Saint-Ex was overjoyed to be with them again and to feel that he was still one of them; this was what he had missed most during the past years.*

* This elite crew was comprised of Leclaire, second pilot—soon to be replaced by Cariou; Comet, the navigator; Néri, Le Duff, and Bouchard,

On the eve of the day set for the return flight of the hydroplane, he climbed aboard while the mechanics were making everything ready, sat down at the controls, gripped them, and stared pensively at the instrument board. The lapping of waves against the hull of the vessel awakened many memories, stirred him almost physically. Guillaumet observed him understandingly and saw the sad smile on his face. For a few minutes Saint-Ex sat there without saying a word. Then he got up slowly, leaned toward Guillaumet, and pressed his arm hard.

"I'm flying back with you," he announced.

And when the *Lieutenant-de-Vaisseau-Paris* left New York for France, Saint-Ex was a passenger on board, having left behind him his publisher and some disappointed journalists, radio commentators, and booksellers. The flight back set a speed record for North Atlantic crossings—twenty-eight hours and twenty-three minutes—and was the first nonstop west–east flight by seaplane. Unexpectedly a tailwind was in their favor. The director of Air France, Monsieur Couhé, returned to Europe in the plane, and alternated with Guillaumet at the controls. Saint-Ex had promised himself that he would pilot the plane for a short time; but he had celebrated this departure too well, and slept for a great part of the journey.

At the beginning of August, he returned to New York, where again he was lionized. For a fortnight he was kept busy with newspaper and radio interviews, appointments with photographers, cocktail parties, and receptions. He may at times have felt cheated of the freedom that was so dear to him, but for the most part he accepted with a mixture of pleasure and shyness the social obligations that are the price of success. And the Americans who met him were charmed by the boyish smile of the big hulking fellow. But soon a look of gravity replaced it.

---

radio operators; and the mechanics Morvan, Chapaton, Roux, Coustaline, and Montaubin. Cariou died in a plane crash in North Africa in 1943; Le Duff and Montaubin were shot down over the Mediterranean in November 1941; and Le Morvan and Coustaline disappeared over the sea in a Laté C–31 in July 1948.

The news from abroad was disquieting to all Europeans who happened to be in the United States. War was obviously near. Another war, while the soil of France was still steeped in the blood of the war that had ended but twenty years before, and while traces of its devastation could still be seen in Belgium and France, from the North Sea to Alsace. Another war, while still the maimed and disabled of the last war could be seen everywhere, and the women who had lost their loved ones, the women with sad, shut faces, who were still living out their joyless lives. Another war that meant more cemeteries to add to the already vast cemeteries, whole cities of the dead, created by the last war. The thought was horrifying.

There were some who were still optimistic, but Saint-Exupéry was not among them. Without much delay, he returned home, and aboard the *Ile de France* he nursed his darkest thoughts. He recalled the last trip he had made to Germany, six months earlier. With his own eyes he had seen the falsity of the French propaganda which depicted a Germany in complete decline, impoverished by the Nazis, a population of underfed slaves, and had realized how dangerous and foolish was that propaganda. For in Germany he found an abundance of food everywhere, factories running at full capacity, a new, young and strong generation. He had been welcomed by Otto Abetz, had visited the famous *Führer Schule,* the National Socialist training centers where leaders were mass-produced, had seen enough to disgust him forever with Hitlerism. At night he had heard the heavy rumbling of tanks in the streets, had felt the houses tremble. He had returned to France as much disquieted by his observations as by the blindness of the French government. From then on he had no more illusions and Munich had brought him no comfort.

In the concluding pages of *Wind, Sand and Stars* he had made his own plea for peace. "There is no profit in discussing ideologies," he had written. "If all of them are logically demonstrable then all of them must contradict one another. To agree to discuss them is tantamount to despairing of the salvation of mankind. . . . There are two hundred million men in Europe whose existence has no meaning and who yearn to come alive. . . . Men can of course be stirred into life by being dressed up in uniforms and made to blare out chants of war. It must be confessed that this is one way for men to break bread with comrades and to find what they are seeking, which is a sense of something universal, of self-fulfilment. But of this bread men die. . . . Civilizations may, indeed, compete to bring forth new syntheses, but it is monstrous that they should devour one another."

Unfortunately, such words could neither stir fanatics nor enlighten fools. As always, everywhere, the politicians turned a deaf ear to the opinions of clear-thinking people. Before 1939 the heads of state in western Europe refused to listen to the most authoritative advice, refused to see what was most flagrantly displayed. Two years before the war, for instance, the well-known French authority on German affairs, Louis Gillet, issued some clear warnings in his book, *Rayons et Ombres d'Allemagne* (*Light and Shadow in Germany*). After predicting that Hitler would settle accounts with France before attacking Russia, he declared: "Obviously, the German army is organized for a sudden attack of unprecedented violence and of prodigious speed, which should disable us in a few hours or days." That is exactly what happened. But Daladier, the Minister of War, blandly replied, "France has the best army in the world."

Saint-Exupéry had never dabbled in politics, but his intelligence and intuition made him aware of certain problems and he foresaw long in advance what would devolve from them.

On August 26, 1939, the *Ile de France* docked at Le Havre. A serious-faced Saint-Exupéry was among the crowd of silent travelers who disembarked and entrained for Paris. One week later, war was declared. And on September 4, Captain Antoine de Saint-Exupéry received his military orders: he was to report to the Air Force station at Toulouse.

There was something about this return to the great city of Languedoc which reminded him of his arrival there thirteen years before. He had been in Toulouse since then, but those visits had nothing in common with these two arrivals which represented turning points in his life. Thirteen years of danger and suffering, of worries and triumphs, of adventure and comradeship had matured him. He had come a long way from that young fellow he had been, sitting on his valise and waiting for the rattling old bus in the cold gray dawn. However, he again had the feeling of abruptly entering a new phase of life, and he entered it without apprehension but with gravity.

A disappointment was in store for him. At the airdrome, he was told that he would not be sent to the front but was to remain in Toulouse as flying instructor, far from danger, outside the struggle. He was at first dismayed, then rebellious. Thirteen years before, he had cleaned spark plugs and engine parts without a murmur, had "taken his place in line" as Didier Daurat put it, because the future was clear and worth waiting for: soon he would be a full-fledged airmail pilot at the controls of a Bréguet. But now he was being asked to stay there and wait. Wait for what? The end of the war? Had he submitted without protest, he would not have been Saint-Exupéry. He protested. He pulled every possible wire in order to get himself transferred to a fighting squadron.

Far from giving him the backing he demanded, his friends only discouraged him. His age—he was approaching forty—and his physical handicap—that shoulder stiffened after the Guatemala crash—permitted him to seek exemption from combat duties, they pointed out, along with certain intellectuals and sports champions and popular singers, men easily replaced. He rejected the idea of seeking exemption. Not a warrior by nature, and hating war, he still wanted to be in the battle, fighting alongside his comrades.

His friend Léon Werth tried to persuade him not to expose his life to danger. "You are worth more alive than dead," he argued. To which Saint-Ex replied: "I can't stand aside while my comrades fight; that would be to act discourteously." He had other reasons, but did not want to argue with his old friend.

Jean Giraudoux offered him a job in the Information Service, but Saint-Ex turned it down, saying, "Apparently intellectuals are kept in reserve, like pots of jam on shelves, to be eaten after the war." He did not consider that he had a greater right to live than a workingman, a schoolmaster, or a shopkeeper.

Didier Daurat, at the head of liaison operations, spoke to the Air Minister, asking to have Saint-Ex transferred to his service. When Saint-Ex received the application form, he tore it up.

The letter he wrote to his friend, Madame X, shows better than anything his state of mind and why he so keenly wanted to be a combatant:

> *I implore you with all my heart to persuade General Chassin to get me into a fighter squadron. I'm buried alive here, the atmosphere is unbearable. Good God, what are we waiting for! Don't see Daurat until you've tried everything else to get me into the fighters. If I don't get into the fighting, I'll have a breakdown. I have a lot to say about what's happening in this war, and I can say it only as a combatant, not as an onlooker. It's my only chance to express myself, as you know.*
>
> *I take a plane up four times a day, I'm in first-rate form, and that makes it all the harder, for they want to make me an instructor, not only in navigation but in the piloting of heavy bombers. And I can say nothing, I'm gagged. Save me. Get me sent to the front in a fighter squadron. You know very well that I've no liking for war, but it's impossible for me to remain at the rear and not take my share of the risks. I'm not like F.... We've got to fight this war, but I haven't the right to say this as long as I'm here, quite safe in Toulouse. It would be sickening to have to stay on here. Give me the right to say what I have to say by putting me to all the tests I have a right to.... It's disgusting to pretend that "people of value" should be put in a safe spot. One must participate if one is to play a useful part. "People of value" are the salt of the earth; then let them mingle with the earth. How can we say "We must fight" if we stand aside? The onlookers who say "We" are swine!*
>
> *Everything I love is threatened. In Provence, when*

there is a forest fire, everyone who isn't a swine grabs a bucket and spade. Everything I love and believe in impels me to fight. I cannot stand aside. Get me assigned to a fighter squadron as soon as possible.

Saint-Exupéry's dogged determination won out over those who worked to save him. Despite a medical report which declared him unfit for combat duties and thanks to the intervention of Colonel de Vitrolles, himself a distinguished airman, Saint-Ex was eventually assigned, with the rank of Captain, to an Air Reconnaissance Group. Although he would not be with the fighters, he would at any rate be at the front in the danger zone.

Group 2–33 of the Air Reconnaissance had been stationed since December 17 in the little village of Orconte in the Champagne district. When Saint-Ex arrived there in November 1940, the tall poplars, which hide the village from travelers on the national highway that runs between Vitry-le-François and Saint-Dizier, were shedding their leaves, yellowed in the first cold nights of autumn. Behind the village stretched a vast plain which provided a natural airfield.

At the mere sight of the bomber planes and the uniformed crews, fresh blood ran in his veins, filling him with a joyful serenity. The officers who would be his comrades welcomed him cordially, proud to have him among them. They were military men, but untainted by the usual defects that he was wont to see in them, perhaps because they had his same passion for flying. He was to describe them in his next book, *Pilote de Guerre* (*Flight to Arras*) as "men of substance"—his highest praise. "As formerly I saw substance in Guillamuet, so now I see it in Gavoille, in Israël."

However, an earlier and less favorable opinion was expressed in a letter to a friend, written from Orcante in 1940: "These comrades with whom I now live don't see the war as I do; they are not fighting to save civilization. Or rather, they have another idea as to what civilization is." 34

One might conclude from these conflicting statements that Gavoille and Israël were the only ones capable of understanding his point of view and of accepting his concept of civilization. But not at all, for they figure among the others mentioned in his book on the war—Vezin, Lacordaire, Gelée, Dutertre, Sagon, Pénicot, Hochedé, and the exemplary squadron leader, Major Alias. All of them, he said in another letter, "posed quite difficult problems." [35] Apparently these problems occurred to him only when he was alone, when that solitude he sought and needed abruptly separated him from his comrades, or rather put a kind of barrier between them. Then he judged them without indulgence. But when, on the contrary, he was with them in the canteen, he could laugh and sing with them, "on the same plane with them, without a shade of condescension, as happy as they to burst into song. With all this good earth for my roots. But a whole sky for my branches, and the winds and the silence, the liberty and the solitude."

He was fond of his comrades and in his war book exalted them. But to a friend he wrote, ". . . their conversation could not possibly interest me, except from a meaning their words contain despite themselves. . . . My heart is touched by all that they do, I feel closer to them than they do to themselves. But all the same, I lack space. And they bore me to tears with their jokes and anecdotes. . . . I must somehow manage to stretch out my branches, but how can I? The presence of these men prevents my tree from growing. And what they have to say about themselves does not interest me at all." [36]

If one did not know Saint-Exupéry, such comments would seem to indicate a lofty disdain. Certainly he felt the lack in this milieu of someone of his caliber with whom to talk. He missed those extremely few thoughtful men he knew in Paris. But also, his peremptory judgments were the result of the growing bitterness he felt in 1940 over the mediocrity of French leadership, civilian and military, and the general chaotic disorder, the "enormous absurdity of present times," as he put it in another letter.

Meanwhile, he sought relaxation in the conviviality of the canteen after the long, dangerous flights. But it was not the same life as before, with the men of the Line, where chance meetings occurred at various posts after months of separation. Then there was so much to talk about, and the hours of reunion were all too short. Afterward, one carried away into the sky some heartwarming tales, the news that had been brought and shared. At Toulouse in 1940, the canteen was the daily meeting place, where meals were taken in common, games played, jokes exchanged. Although, at times, it was also a place of anxious waiting when a plane was late in returning to base.

Despite all the complaints in his letters, Saint-Ex recovered his old gaiety, his youthful smile, during those months at Orconte. And the others listened attentively to his tales or marveled at his card tricks. Even so, Saint-Ex was glad to return at night to the humble bedroom he had taken at a nearby farmhouse situated on the village square opposite the church. Once the heavy street door was opened, you entered quite a big porch where the farmer and his family took their meals in warm weather. To the right, off this porch, was the kitchen, to the left was the room occupied by Saint-Ex. He had taken the room almost immediately upon arriving in Orconte.

The farmer's wife had opened the door and had led her guest to his room. Saint-Ex glanced around, felt the bed, put his suitcase on it. Then he turned toward the woman and was surprised at the unfriendly expression on her face.

"It's all I have to give you," she said.

Saint-Ex smiled. The face of the farmer's wife lost its hard lines.

For three days she had anxiously been expecting his arrival. When Jouve, the canal watchman who had been mobilized on the spot as quartering officer, had announced to her that a captain of the Air Force was to be quartered at her house, she had grumbled, "I don't need an officer here."

"Oh," said Jouve, "you're wrong; you don't know who this one is! He's a famous writer."

"What's that to me?"

"He's called M'sieu de Saint-Exupéry."

"Well, you can just put him up somewhere else."

Jouve stuck to his guns, and so now there was M. de Saint-Exupéry, aviation captain and famous writer, standing in the bedroom, facing her, bulky and carelessly dressed. He liked the farmer's wife. She was good-looking in a plump way; everything about her radiated physical and moral health. It was she, he discovered, who ruled this household.

One day he described her in a letter—which he left open on the table before sending it off—"She has the face of Minerva." The farmer's wife, who of course read the letter, was not very flattered until, looking up the word in the dictionary, she learned that Minerva was a goddess.

I have talked to this woman about Saint-Exupéry and she recalls how she questioned him that first day. "Why didn't you go to lodge at the château?" she asked.

His face became melancholy and his eyes clouded. Her question flooded him with poignant memories of the château where he had spent his childhood, the games played in "the dark and golden park" which he and his sisters and brother had "peopled with gods"; and of "the cool breath of the vestibules" where they had sat at nightfall, waiting for the lamps to be brought. But now all this was in the past. The château had been sold, his mother could not afford to maintain it. Now the old home he had loved sheltered a vacation colony. He had visited it not long since, without entering, keeping "outside of its little wall of gray stone, marveling that within a space so small we should have founded a kingdom that had seemed to us infinite." But he told the farmer's wife nothing of these thoughts. Instead, he replied simply, "You see, I like it better here with you."

He was speaking the truth. Saint-Exupéry did prefer the farmhouse of the Cherchell family to the Château d'Orconte, and apparently liked to share the simple life of these farmers. They recall how he often returned home from a mission and lingered to chat with them, or to sit down quietly with them at their supper table. In *Flight to Arras* he has described one of these evenings. "Silently my farmer broke the bread and handed it round. Unruffled, austere, the cares of his day had clothed him in dignity." And Saint-Exupéry fell to thinking of what that bread symbolized, of the golden fields that had produced it, those fields that, next day perhaps, would be invaded by the enemy, and he turned to look at the young niece sitting beside him. And he said to himself, "Bread, in this child, is transmuted into languid grace. It is transmuted into modesty. It is transmuted into gentle silence."

But there was something ominous in the silence of the peasants of eastern France. These people had experienced the German invasion of 1914, and their parents had suffered the Prussian occupation in 1870. Now, once more, they were under this menace, the enemy was near. Saint-Exupéry knew this better than anyone. But he gave no sign of it, and at table with them he talked about things far removed, about his peacetime flights, about the desert; about Argentina and the Andes; about Guillaumet, who was a native of the Champagne district as these peasants were.

The youngest child, Cécile, was then four years old, a well-behaved and appealing little creature. Saint-Ex made much of her, often took her on his knee while he talked. He had "a great deal of paternal love stored away," as he had written to his mother when he was only twenty-four, adding that he wanted "some little Antoines."

This love of children was deep and persistent. When he visited his sister Gabrielle at Agay he played games with his nephews and nieces. Wherever he went, he seemed to attract youngsters. A friend who was with him in Camargue but had entered, alone, the church of Saint-Gilles, was intrigued by a sudden silence in the town square outside, where a few minutes before there had been the clamor of children. When he sought the cause, he found the square empty of children and, looking farther, he discovered Saint-Ex in a pastry shop "surrounded by twenty urchins licking the remains of cakes off their fingers. Saint-Ex's face was radiant with pleasure." [37] When he was at the desert post of Juby, swarms of little Arab boys were often at his heels. "Every day I give chocolate to a gang of charming, roguish little Arab boys," he wrote to his mother, adding the boast, "I am popular with these brats of the desert." According to Pierre Chevrier, "a well-washed and curly-headed infant" did not always stir this paternal love in him; he had to feel "the presence"—or personality—of a child to have that heart-pang. During the war, he was often to be seen in a street of Algiers or Naples, surrounded by youngsters enchanted with the small paper helicopters he fabricated and launched for them, watching spellbound as the fragile craft flew along the walls or rose, spinning, into the air. All his life he remained close to children, and they sensed it; there was an understanding between them.

The little Cécile that he used to take on his knee of an evening, now grown to girlhood, remembers him with great affection. She especially recalls a gift he once gave her.

It happened one Sunday when the Orconte churchbells were ringing after the morning service. The congregation did not linger to gossip that day in the square, for rain was beginning to fall. The farmer's wife dragged Cécile along by one hand, holding an umbrella with the other, not noticing that the child was trying to reach the umbrella handle. But Saint-Ex, looking down from his window, did notice it, and he came out of the house just as the mother was angrily opening the door and the little girl entered.

"What's wrong?" he asked, bending over the sad little face streaming with tears.

The child's throat was too contracted by sobs to reply, but her mother answered for her: "She wants an umbrella! And there aren't any umbrellas for children! Isn't that so, M. de Saint-Exupéry?"

"I don't know, I'm not sure," he said thoughtfully.

Next day he returned to the farm with a small umbrella which he had bought in a bazaar at Vitry-le-François. He held it out to Cécile. It was the prettiest umbrella he had been able to find; it was in waterproofed canvas on which flowers and birds were painted.

Cécile herself told me this story eight years afterward, as we sat at the big table that had been brought out especially, and as the farmer uncorked a bottle of champagne. This was the porch where Saint-Ex paused every day to glance into the kitchen and greet his friendly hosts with a word or a gesture. It was a warm summer day.

"You must show me that umbrella," I said to Cécile, who was sitting beside me.

She turned to look at me in silence.

"You still have it, I hope?" I asked doubtfully.

"When we came back after the exodus," said the farmer, replying for Cécile, "we found it, all torn. I threw it out."

"Oh, what a shame!" I said. But then I noticed a strange light in Cécile's eyes.

"I still have it," she announced.

"But I threw it out, behind the barn," said the farmer, making a wide gesture.

"Yes," said his young daughter. "But I went out and got it."

"Where did you put it?" asked her father, suspiciously.

Cécile pointed towards the top of the big armoire. "Up there," she said.

The farmer climbed upon a chair and took down from its hiding place, where it had lain for more than seven years, the dusty and cobwebbed little umbrella.

In *The Wisdom of the Sands,* there are some lines reminiscent of this story which seems to show that Saint-Ex thought of Cécile years later. The passage refers to a little girl the desert chief saw leaning against a fountain, crying. He paused, caressed her hair lightly, and turned up her face that he might see it. The chief, like Saint-Exupéry, was haunted all his life by the memory of that weeping child, since, "If a little child's tears move you, they are windows opening on the vastness of the sea; for not those tears only, but the whole world's tears, are quickening your compassion, and that child is but one who takes you by the hand and shows you the sorrows of mankind."

At night, when he returned to his room at the farmhouse, he shut himself in, alone, and meditated or wrote while the village slept. Doubtless he noted down the impressions of that day's reconnaissance flight, the thoughts inspired by the burning towns and battles he had seen, the rout he had witnessed of armies, the street fighting, the roads filled with a fleeing population, sometimes whole villages evacuated upon the roads, blocking the movements of the armies. These descriptions and reflections, which we find in *Flight to Arras* and also in his notebooks, were for the most part written in the farmhouse room in Orconte. Occasionally he wrote to friends. A letter to Léon Werth about this time recalls passages in his *Letter to a Hostage* published in the war years still to come. In part it reads:

> *I believe I understand things a bit as you do. And I often have long arguments with myself. In these arguments I am not biased, for I argue from your point of view almost always. But oh, Léon Werth, I like to remember drinking a Pernod with you on the banks of the Saône, while biting into a sausage and a good loaf of country bread. When I recall that afternoon, I have a feeling of plenitude. No need to tell you, since you feel these things as I do. I was very happy. I'd like to experience that whole afternoon again. Peace is not something abstract. Nor is it the end of danger and cold—those things don't bother me. But peace—peace means contentedly eating bread and sausage with Léon Werth on the banks of the Saône. And I am sad when I think that the sausage no longer has any taste. . . .*

Sometimes he wrote late into the night. Then the farmer's wife, an economical woman, cut off the electric current. And Saint-Ex, who never suspected her of such a thing would say, when she wakened him next morning, "There certainly are a lot of power failures in this part of France!"

Those who knew him well recall how soundly he slept and how hard it was for him to wake up. Léon Werth gives us a vivid description of that sound sleep: "No one who hasn't tried to wake up a sleeping Saint-Exupéry has any idea of what sleep is. One day I had agreed to wake him up for an early departure. I called him. It was quite in vain. I gave him a slight shake. He replied with a muffled moan. I persisted. The moan became a guttural growl, which sounded like the roar of the distant sea. Then, propping himself up, he looked at me with mingled indignation and astonishment. And then again he lay down in bed, entering once more a realm of sleep so vast and shut that one was horrified at the tons of dream and unconsciousness that it could contain. And while he plunged again into sleep, one marveled that the whole world, sea, earth, and the other planets were not caught in the contagion of sleep and brought to a standstill." [38]

In *Flight to Arras,* Saint-Exupéry fondly recalls that clay-walled farmhouse bedroom in Orconte, which had been, perhaps, his "one great adventure" in the war. At least, getting up early in the morning in "the bitterly cold winter of '39" was an adventure, the way Saint-Exupéry tells it. "The temperature would drop during the night low enough to freeze the water in my rustic crock, and the first thing I did in the morning was of course to light a fire. But to do that I had to get out of a bed in which I lay snug and warm and happy. . . . This body, which during any daylight hour might reveal itself my enemy and do me ill . . . was still my obedient and comradely friend as it snuggled under the eiderdown; it had to be washed in freezing water, shaved, dressed, made respectable before presenting itself to the bursts of steel. And getting out of bed was like a return to infancy, like being torn away from the maternal arms, the maternal breast, from everything that cherishes, caresses, shelters the existence of the infant. So, having pondered and meditated and put off my decision as long as I could, I would grit my teeth and spring in a single leap to the fireplace, drench the logs with kerosene, and touch a match to them. Then, when the oil had flared up, and I had succeeded in crossing back to my bed, I would snuggle down again in its grateful warmth. With blankets and eiderdown drawn up to my left eye, I would watch the fireplace. . . ."

The truth varies slightly from this account. As usual, when

Saint-Exupéry gave full rein to his imagination, he described an event as he would have liked it to be. But he did, at times, confess to having invented a scene. In his war book, he recounts navigating at 35,000 feet, with his plane leaving behind it "a pearly white scarf, like a bridal veil. . . . We bank, and a whole sky of suitors banks in our wake." To imagine the enemy fighter planes as a swarm of impassioned suitors is certainly an original metaphor. But a few pages farther on, he revises his story: "It is hard to believe that I invented that disgusting literary image. . . . For one thing, I fit like a pipe in its case, I can see nothing behind me. I see behind me through the eyes of my gunner . . . if the intercom is working. My gunner never called down to me, 'Adoring suitors aft in the wake of our train!' "

Right or wrong, it was a vivid description, as was his description of rising in the morning at Orconte.

The truth is that every morning the farmer's wife knocked at his bedroom door. She knocked hard. He uttered a growl. She entered the room. From the bed, a bleary eye observed her. She heard another groan and saw the great body turn over suddenly toward the wall. Then she lit the wood fire in the fireplace. Soon its warmth would fill the room. Back in the kitchen, she heated a big pot of water which she took back to his room, to wake him up again. Again that groan, again that half-shut eye looking at her. On most mornings she had to return three or four times. At last, the bedroom door would open, Saint-Ex would come out, his face still puffy from sleep, and would call out to the farmer's wife, "Madame, do you happen to have some hot water for me?"

His body washed, shaved, dressed, suitably arrayed to be exposed to shell fragments, Saint-Ex went through the glacial morning to the airfield. The smoke from his cigarette was blue in the dim light and condensed in the cold air. The frozen ground rang beneath his steps. In the operations room his comrades were sitting or standing about, some talking seriously, others joking, while still others were studying a map, preparing a mission.

Group 2–33 was the second group (there were only two) of the 33rd Reconnaissance Squadron. Their total of seventeen aircraft were Potez 63, two-engine planes with a crew of three men, pilot, observer, gunner. The Potez 63 was a smooth-running machine with pure lines. Unfortunately, destined to fly alone, it lacked by sixty miles per hour the speed needed if it were to escape the German fighters. It was armed with machine guns forward (operated by the pilot), machine guns aft (operated by the gunner). Its gunpower was also inferior to that of the enemy planes. Shortly after Saint-Exupéry joined Group 2–33, these machines were replaced by a faster and better-armed aircraft, the Bloch 174. But the controls of this plane, though destined for high altitude flying, froze at high altitudes, as did the guns. This partly explains why there were such heavy losses in reconnaissance flying during the campaign of 1939–1940.

Each crew set forth alone on long flights over enemy territory to gather information and bring back photographs. The missions of Group 2–33 took the planes over the regions of Trèves, Cologne, Aix-la-Chapelle, Euskirchen, Düsseldorf. Had Saint-Exupéry's plane trailed a bridal veil behind it, the enemy aircraft would soon have spotted it. In the latter part of the 1939–1940 campaign, during the German offensive, the Bloch 174, flying low, would join in the battle of the ground troops and many received direct hits from German antiaircraft guns.

The missions over Germany, dangerous though they might be, did not, of course, have the murderous character of a battle. Each crew took its turn, and at times remained several days without flying.

Saint-Exupéry's existence during this period was in most respects like that of his comrades. Father Guy Bougerol, who was an observer in this Group, has given us an account of this period, in his book *Ceux qu'on n'a jamais vus*. He pictures Saint-Ex mingling with the others in the operations room, fraternizing with everyone, seeking out particularly a few, Gavoille, Israël, and others. When

Saint-Ex was not flying, he was apt to go, at the end of the afternoon, to Vitry-le-François for a chat with the bookseller Ruet, or to browse among the books. This bookshop was a meeting place for some officers who would pick him up there before going on to a café for a drink. Or sometimes Mme. Ruet persuaded them to have a glass of Pernod right there. Her husband liked Saint-Exupéry's conversation, and she was proud to have him as a guest.

One evening, at Ruet's, he did not disguise his anxiety over the strength of the Germans and the weakness of the French. For some, this period was still referred to as the *drôle de guerre*—the funny war, the phony war. But it was serious enough, this war, for Group 2–33, which had already lost several crews.

"For the time being," he said, "their strength is of little importance. But just wait. When they let loose. . . ."

Early in the morning of May 10, 1940, the Germans finally did let loose. The *blitzkrieg* was on. And before the brutal force and size of the German attack, the French defense was shaken. What did we have with which to oppose the Germans? Their supremacy in the air was immediately apparent—only a short time later we learned we were outnumbered six to one.

Reconnaissance flying became more than ever important in this war of swift movement, but our impotence became all too apparent, reflecting the criminal lack of foresight on the part of our statesmen who, before 1939, were responsible for the destiny of France. The Germans began their offensive, as they had done eight months earlier in Poland, by massive bombing of our airfields. After the first attack on their field, Group 2–33 practically disintegrated: there remained only seven aircraft: five Potez 63s, two Bloch 174s. With seven machines, the squadron leader, Commandant Alias, was expected to explore the sector extending from the English Channel to Luxembourg. Here and there, on various airfields at the rear, there remained a few Bloch 174s, which were brought up; but the number of planes available to Commandant Alias remained unchanged, for in this absurd enterprise, "crew after crew was being offered up as a sacrifice. It was as if you dashed glassfuls of water into a forest fire." In three weeks, Group 2–33 lost seventeen crews out of twenty-three.

In the very first pages of *Flight to Arras,* we see Commandant Alias issuing orders to a crew—Saint-Exupéry's—for a dangerous and quite useless reconnaissance mission. Any information they would bring back could not be transmitted to headquarters, for headquarters was constantly on the move, nor even to base, which was also retreating inland steadily. And even had it been possible to transmit information, it would be of no use, for the enemy was advancing with horrifying speed. The missions sent out were openly called "sacrificed missions." But the war had to be carried on, even though defeat was inevitable. In the terrible gamble, all the cards were stacked against us.

"I am off on an 'awkward' sortie," writes Saint-Exupéry, for that was the word Major Alias had used when giving him orders for the mission which would take him over the town of Arras, and he recalls his feelings as he set forth. "Is my mind filled with the thought of the war of the Nazi against the Occident? Not at all. I think in terms of immediate details. I think . . . of the absurdity of flying over German-held Arras at two thousand feet. Of the futility of the intelligence we are asked to bring back. Of the interminable time it takes to dress in these clothes that remind me of men made ready for the executioner. And I think of my gloves . . . I have lost my gloves. I can no longer see the cathedral in which I live. I am dressing for the service of a dead god." And again, recalling the neutral tone of voice used by Major Alias in issuing these useless orders: "Had I been Alias, I should have said without a change of voice, 'Captain Geley, you are to be shot at dawn,' and waited for the answer."

Like his comrades, he continued to risk his life in vain. Yet he had no regret at having entered a combat unit. He did not preen himself on serving in one of the most dangerous of the fighting services, but derived a feeling of *being,* and of having the right to speak his mind if and when he returned to base. Death seemed to him "neither august, nor majestic, nor heroic, nor poignant." Death was "a mere consequence of disorder." He accepted it, but risking one's life had not the same meaning as in former times on the Line. It had no meaning whatever. All the crews "accepted the expectancy of death." It was the common lot.

In this dangerous life his development, arrested for a time, continued. For him, living dangerously was to live. And "to live is to be slowly born. For borrowing ready-made souls would be too easy!"

But this is not to say that he accepted death and the disorder of war as a fatality. He suffered over all those useless deaths and the chaos into which France had fallen. He burned with indignation against the political and military leaders, but still reflected in *Flight to Arras,* "One's impulse is so strong to make somebody responsible for disaster, and to believe that by putting him out of the way all can be saved."

In the second week of May 1940, he had a short leave of absence to go to Paris, where he managed to see Paul Reynaud, the prime minister of the disintegrating government, and asked to be sent to the United States so that he might try to persuade Roosevelt to release some American aircraft for use in France.

Reynaud listened to him absent-mindedly. He was in a hurry to get rid of this bothersome guest, for he was to broadcast once more a message to the French people, telling them, "We will defend Paris street by street, house by house"—and then flee to the south.

"I'll see what can be done about it," he said, and from his tone Saint-Ex realized that his *démarche* had been useless. Reynaud might as well have said, although not in Major Alias' tone of voice, "Captain de Saint-Exupéry, you are to be shot at dawn."

Saint-Ex rejoined his unit, and the lost-cause missions continued to be sent out. Once more he flew planes whose guns and controls froze at high altitudes. And again beneath his wings he witnessed the defeat: burning villages, roads black with refugees, "that interminable syrup flowing endless to the horizon," the enemy's armored tanks sometimes entangled in this crowd of fleeing people, all moving toward the south. And he felt discouraged to the very marrow by this universal ruin.

Group 2–33 was also moving gradually to the south. They were stationed at Orly, then Nangis, then Chapelle-Vendômoise, then Châteauroux, then Jonzac. And each day the Group dwindled, so that the remaining crews were constantly in the air, exhausted for lack of sleep. Finally, orders were received by Major Alias to retreat to Algiers, and on June 17, a four-engined Farman bore the officers to that North Algerian port.

A few days later, the Armistice was signed. Fighting ceased on French soil, two thirds of which had been invaded by the enemy.

In the relative calm of Algiers, Saint-Exupéry had time to meditate upon the defeat of France, which to him seemed irremediable. All the sacrifices and risks of the war now appeared to him glaringly futile. He had seen the incapacity, sluggishness, and egotism of the leaders of France, the collective cowardice of those who thought only of living well while millions of French people, among them old men, women, and children, were suffering and dying like hunted animals on roads so blocked with broken-down cars and fleeing crowds that they had become impassable. At Bordeaux he had seen ministers and deputies and superior officers, often accompanied by their wives or mistresses, eating in expensive restaurants and behaving as if nothing were wrong or as if they had no reason to feel disturbed by these events. And at Algiers he had learned of the far from brilliant behavior of certain statesmen at the time of the debacle.

Against all this, he weighed the sacrifices of the combatants. He who had wanted to participate, who had refused to be exempted, who had turned down a relatively safe post in Toulouse, because he wanted to fight in this war, while detesting war, was now filled with disgust. He who had risked his life because everything he loved was menaced, now waited impatiently in Algiers for his demobilization papers. He had them in August.

On August 5, Saint-Exupéry landed at Marseilles and immediately went to his sister Gabrielle's house at Agay, where his mother was staying with her daughter and son-in-law, Pierre, and their children. It was a happy family reunion and, as always in Provence, he felt truly alive again "in that part of the world where even the dust is perfumed, as in Greece."[39] The olive trees, the sheep browsing in the meadows, the family life, the beautiful old house, all recalled his childhood. He was fond of the venerable old mansion of the Agay family—it dated from the time of Louis XIV—standing at the end of a rocky cove, its walls and foundation, solid as ramparts, lapped by the sea waves, sheltered from the north wind by ochre-colored cliffs which flamed in the rays of the setting sun. This place revived some of his happiest memories.

At Agay the days passed calmly. Saint-Ex had long talks with his mother and sister and brother-in-law, or entered into the games of his nephew and nieces. Then, at night, when everyone else was in bed, he remained alone in his room, writing or meditating. He liked to stand at the open window on a starry night, listening to the murmur of the sea, and letting his memory drift. That sea murmur, how often he had heard it at Juby. And the same stars shone there, above the great nakedness of the desert. And he, too, had felt naked and open to the sky at Juby. He had often been alone then, as now. But more often than not his thoughts turned to suffering mankind.

In the morning his sister Didi could see by the overflowing ashtray, the empty teapot and the pages covered with his handwriting that he had worked late into the night.

"What are you writing?" she asked him one day.

"I'm working on my posthumous book," he replied.

He was writing *The Wisdom of the Sands.*

Naturally, this peaceful life could not hold him for any length of time. Two months was as long as this nomad could remain anywhere. The respite at Agay merely enabled him to get his bearings and recover his desire, or rather need for action. Later on, recalling this short stay in Provence, where the sounds of horses' hooves and carriage wheels brought him back to a simpler life, he declared in a nostalgic letter, "And it seemed to me that all my life I had been an imbecile. . . ." This thought occurred at a moment of disillusionment, for he had no real regret and he was not ripe for a life of retirement. But what was there for him to do in this peaceful portion of unoccupied France? And where could he go?

At this time he apparently decided that the best course open to him was to leave for the United States. Although his motives for going there are easily explained, they gave rise to misunderstanding and considerable debate. Some commentators have suggested that the Vichy government sent him to America, where his prestige and intelligence could be useful to France. But Saint-Ex emphatically denied this later on and there is no reason whatever to doubt his word. Yet, the rumor persisted that he was an official emissary, and specious arguments were circulated to support this theory.

When he landed at Marseilles on August 5, 1940, he was practically penniless, it was said. But on November 5 he had enough money to embark for North Africa (sailing on the *Ville d'Alger*) whence he sailed to Lisbon, arriving there the sixteenth, with the intention of going on to America. Now, when he left Agay, it was to go to Vichy, where he remained a week. Why? In Vichy, he met his old acquaintance, Drieu La Rochelle, an alleged "collaborator," and went with him by car to Paris. Later on, in North Africa, while waiting to sail to Lisbon, he met Father Théry, whom he had often encountered in Paris along with his friends Monzie and Werth, and with whom he liked to discuss philosophical questions. Father Théry has written that Saint-Exupéry left for America "with the conscious intention of serving France." [40] In addition to all this, there is the fact that *Flight to Arras* was published in 1942, with the authorization of the Germans.

The truth is that his American publishers had cabled him proposing to arrange for his visa and to facilitate his passage to America, where he had friends and a great reputation. At Agay, in unoccupied France, there was nothing to do, no way he could earn a living, while in the United States his financial problems would be solved. He could collect royalties on his published work and could write again far from "the black night of our cities."

His trip to Vichy is also understandable. It was imperative that he go there to procure a passport. His encounter with Drieu La Rochelle was fortuitous; Drieu, as a contributing editor of the Gallimard periodical, *Nouvelle Revue Française,* was one of his old literary acquaintances. And since Drieu was leaving by car for Paris, Saint-Ex was glad to have a lift.

Father Théry's assertion that Saint-Ex went to the United States with the avowed intention of serving France indicates that he hoped to acquaint Americans with the true situation in France, the sacrifices that were being forced upon her by the German military power. He was to say as much in *Flight to Arras.* As for the German authorization to publish this book in France in 1942, there is nothing unusual in the circumstance. At the time it was impossible to publish anything without German permission and this book was not the first to show how easy was the German victory. *Flight to Arras* was a cry of anguish for his defeated country and a powerful plea for her resurgence, so the Nazi censors could not have read it very carefully. In fact, they banned the book after the United States entered the war because it was well known that Saint-Ex was there and would no doubt rejoin a fighting unit.

Had Saint-Ex left France as an official envoy, the government would have procured a Spanish visa for him. But he had no Spanish visa and therefore was obliged to go to Lisbon by way of North Africa. Spain had refused to grant him a visa because he had been on the "Red" front in 1937; he was even accused of convoying planes to the Republicans in the Spanish Civil War. This accusation had originally been made by the French fascist group led by Colonel La Roque.

Undoubtedly, Saint-Ex left France, as so many of his compatriots did after the Franco-German Armistice, because he was overwhelmed by the French defeat. Blind optimism was not characteristic of him; it is doubtful that in 1940 he had much hope of a possible change in the situation. He had seen German military strength, had seen it for months beneath his plane when on reconnaissance flights over enemy territory. And now Russia, with its two hundred million inhabitants, was an ally of Nazi Germany. Hitler was the ruler of Europe. France was crushed and alone. The English—what few troops they had on French soil had quickly returned to their island shortly after the beginning of the *blitzkrieg*—were waiting beyond their girdle of water. What else could they do? As for the United States, Saint-Exupéry had expressed his disbelief in any help coming from there at several points in *Flight to Arras*. "After all," he asked, in one eloquent passage, "why do we go on fighting? For democracy? If we die for democracy then we must be one of the democracies. Let the rest fight with us, if that is the case. But the most powerful of them, *the only democracy that could save us,* chooses to bide its time. Very good.... Why, then, do we go on dying?" [The italics are mine.] It is clear that with four thousand more planes than she had, France could have stopped the Germans at Sedan. Four thousand planes represented two months' production in the United States. We could have supplied the crews for those planes.

While America remained outside the war, Saint-Exupéry feared the eventual triumph of Germany, as did a great many others who were not brave enough to admit it. Pierre de Lanux, who saw a good deal of Saint-Ex in New York in 1941, has this to say of his attitude: "He saw no possibility of the Allies' winning the war, and he condemned faith in such a victory as being the result of idle optimism—as indeed it was, with some people." [41] But when the Americans landed in North Africa, he spoke enthusiastically of "the miracle of the American landing" in letters and newspaper interviews. It was this miracle that gave him renewed hope and impelled him once more to enter the fight.

But in 1940 he had no wish to go on fighting. After the Armistice, when he was waiting in Algiers for his demobilization, he thought only of hurrying back to his family at Agay. There were no Germans at Agay, and he saw none at Vichy. The first he saw of the German conquerors was at the demarcation line between occupied and unoccupied territory. But when he reached Paris and heard their hobnailed boots hammering the pavements and saw their uniforms blemishing the Paris scene, he was filled with despair. Life in occupied France, he realized, was not to be thought of.

"I have never known a man as little made for neutrality, for emigration, for exile," his translator Lewis Galantière has said. "Saint-Exupéry was obsessed with the notion that France must stay in the war. He wanted passionately to serve his country, but as a soldier, by fighting for it." After the invitation came from his American publisher he borrowed a plane or hitched a ride to Tunisia to see the old comrades of his reconnaissance group. "I wanted to know if they could go on fighting," he told Galantière. "They looked at me in astonishment. You're out of your mind, they said. We have no reserve planes, no fuel, no tires, no spare parts. How many missions do you think a plane can fly without spare parts? The best that we can do is hide as much equipment as possible from the enemy Armistice inspectors—bury it—and hope to use it another day." [42]

And yet, he hesitated to leave his comrades, to abandon his mother and "poor little forsaken Consuelo," as he referred to his wife in a letter written to his mother from Orconte in May. "If one day she takes refuge in the Midi, do welcome her, mother, for my sake." But Consuelo refused to go and live with her mother-in-law. Apparently he still hesitated in Lisbon and was torn between sailing for America and going back to France. "Tell me that I should return," he wrote to his Egeria, "and I'll return." She advised him to leave. For she was quite aware that were he to remain it would be for a temporary stay and that his situation would be hopeless. Later on, she was to join him in New York, returning only when Consuelo finally went to America to be with her husband again.

With the aid of his American publisher, Saint-Ex obtained a visa and passage on a small Portuguese vessel which sailed from Lisbon, the only gateway left open in Europe, in December 1940. It was the beginning of a restless, anxious period for him, as he was obsessed by the plight of his country and could think and talk of little else for a time. Yet the next two and a half years proved to be a productive period too, for he was to do some of his best writing in America.

11

Yet, dark as was the hour, I found strength to take up life again. "I have broken through my last husk," I told myself, "and now I shall step forth the purer."

—The Wisdom of the Sands

When Saint-Exupéry landed in New York, the terrible year of 1940 was ending. In France, Belgium, Luxembourg, Holland, Denmark, Poland, almost throughout a defeated and subjugated Europe, people were living a desperate and harried life, some of them subsisting in the ruins of their houses. A particularly severe winter was to kill off thousands of children who were deprived of warmth and sufficient food. Craftily, the war continued its work of destruction.

On looking up his old friends, Saint-Exupéry found that some of them were indifferent to the misery of Europe—as most people are indifferent to suffering which they cannot actually see and touch. In America, people were living exactly as before, as if nothing had occurred on the planet. They were merely puzzled, unable to understand the sudden defeat of France, surprised that the heroic French soldiers had not held out longer against the German onslaught. In short, they were not yet affected by the war and did not wake up to facts until the Japanese bombed Pearl Harbor and their own security was threatened.

Saint-Exupéry had never liked living in New York, and upon his arrival in December 1940 found little changed. His first visit had occurred in 1938, when he made the ill-fated attempt to fly to Tierra del Fuego.

In a letter to a friend at that time he wrote: "I'm living on the twenty-fifth floor of a hotel of stone, and I hear through my window the voices of a new city. And that voice has a harrowing sound. . . . It reminds me of the tumult in mid-ocean, the hubbub of a ship in distress. Never before have I felt so strongly this piling up of men in their stone pyramids and making all these sounds of departure, of traffic, of shipwreck, an embarkation of men without a captain, making they know not what voyage between their planet and the stars. . . . All these crowds, these lights, these spires of the buildings seem to state, overwhelmingly, the problem of Destiny. No doubt it's idiotic, but I feel here, more than elsewhere, as if I were on the high seas." [43]

It must be remembered that in 1929, when he had just landed in Buenos Aires and was homesick for his life in the desert, he had showered the Argentine capital with abuse. Now in New York he doubtless missed the tranquility and family life at Agay, a calm island in a wartorn world. On the island of Manhattan he was again living in a high stone tower above the hubbub of the city. Mrs. Eugene Reynal, the wife of his publisher, had found an apartment for him on the twenty-first floor of a skyscraper facing Central Park, for he insisted on having a view. It was a handsome, spacious apartment with a terrace at 240 Central Park South. André Maurois recalls visiting him and being impressed by the size of the apartment and its view. Saint-Ex was rarely alone there; though he dined out occasionally, he usually preferred to have friends in for lunch or dinner, sometimes taking them down to the restaurant in the building or having a meal sent up.

After his arrival he was too tense and preoccupied to settle down to work. The war was so much on his mind that he talked of it constantly, and he frequently expressed concern for the welfare of his wife and family. His friends recall that he spent hours discussing strategy and weapons with scientists and engineers, plotting and planning means of getting France back into action and of securing American intervention. After a period of adjustment his publishers urged him to start writing again. "It is your duty," they said, "to explain France, to explain her defeat." But he resisted any semblance of pressure, for he was no hack writer who could turn out books on order; he had spent four years of laborious work on *Night Flight*, seven years on *Wind, Sand and Stars*. At last, a sense of duty drove him to begin a war book, but progress was slow because of his own state of mind and constant interruptions from French relief and cultural agencies, lecture bureaus, newspaper and magazine editors who telephoned incessantly, making demands upon his time.

All was not gloom and depression, however. Saint-Ex knew congenial people in New York, though his closest associates were those who spoke his language and shared his interests. He did not speak English and refused to learn the language. Indeed, Pierre Chevrier quotes him as saying "I don't want to speak another language. It's impossible to write one language well if you employ several languages." Georges Pélissier reports a similar comment and describes Saint-Ex shopping in a Fifth Avenue store, surrounded by a swarm of pretty salesgirls trying to understand what the Frenchman was saying. The truth is that, despite his supposed prejudice against learning languages, he did speak Spanish, which he had learned in Argentina and found very useful when he reported on the Civil War in Spain. As for his opinion that knowing other tongues is a handicap to the writer, there are many instances to refute this—André Maurois, André Siegfried, Joseph Conrad, among others. The truth is that Saint-Exupéry was lazy about studying English—not unlike many of his compatriots. At school in Fribourg, he would certainly have had to study a foreign language. And from Strasbourg he had written to his mother, "I'm learning the language"—German of course. Though not vainglorious, he did not like to feel inferior to anyone. Because of the type of people he met in New York he thought that he would have to speak English perfectly or not at all. His views recall those of Paul Fort. This poet, arriving without money in Moscow, to which he had taken his fiancée in 1914, went to the French embassy to ask the diplomatic corps to arrange some lectures for him. When the cultural attaché rather dubiously asked whether that prince of poets spoke Russian, he replied: "No, but people everywhere understand French—at least, the best people."

Even without English, Saint-Ex was able to communicate and soon knew the opinion Americans had of France. Having traveled a good deal, he was aware that France continued to enjoy an intellectual prestige abroad, as she had for a long time, thanks to her writers, artists, and scientists; but the attitude of French politicians had somewhat damaged that prestige. "Why does one discover, every time one leaves France," he complained in a letter, "that there is something slack in the French political system? Why is the electorate so dully complaisant? Why do Frenchmen take so little interest in their functions and so little interest in human welfare?" The defeat of her army had further damaged France's reputation, which was in no way improved by the behavior of certain émigrés in America. In their dissensions and jealousies, which had split them into several incompatible groups, they exhibited the worst features of France to Americans.

But was it the true image of France that they presented? It was certainly not the nation that had fought and sacrified. Sacrificed for what reason? This was the question that Saint-Exupéry found himself asking in *Flight to Arras*. "Why is it that more Frenchmen are not being killed?" men in the outside world were wondering. But he, for his part, as he watched the crews go off to their death, was asking, "What are we giving ourselves to? Who is still paying the bill?" It is tempting to quote the entire passage from the book, so eloquently does it present the case for France in the last dreadful part of the 1939–1940 campaign:

> *For we were dying. For one hundred and fifty thousand Frenchmen were already dead in a single fortnight. Those dead do not exemplify an extraordinary resistance. I am not singing the praises of an extraordinary resistance. Such a resistance was impossible. But there were clusters of infantrymen still giving up their lives in undefendable farmhouses. There were aviation crews still melting like wax flung into a fire.*

Look once again at Group 2–33. Will you explain to me why, as I fly to Arras, we of Group 2–33 still agree to die? For the esteem of the world? But esteem implies the existence of a judge. And I have the impression that none of us will grant whoever it may be the right to sit in judgment. To us who imagine that we are defending a cause which is fundamentally the common cause, the cause of Poland, of Holland, of Belgium, of Norway; to us who hold this view, the role of arbiter seems much too comfortable. It is we who sit in judgment upon the arbiter. I invite you to try to explain to us who take off with a "Very good, sir," having one chance in three to get back when the sortie is an easy one; I invite you to try to explain to a certain pilot out of another group, half of whose neck and jaw were shot away so that he is forced to renounce the love of woman for life, is frustrated in a fundamental right of man, frustrated as totally as if he were behind prison walls, surrounded inescapably by his virtue and preserved totally by his disfigurement, isolated completely by his ugliness— I invite you to explain to him that spectators are sitting in judgment upon him. Toreadors live for the bullfight crowd: we are not toreadors. If you said to another of my friends, to Hochedé, "You've got to go up because the crowd have their eye on you," Hochedé would answer: "There must be a mistake: it is I, Hochedé, who have my eye on the crowd."

No other French voice at the time was raised so passionately and candidly. He honestly faced our defeat and spoke out against our impotent leaders who had declared war without preparation, and against the democracies, especially the most powerful democracy, which could have aided us. He voiced a plea for those who had fought, and even dared to be ironical about the phony war, or what the French called the *drôle de guerre*. As he said in *Flight to Arras*, "After all, it is we ourselves who call this a funny war. Why not?

I should imagine that no one would deny us the right to call it that if we please, since it is we who are sacrificing ourselves, not those others who think our epithet immoral. Surely I have the right to joke about my death if joking about it gives me pleasure."

Flight to Arras, the English version of *Pilote de Guerre,* was published, like the French original, in 1942. It created a great stir in the United States and served to clarify American ideas about the war. "The young people who were then entering the war," writes Pierre de Lanux, "seized upon this book, and the vocations that it determined or released cannot be counted. I believe this book rendered a unique service to the French cause in America." [44] But in some quarters the book was misunderstood, for it appeared two months after Pearl Harbor when, according to Lewis Galantière, "Americans wanted to be told what to do, not what to be, wanted a book on Democracy, not on Man." [45]

In France the book was enthusiastically received by some readers, while others, out of servility to the Germans, disparaged both the work and its author. This was to be expected. What was surprising and saddening was the attitude of certain French refugees in America, who attacked the author virulently, labeling him a "Vichyite"—a grave injury in their eyes. Had not Saint-Exupéry dared to say—what all reasonable men still believe—that the government of Marshal Pétain was the consequence of the defeat, and that blame for this defeat belonged essentially to the governments which preceded it? Fundamentally, they sought an excuse to injure a famous compatriot who had spoken the truth.

Saint-Exupéry had seen these same exiles in Portugal, at the Estoril Casino, near which he had lodged for a while. "Those refugees," he wrote later on in *Letter to a Hostage,* "were not proscripts seeking a refuge from persecution; they were not immigrants seeking a land to enrich by their work. I'm speaking of those who expatriated themselves far from the misery of their own people, in order to put their money in a safe place." These "superpatriots," as Saint-Ex called them, who had not fought and would never fight for their country, became the worst detractors of the author of *Flight to Arras.* The book served merely as a pretext.

What they really objected to was his refusal to align himself with the Gaullists.

Saint-Exupéry had no doubt of General de Gaulle's integrity or that of the Free French combatants who had rallied around him in England. But he refused to join them because he believed that de Gaulle was asking the French to fight a fratricidal war at a time when unity was of the utmost importance. "I should have followed him with joy against the Germans. I could not follow him against Frenchmen." [46] He was also repelled by the political scramblings for position, the petty squabbles of the Gaullists in America. "They glare at each other like dogs round a feeding-trough."

He refused to recognize the right they ascribed to themselves of representing France, of *being* France—any more than he recognized his own ability to represent or be France. That privilege, he felt, belonged to those who had remained at home. "For us Frenchmen outside France," he wrote in *Letter to a Hostage,* "there is a job to do in this war, and that is to raise the blockade on the seed-corn frozen by the German presence on the soil of France. We must bring succor to you, the hostages in France. We must free you in the land where you have the fundamental right to put down roots. You are forty million hostages. And it is always in the cellars of oppression that the new verities are prepared: forty million hostages are evolving their new verity in France. We submit in advance to that Truth."

It must be recalled that Washington at this time refused to recognize General de Gaulle as head of the French government. Saint-Exupéry's unwillingness to join the Gaullists, his unfriendly attitude and comments about them, repeated to their leader, could not but make General de Gaulle an enemy of the airman and writer; and de Gaulle was a stubborn enemy who would not refrain from taking action when the time came.

While his ignorance of the language kept him from expanding his contacts, Saint-Ex was liked by Americans, who appreciated and admired him not only as a writer and philosopher but also as a man. His appearance, demeanor, and originality made a favorable impression. He was much talked about; his reputation was widespread, his prestige great. The American press described in detail his likes and dislikes, his habits and attitudes.

One reporter portrayed him rather pitilessly as not notably distinguished in looks, more than six feet tall, "round-faced, with an expressive but ordinary mouth, thinning hair, an impertinently turned up nose," but exclaimed over his "marvelous hands, capable of as much grace and eloquence as his speech." When he shook hands—as Frenchmen do on every occasion—his handshake was so vigorous that you "felt there was enough strength in it to wrench off your arm." [47] These descriptions, while a little farfetched, in any case prove that Americans observed him, took pleasure in meeting him, and in presenting him to the public. René Delange quotes one reporter as saying, "He likes to write, to talk, to sing, to gamble, and to speculate on the meaning of life, and to be with women." And Mme. Lecomte de Noüy, an American by birth, commented: "He combines a very real and profound mysticism with a great appetite for all the pleasures of the senses and a total irresponsibility in his daily life, which is rather disconcerting upon first acquaintance." [48]

Indeed, he was talked about more in America than he had ever been in his native France. But his friendships were limited to a few close associates whom he saw regularly. Among them, oddly enough, were several fervent and official Gaullists, including Hervé Alphand (later the French ambassador to the United States), M. Monzéarly, and Colonel de Chevigné. He saw a good deal of his publishers, Eugene Reynal and Curtis Hitchcock, his translator, Lewis Galantière, Bernard Lamotte, illustrator of *Flight to Arras,* and Pierre de Lanux.

Among his good friends were the Lecomte de Noüys, whom he had known in France. Mme. Lecomte de Noüy recalls that he arrived at their home at unexpected hours to read aloud passages of his latest work. Lecomte de Noüy, author of *Dignité humaine,* naturally had much in common with the author of *Wind, Sand and Stars.* Their viewpoints on the major problems of humanity and their firm belief in the perfectability of man, in man's incomparable destiny, brought them close.

However, it wasn't all serious talk about philosophy and war. Saint-Ex knew how to relax and laugh with his companions; as in the past, he held them enthralled with his tales and amused them with his card tricks. With the artist, Bernard Lamotte, whom he had known in the old days as a student at the École des Beaux Arts, he established a close, sometimes rough camaraderie which concealed a warm affection. During heated discussions Saint-Ex would poke a forefinger at him and exclaim, "Idiot! Do you understand what I am saying? No, I see you don't understand." As absent-minded and abstracted as ever, he would turn up at Lamotte's studio without warning at any hour of the day or night, and would mutter like a forlorn child, "I saw your light on and thought you were at home."

After welcoming him, the artist would return to his easel, where he was working on an illustration for *Flight to Arras* or perhaps completing a commercial art assignment. Saint-Ex would settle down to write quietly at a table, but in a few moments he would interrupt Lamotte by reading to him a passage he had just written. Or he'd get hungry and ask for a bite to eat. Lamotte pointed to the refrigerator and said, "You know where the food is. Help yourself." But Saint-Ex was helpless in the kitchen, so his friend dropped his work to prepare a snack, or a pot of tea—"I don't want a little cup, but a big potful of tea," said Saint-Ex, indicating with a gesture the gargantuan size of the pot. And he'd swallow quantities of the beverage as he continued writing. At times, overcome by fatigue after a sleepless night, he would lean his head against the table and fall fast asleep.

"He was always welcome. After all, he was my brother," said Lamotte, with a casual shrug that belied the devotion in his voice, as he reminisced about his friend. "He was like a cathedral—so large and powerful physically, and mentally too. How he could talk! He was as great a talker as he was a writer. I remember one night how we listened to him from eight o'clock in the evening until about two in the morning. No one else said a word, or wanted to, while Saint-Ex told us about his experiences in the desert or flying through a typhoon. When he described how he crawled along in the desert, almost dying of thirst, his tongue swollen, we felt that we too were dying of thirst—so vivid was it that we had to reach for the wine bottle!"

Lamotte's studio represented a little corner of France to Saint-Ex. It was in a penthouse atop an old brownstone house on West 53rd Street, next door to the Museum of Modern Art. Because it was surrounded by glass skylights it looked like a goldfish bowl and was nicknamed *Le Bocal.* There were paintings on the walls and sausages strung from them. Lamotte had built a brick barbecue on the roof and had constructed from rough wooden planks a large table on which his friends proceeded to carve their names. Above it hung a kerosene lamp and around this table, which became famous in the French colony, gathered at impromptu dinners Saint-Ex, Marlene Dietrich, Jean Gabin, Charlie Chaplin, or any one else who happened to be in town. Two ducks, called Théodule and Julie, had free run of the roof and drank wine, especially with strawberries in it, as freely as the guests. Sometimes the ducks waddled around tipsily, to everyone's great amusement. One day, Saint-Ex arrived to find Théodule with a bandage around his beak. Asking what had happened to his favorite pet, he learned that, while Lamotte was shucking corn for the ducks' lunch, Théodule had stuck his inquisitive beak too close to the knife and the cut had bled as profusely as one on a human proboscis.

Friends recall with nostalgia the gay parties at *Le Bocal,* and how expansive Saint-Ex became in this home away from home. When Consuelo first arrived in New York, Lamotte gave a cocktail party for the Saint-Exupérys. Eugene Reynal, his publisher, noticed that Saint-Ex seemed more subdued than usual, and soon he drew Reynal aside and asked him not to leave him alone with Consuelo. Later, the Reynals went out to dinner with the Saint-Exupérys. At one point, Saint-Ex whispered to Mrs. Reynal in French, "Well, she'll be gone tomorrow. I can stand it as long as I'm not alone with her." Meanwhile, Consuelo murmured to Mr. Reynal in English, "He doesn't know it, but I'm here to stay." Presumably she had stopped off en route to visit her family in South America. But she did stay on and Saint-Ex rented a separate flat for her in his building. Later, they both moved to a brownstone house on Beekman Place, with high-ceilinged rooms and probably enough space to give each of them privacy.

Despite Saint-Exupéry's dismay over Consuelo's arrival, his old need to look after her apparently reasserted itself. When he had been on his own in New York, his friends noted that he was usually drawn to small, frail women—Consuelo's type—who appealed to his masculine tenderness. "He was a man of great breeding and distinction, but unworldly," Lewis Galantière has said. "When he met a woman he liked, he blushed. And he would offer to read her his writing or explain a fascinating theorem. He never sought to make himself interesting by talking of his adventures. . . . He was no Puritan, but he had a horror of anything that smacked of depravity or morbidity." [49]

Sometimes women who were quite different from Consuelo, aggressive women who tried to manage him and arrange his life, attached themselves to him, and he was not brutal enough to get rid of them.

Those who had met Madame X during her stay in New York were impressed by her attractiveness—"a woman of great breeding, genuine heart and honorable nature" was the consensus. But they also remarked that it was Consuelo who called forth his tender regard. "He had a particular feeling that she needed to be looked after," said Galantière. "He would have left any other woman to go to her if she were in a bad way."

This same friend feels, however, that women were not too important in Saint-Exupéry's life. What he needed most was comradeship. The day he gave a lunch for some old flying companions he was radiantly happy. In his element, Saint-Ex exchanged reminiscences with them of old pioneering days. The lunch was long and noisy, the talk inexhaustible.

Subconsciously, though he led such a full active life in New York, he must have longed to fly again. Sometimes, just for the fun of it, he launched from the high windows of his flat small paper helicopters he liked to make, and reflectively watched them mount toward the sky then suddenly, borne away by a current of air, disappear behind another building. When one of them by chance entered an open window, he was delighted as a boy would be at imagining the surprise of the people in that room.

He also took a childlike pleasure in American gadgets, such as the recording machine he impulsively acquired. One day he turned up unexpectedly at Lamotte's studio, and said, "You must come out with me and see an organ I want to buy."

"An organ!" exclaimed Lamotte. "Are you crazy? What will you do with an organ?"

"Play it, of course," said Saint-Ex.

Lamotte, who had not realized that his friend possessed this talent, had to drop his work and accompany Saint-Ex to Aeolian Hall on West 57th Street, where a huge organ was on display. Saint-Ex began to pound the keys, and the instrument emitted a cacophony of grunts, puffs and squeaks. He still spoke no English, of course, so he asked Lamotte to find out the price. "What will you do with this monster in your apartment?" demanded Lamotte. Meanwhile, the salesman, convinced that these two mad Frenchmen were wasting his time, named a price of about $18,000. "Ah, you see!" said Lamotte, translating the outlandish sum. "You can't afford it." As he turned reluctantly away from the coveted organ, Saint-Ex's eye lighted on a large recording machine. "What's that?" he demanded. The salesclerk had to demonstrate the device, and Saint-Ex was so intrigued that he bought it on the spot, peeling off the $700 price in twenty- and hundred-dollar bills, to the clerk's amazement.

This machine became a favorite toy and on it Saint-Ex would record anything that came into his head. Perhaps it would be a Mozart symphony conducted by Toscanini over the radio. Then he and his friends would read classical French verse for the same disc, with the music serving as background. Claude Alphand would record Breton and other charming folk songs, while her husband did imitations of dialogue between the doddering Pétain and Hitler or a certain senile general.

Saint-Exupéry's handwriting was so illegible that no one could transcribe it. His publishers persuaded him to get a dictaphone; characteristically, he bought a large, expensive machine. Usually, he started writing late at night after his friends had gone. Either he worked at the dining-room table with a big pot of strong tea nearby, or when he got hungry, he would go to Reuben's, an all-night restaurant on East 58th Street. He would sit in a booth, order a steak *tartare* and write until dawn. Then he would go home, record what he had written on the dictaphone, revising as he went along, and go to bed at six o'clock. Arriving at nine, his secretary transscribed the night's work while he slept.

Like the dictaphone, the telephone played an important role in his life. He would call one or another of his friends, usually late at night, and say that he would like them to come over, or he wanted to see them. Usually, it was: "I want to read you a page I've just written."

Though he "wrote like an angel," according to Lewis Galantière, "he needed constant reassurance, and was convinced that he did not know how to write." Galantière was translating *Flight to Arras*, chapter by chapter, as it came from Saint-Exupéry's hands. Often he was awakened by the phone at two in the morning, and Saint-Ex would read a passage to him and wait expectantly for his comment. Half-asleep, unable to understand what the rapid, muffled voice was reciting, he would murmur, "That's good, that is!" or "Magnificent!" Then Saint-Ex would say, "Sorry to disturb you. Good-night," and hang up.[50]

He was always calling not merely friends in the city where he happened to be or even on the same continent, but across the ocean in the most distant lands. Before the war, when he was stationed in Buenos Aires, or in New York, he not infrequently called his mother or his wife or a friend in France, for the sheer pleasure of talking to someone thousands of miles away. Once, from the *Normandie* in midocean, he called his sister Gabrielle, merely to say, "Isn't it wonderful to be able to telephone from the middle of the ocean!" He spent a small fortune on telephone calls.

Sometimes friends living in one of the free countries of Europe telephoned him; and occasionally he received a call from his good friend, Madame X, from Geneva. In order to telephone him, she had had to cross the border disguised in men's clothing. The conversation would be short, but at least he had news of France and heard a beloved voice. Then the Swiss frontier was closed and these calls became impossible. When all of France was occupied by the Germans, he began to feel ever more keenly his exile, and to visualize the sufferings of those who had not fled their country but had remained. He felt impotent to do anything for them, and sometimes he was ashamed of having left France.

It was in this desolate mood that he wrote his *Letter to a Hostage,* addressed to his old friend Léon Werth, who was living in hiding to avoid deportation as a Jew. Saint-Exupéry realized that his letter could not reach its destination until much later, and would perhaps be read in France only after Léon Werth had vanished from the world. But he wanted people to know what his thoughts as an exile were. "France has been occupied by the enemy," he wrote, "the whole country has entered into a world of silence, like a ship with all fires banked, so that we have no way of knowing whether her passengers and crew have survived the perils of the sea, and the fate of each loved one torments me more gravely than a deep-seated and devouring disease."

At that time he believed he was suffering from a serious illness. As a result of his series of crashes he had injuries that had healed badly and still caused him pain. Sedatives proved ineffectual and he often could not sleep. During a visit with the noted film producer Jean Renoir and his wife in California he became ill and had to undergo an operation. While convalescing he continued to work on what he always referred to as his "posthumous book"—the notebooks he had kept for years of all his meditations and observations. Eventually these notes covered more than 1200 pages. From them sprang the idea for his great war book, *Flight to Arras*, and later, portions of his notes were condensed in *The Wisdom of the Sands*.

During the melancholy period immediately preceding the war, when he had been briefly in New York, he no longer wrote, or almost not at all. The present years in America were saddened by anxieties over the plight of his country and his family. But at least he had no serious financial worries, for he was kept solvent with royalties on his published work and advances on future books, and he was writing a good deal. In less than two years he produced *Flight to Arras*, the *Letter to a Hostage*, *The Little Prince*, and part of *The Wisdom of the Sands*.

Of all this writing, *Letter to a Hostage* is perhaps the most personal. It is an expression of moods, "marvelously condensed and radiant" and displaying the "qualities that are most exclusively human," as Daniel Anet has said in his life of the writer. The *Letter* is a natural sequel to *Flight to Arras*. The book that followed it, however, came as a surprise, although it is enchanting. Referring to this remarkable book, *The Little Prince*, Father Barjon, a onetime classmate of Saint-Ex, calls it "a bouquet of images, like those clumps of flowers found growing in a cleft of a rock, which arouse our curiosity and make us wonder how the seeds were brought there." [51]

This little book had a curious genesis. When Bernard Lamotte began to illustrate *Flight to Arras*, Mrs. Reynal asked if she might keep the first drawing. Saint-Ex wrote a droll inscription across it: "For Elizabeth. Anyone else who has this in his possession is a thief," and in one corner he drew a small winged figure. He kept on "doodling" with these little flying creatures; and his friends commented that they were so good, why not put them into a book. Eugene Reynal suggested that he try coloring them. Intrigued, Saint-Ex bought a set of paints—typically, the most expensive water colors he could find. And so the pictures and story of *The Little Prince* were evolved simultaneously. Bernard Lamotte was often with him when Saint-Ex was doing the illustrations, and Lamotte gave him advice which Saint-Ex made an admirable effort to follow. Certainly he must have enjoyed writing this little book; escaping the dissensions of his fellow men, he entered the pure realm of childhood. It also offered him a new method for expressing his general philosophy.

While he was working on this book, an important event occurred: the United States entered the war. The "miracle" that he had so long doubted had at last been accomplished. He would be able to have his plane again, would fly to the rescue of his oppressed comrades, would help free the hostages. "The essential is to live for the return," he had written in *Letter to a Hostage*.

He had been waiting for that hour. He had even advocated, before the event, the landing of American troops in North Africa. In mid-1942, he had conceived the idea and Lewis Galantière had discussed it with friends in the Office of Strategic Services in Washington. The officers had replied that Saint-Exupéry might well be a great poet but he was certainly not a military genius, and pronounced the project absurd. When Galantière reported these remarks, Saint-Ex said, with a smile, "Oh, so they're cleverer than I thought!" This "absurd" idea, unknown to them both, had already blossomed as a plan in Washington and been agreed to by the British. Pierre Chevrier, who reports these facts, concludes: "It is easy to see why Lewis Galantière's proposal was so badly received in Washington."[52]

At the very first news of the landing of American troops in North Africa, on the seventh of November 1942, Saint-Exupéry began making efforts to rejoin a fighting unit. As in 1939, he was again in serious difficulties—which would not be his last or worst. He persisted, however, until he had what he wanted.

In April 1943, a few friends saw him off at Grand Central Station where he was taking a train to Baltimore in order to embark on a ship sailing from that port. Bernard Lamotte, who was saddened by the departure of his old companion, tried to put a brave face on it and voiced what he called "the usual banalities in saying good-by." Just before the train pulled out, he said, "We'll be seeing you back here soon." Saint-Ex shook his head and said, with a melancholy smile, "No, I won't be back."

Was this a premonition of his ultimate fate? Or was he merely saying that he would not come back to America and hoping that Allied victory would make it possible for him to return to France? Lamotte never knew the precise answer and believes it is only hindsight that led him to interpret the parting remark as an evidence of psychic intuition.

When finally Saint-Ex was a passenger on an American military convoy that was taking him to the coasts of Africa, he was both glad and grave. He would rejoin his old Group that was being reformed in North Africa; he would fly again; he would soon be in the skies above his native land. The vast sea and the open sky were reviving his love of wide horizons. The thirty ships of the convoy moving slowly across the Atlantic were laden with 50,000 soldiers and great stocks of war matériel. These ships tirelessly plowing the ocean were making the first lap of the long road that would have to be traveled before the liberation of the hostages could be achieved. And Saint-Exupéry was determined to participate in that liberation.

12

. . . the one thing needful for a man is to become—*to* be *at last, and to die in the fullness of his being.*

—*The Wisdom of the Sands*

The landing of American troops in North Africa rapidly transformed the atmosphere of Algeria. The calm of former times had been succeeded by a feverish activity. Ships were unloading soldiers and supplies in all the ports, the roads were filled with noisy trucks, the sky was scored by fast airplanes. The towns, even the smallest of them, were humming with activity, and men in various kinds of uniform milled about; the French troops had quickly thrown in their lot with the Americans who brought them at last the means for liberating the French capital. French aviators were especially eager to use modern planes, their own being obsolete models in need of repair. And they were anxious to resume the war in the air that they had courageously sustained in 1939–1940 against such tremendous odds. The wait had been long. For some of them it had been too long, had shaken their faith.

Then, one day in May 1943, the French aviators who were waiting at Laghouat for the arrival of new machines, heard that Saint-Exupéry had come to join them. "And from that moment, I began to hope," writes Jules Roy, who was among the anxious airmen.[53] According to Roy, everyone felt the same way: the knowledge of Saint-Exupéry's presence had a tonic effect. Among these men were some who had doubted him, who had unjustly and severely judged him, and who were in part responsible for the moral sufferings he had endured in New York. There was one in particular who had called him a scoundrel for not having rallied to the Gaullist banner, and had said, "We will make him answer for it" if ever they met again. They met at Laghouat, and Saint-Exupéry's accuser felt nothing but remorse.

The first squadron of his old Group 2–33 was stationed at Oujda, to which Saint-Ex, after some conniving, managed to get sent. He had not come to North Africa to remain on the ground; he was a pilot, and he intended to fly. In New York, when he had heard of the landing of American troops, he had told his compatriots, "Now there will be guns for everyone," and had thought there would surely be an airplane for him. Thanks to the intervention of Colonel Elliot Roosevelt, the President's son, the Group had been equipped with Lockheed Lightnings—or P–38s as they were generally called. But the P–38 which Saint-Ex expected to pilot, and which attained a speed of more than 400 miles an hour, was to be used for high-altitude reconnaissance photography—it generally flew at 35,000 feet. The Americans had fixed thirty-five as the maximum age for a Lightning pilot, and Saint-Exupéry was now forty-three. One must realize how strictly the Americans applied their rules to appreciate the tenacity needed to persuade them to relax the regulations in this instance. Saint-Ex brought all his obstinate determination to bear, and at last obtained authorization to train on Lightnings for operational flying.

"I've just flown a Lightning," he wrote enthusiastically to Dr. Pélissier. But this did not satisfy him. He had not come to North Africa to fly for fun. He wanted to take his place in combat, to be a war pilot. Something else was involved, and it is explained in the letter he wrote to President Roosevelt's special envoy in North Africa, Robert Murphy. This letter, which is dated June 17, 1943, reveals along with the mature Saint-Exupéry the young Antoine, with all the charm that was so hard to resist.

Addressing Mr. Murphy as "Dear friend," he spoke of his Franco-American reputation as a writer, excusing himself for doing so by saying he hoped this might enable him to render some service to his country. He referred to his career as an Air Force pilot in the campaign of 1939–1940, when he had been a member of an aviation

Group which had fought hardest and suffered most; he then mentioned that he had "refused to join the Gaullists in the United States," and as a result had been called a fascist, and said that he had taken calmly what was clearly a libel by "that unique party." He had made efforts to rejoin a battle squadron as soon as he heard of the American landings in North Africa. "I believe I am the first French civilian to return to North Africa from abroad." Venturing to suggest that the way to bring most efficient help to France was not through bloody reprisals, as "the unique party" fanatically advocated, he now stated his main reason for writing the letter, which was to be granted "the right to participate in the combat as soon as possible." He added that only when he and his comrades had risked their lives would he have the right to speak his thoughts and be listened to. If he were allowed to fight, he said, then he would "write another *Flight to Arras*."

The letter had the desired result, and soon Saint-Ex rejoined his squadron on La Marsa airfield near Tunis, from which he made his first operational flight over France. The islands of Sardinia and Corsica had to be avoided, since they were still in enemy hands—normally a plane that developed engine trouble could have made an emergency landing on either of these islands—which increased the danger of the flight. His mission was to photograph the Rhône valley and a portion of the coast almost as far as Toulon.

He took off in his 2600-h.p. Lightning at midday in the full heat of the North African summer. The sky was unclouded and the sea beneath his wings was a bright shimmer of silver. As he looked down at that sea in the moments he could take his eyes away from the complicated instrument panel, he may have recalled the last time he had flown over it, three years earlier, at the controls of a cumbersome Farman, when he and some of his comrades had left a France crushed by the German armies. Now he was returning to prepare for her liberation.

Soon a vague line indicated the horizon: the coast of France, the coast of Provence, where his mother waited with Didi and her family. At his altitude of 35,000 feet, he could not see where Provence began or ended, but there it was, an immense stretch of grayish-green land. And then he was almost immediately above the delta of the Rhône. He turned on the photographic apparatus which began to register what the eye could not see but which would be interpreted in the laboratory where, as he put it in a magazine article, "the interpreters of these photographs work exactly like bacteriologists. They seek on the vulnerable body of France traces of the virus which devours her. One can die from the effects of these enemy strongholds and depots and convoys which, under the lens, appear like tiny bacilli."

Six hours later he was back at La Marsa, with mixed feelings of joy and sadness. He had rejoined his squadron, he was once more an Air Force pilot. But he had also seen a France which was "near, and yet so far! One feels separated from her as though by centuries. All one's tender memories and associations, indeed, one's very *raison d'être,* are to be found there, stretched out, as it were, 35,000 feet below, in the clear glint of the sun; and yet, more inaccessible than the treasures of the Pharaohs under the glass cases of a museum."

Only a few days later, he took off on his second operational flight, but unfortunately, upon his return, he was unable to pull up short as he touched down, and crashed into a vineyard, suffering minor damages. This trifling accident caused the American command to withdraw the exceptional rights they had granted him to pilot a Lightning.

The decision had catastrophic effects upon him. To be grounded after all the efforts he had made to be put on operational flying was more than discouraging. And what efforts he had made, through influential friends, letters to important officials, and even a lavish dinner for the American officers! The dinner, by the way, had no effect except to give the colonel indigestion. Now all those efforts had been made in vain. Orders were orders, and he could only obey. His hand lingered lovingly on his damaged Lightning, then he left La Marsa airdrome and went to Algiers to stay with Dr. Pélissier. There he was to spend eight of the most painful and melancholy months of his life.

Never before, not even in his blackest moments, had he descended so far into the pit of despair. Léon Werth refused to admit that a man of Saint-Exupéry's stamp could ever experience real despair: he was too full of life, too courageous. "I reject this image of a Saint-Exupéry giving up to despair," Werth said. "The writings and the declarations of witnesses denying it are no less trustworthy than those that confirm it." [54] But we who knew him have his own statements on this subject, and while allowing for the exaggeration he was led into by his hypersensitivity, we believe them.

He was deprived of his wings. He had been relegated to the reserve force. He could believe that henceforth he was separated from his comrades of the air, who would take part in the imminent liberation of France. He could believe that he was banished because of his age—the Americans had again used this as pretext to justify the enforcement of their ruling. Moreover, he was again feeling the effects of the hatred of his enemies, who had pursued him even into North Africa.

For Algeria was now the headquarters of the Gaullists, who were soon to form a provisional government of France. And the place was a nest of intrigue, both military and political. Typical of France in her darkest as well as her most glorious moments, there were plotters and schemers struggling for position and rewards, side by side with the combatants.

It was against this sort of situation that Saint-Exupéry had issued a stirring call in November 1942, upon hearing of the first American landings in North Africa. His appeal had first been broadcast over the radio and afterward printed in *The New York Times Magazine* as "An Open Letter to Frenchmen Everywhere." *

This article strongly urged that political differences be resolved

* Published in *The New York Times Magazine*, November 29, 1942, and reprinted in full in Appendix II.

and that Frenchmen of every belief and shade of opinion unite for the liberation of their country.

It is perhaps regrettable that General de Gaulle and Saint-Exupéry never met. However, the head of the provisional French government did nothing to bring about a meeting, and indeed took occasion to cast aspersion on the airman and writer who had refused to rally to his cause. General Chassin has reported that when de Gaulle delivered a lecture before the Forum of Algiers in 1943, on the subject of French thought, he mentioned several second-rate writers along with the great, but pointedly omitted any mention of Saint-Exupéry.[55]

The hostility encountered by Saint-Exupéry ranged from the silliest to the most solidly entrenched. When, in desperation, he asked to be sent on a mission to the United States, where he believed his prestige would allow him to procure more arms and planes for the French forces, his request was turned down. And he was again refused when he asked to be allowed to go to England. Taking pity on his friend who was chafing at the enforced inaction, Chassin suggested that he might be allowed to go to China on some mission or other. Saint-Ex agreed to the idea, and Chassin drew up a report highly recommending him, recalling his brilliant qualities and world renown, adding that he was actually suffering over being unable to render some service, but that he was still kept on the reserve list in Algiers. General de Gaulle wrote with his own hand in the margin: "Good. Let him stay on the reserve in Algiers."

Some of Saint-Exupéry's influential friends tried to intervene in his behalf, and spoke directly to General de Gaulle or a member of his entourage, praising his qualities as writer, aviator, and man. They were met with this response, "I have heard that he's quite good at card tricks!"

Then came the worst blow: Saint-Exupéry's books were banned in North Africa—that sole part of "free France."

A few months later when, thanks to his American friends, he

was again undertaking flights over France, he wrote bitterly to Madame X, referring to the suppression of his books, and he also wrote to Pierre Dalloz on the subject, this time sadly ironical. "While I made my way over the Alps at the speed of a tortoise, and at the mercy of swarms of German fighter planes, I smiled to myself at the thought of those superpatriots who ban my books in North Africa. It's really funny." [56]

Saint-Exupéry's reaction to this kind of persecution becomes apparent in the letters he wrote at that period. He must have been hurt to the quick to have declared: "The factory turning out hate, disrespect, and muck which calls itself the Reestablishment of France . . . you can have it. I am now exposed to the most naked and absolute dangers of war. Some German fighters almost got me the other day. It did me good. Not that I experienced any of that delirium of the sportsman or warrior, but because my enemy was visible and tangible. I don't understand anything except what has substance. All these phrases and formulas sicken me. I'm sickened by their ignominy. I'm fed up with their polemics, fed up and baffled by what they call their valor. . . . The way I see it, valor means to save the French spiritual heritage by continuing throughout the occupation to keep open the library of Carpentras. Or it means to fly a plane in the face of naked danger. Or to teach children to read. Or it means agreeing to die as a simple carpenter. And those others say they are France! Well, I don't think so, and I'm a native Frenchman. Poor France."

Clearly, the letters of this period of enforced inaction were written to relieve an almost unendurable frustration. "I can no longer tolerate this defamation and injury and this preposterous inactivity," he said in one of them. "I love my country, all by myself, more than they love it, all of them. They love only themselves." To Dr. Pélissier he wrote, "I can't go on forever arguing about myself. I cannot endure explaining, I have no accounts to render, and people who misunderstand me are strangers to me. I'm too tired, too tired to change! I have quite enough enemies to instruct me. What I need are friends who would be gardens where

I could rest. . . . Dear old friend, I feel I'm at the end of my tether tonight. It's sad, for I so much want to love life a bit, but I don't like it at all." [57]

He also wanted to work. The manuscript of *The Wisdom of the Sands* was with him in his room; from time to time he added a few lines. But, as he wrote to a friend: "I try to work, but work is difficult. This atrocious North Africa rots the heart. I am at the end of my tether. How easy it was to fly a Lightning on operations!"

Everything overwhelmed him. His room was gray and sad, it was "a stupid room," "like a cell," but a cell in which he lived "without religion." The stairway that led to it was steep and dark; one night he fell down it and was convinced that he had fractured a vertebra; he was even sure it was the fifth lombar vertebra: "It hasn't any marrow, it's an inedible vertebra."

Dr. Pélissier, who gives us the details of this accident, examined him and refused to accept the diagnosis. Saint-Ex was a difficult patient. He went to see two other doctors, who held different opinions. The X-ray specialist, "very much under Saint-Ex's influence," says Dr. Pélissier, who had unfortunately been unable to accompany him on that visit, "concluded that there was indeed a transverse fracture of the fifth lombar vertebra." However, the X-ray plates merely showed something resembling "morning mists in a Japanese landscape. Something which might be either a hill or a vertebra." In his distress, Saint-Ex took refuge in imaginary illnesses. At about this same time he believed he had cancer. As Pierre Dalloz has put it, he "exiled himself from his exile," and not merely in hypochondria, for sometimes he would lose himself in working out difficult problems in mathematics or calculus, in theories of aerodynamics, and sometimes he would invite a friend in for the evening.

The friend would find him in his wildly disordered little room, and Saint-Ex would summon Dr. Pélissier's housekeeper, Séverine, and ask her to serve some dried figs or dates or oranges. Séverine took a motherly attitude towards Saint-Ex, but at times she would become exasperated. "She is both my mother and my stepmother," he would say, when she scolded him. Séverine was not as patient as Paula had been; she was too old to tolerate some of the eccentricities of Dr. Pélissier's guest, who disturbed the calm of the house and, to amuse the friends whom he sometimes entertained in the sitting room, rolled oranges up and down the keys of the piano, while working the pedals, "thus producing a succession of sounds in which, with an effort, one might discern the water-music of a fountain." [58] But this game made the keys sticky and upset Séverine, who took fond care of the grand piano.

Sometimes he met Frenchmen newly arrived from still-occupied France, having made the journey at great risk. He was always eager for news of what was happening in France under the German occupation. He wanted to hear about the hardships and hopes of his oppressed countrymen. The tales of courage and sacrifices of the underground fighters brought tears to his eyes and momentarily distracted him from his personal troubles. But nothing could heal the wound inflicted by spite and calumny. For one thing, he kept it open by continually thinking of it and referring to it in his letters. And the flying comrade who saw Saint-Ex secretly weeping with rage and grief was not mistaken about those tears.

Saint-Exupéry wept not only for himself, but for all mankind. "I hate my epoch with all my strength, for my generation is dying of hunger and thirst," he wrote in one letter. "I am profoundly sad today. I am sad for my generation, empty as it is of all human content . . . a generation which thought only about Bugattis and bars and calculating machines, now finds itself caught up in a strictly gregarious and colorless life. . . . The man of today is kept pacified with bowling or bridge, depending upon his social rank. But we are all castrated, and with amazing thoroughness. . . . I have the impression that we are heading for the darkest period the world has ever known." This letter, dated July 1943, was never posted and is referred to in the bibliographies as "the Letter to a General." (It was published in *Figaro Littéraire*, April 10, 1948.)

The same thoughts, the same apprehension and despair, are apparent in other letters written in 1943 and 1944. "If I'm shot down," he wrote to Pierre Dalloz, "I'll have absolutely no regret. The anthill of the future horrifies me, and I loathe their robot-virtues."

Obviously, he was dismayed by the ever-increasing moral aridity of our epoch. But he kept thinking about the message he felt he had to give humanity, a message which would help restore to mankind a spiritual significance. Time and again he repeated phrases such as "We must give mankind something resembling a Gregorian chant!" He had tried to do this in all his books, each one of which revealed a steady ascent in the nobility of his thought, as indeed his life had represented a steady ascension. But it seemed to him that his ideas had not been understood or had been willfully misinterpreted. He had preached love—and he was hated. He had shown grandeur—and mud was flung at him. He was of course mistaken in lumping all men together, but he was blinded by his distress. A handful of individuals had injured him unjustly; and because of them he rejected all men and saw "the darkest period the world has ever known" approaching.

He had given too much of himself and had climbed the heights too far, alone. From such a height and such solitude he could not but have a disillusioned view of the world. Man was still very far from being what could be wished. Man was also very far from what he would be one day.

Saint-Exupéry did not rest in his efforts to get back into operational flying. As he had done in 1939, he turned a deaf ear to the friends who advised him to give up flying, to abandon a life of danger. He must have had this in mind when he wrote, in *The Wisdom of the Sands,* "Therefore hearken not to those who seek to help you by bidding you renounce one or another of your aspirations. You are conscious of a driving force within you, the thrust of your vocation. If you play false to it, you are mutilating yourself; yet bear in mind that your truth will take form slowly, for it is the coming to birth of a tree and not the finding of a definition, and therein Time plays an essential part. The task before you is to rise above yourself and to scale a difficult mountain."

Early in 1944, his old friend and former teacher, Colonel Chassin, came to his rescue. Chassin was in command of the 31st Squadron of bombers, based at Villacido in Sardinia, and he somehow managed to have Saint-Ex assigned to this base.

Thus he went out as bombardier on some operational flights over northern Italy, still occupied by the Germans. He brought no enthusiasm to this task; indeed he was revolted at the idea of dropping bombs, even on railways, bridges, and airdromes. But he was flying again and, more important still, he had been rescued from the depressing atmosphere of Algiers. And in Chassin he had a friend with whom he could discuss the scientific or philosophical problems that were more and more preoccupying his mind. For his part, General Chassin had the satisfaction of seeing Saint-Ex recover some of his normal energy and enthusiasm. But upon his arrival at the base, we are told, he showed shocking signs of fatigue and looked prematurely aged.[59]

Of course—and Chassin realized this—the only thing that could restore Saint-Exupéry's delight in living would be to fly a Lightning again with his old unit, Group 2–33, which happened to be stationed not far off, at Alghero in Sardinia. This had been his cherished wish from the minute he had landed in Algiers, as may be seen from his "Letter to a General." "If I endure this speed and altitude at an age considered patriarchal for the job, it is more out of a desire to share the cares and vexations of my generation than from any hope of finding the satisfactions of the past," he said. The letter was written on June 1943, in Oujda, where he had had to accustom himself to American army ways, sharing a room with two other men, lining up for "chow" and eating his meals standing up. "I am so weary of all these comings and goings in this big camp in the heat of the sun," he wrote to Dr. Pélissier at about the same time, adding, "sometimes I just feel like leaning against a tree and crying with rage."

But now, as bombardier on one of Colonel Chassin's "Marauders," he was certainly participating and therefore had a right to speak his mind, since, as he had said in his letter to Robert Murphy, "If I do not take part in the combat, I can but remain silent." He was participating, but his hands no longer gripped the controls of a plane, and he was no longer alone with his thoughts, high above the earth. His reason for wanting to pilot a Lightning again may be glimpsed in an article published by *Life* Magazine: "High-altitude flights in that light monster," he declared, were "like a diver's plunges into the depths of the sea. One enters forbidden territory, decked out in barbarous equipment, encased in a framework of dials and instruments and gauges. . . ."

Saint-Exupéry was to have his wish, thanks to Chassin's intervention and the unexpected aid of an American photo-journalist, named John Phillips, who had turned up in Algiers in the winter of 1944. In a book of reminiscences called *Odd World*,[60] Mr. Phillips devotes a chapter to Saint-Exupéry in which he recounts how he first became aware of the aviator–writer. In 1939, Phillips, then at the beginning of his career, was bound from Buenos Aires to Patagonia, en route to Cape Horn, which he was assigned to photograph.

In July it was deep winter in Patagonia, and while waiting for a plane he sat in the cold airport reading a book which a friend had given him the night before. " 'Isn't this a coincidence!' had been her greeting," Phillips said. " 'I have just received a book from Paris by an old friend who used to fly to Patagonia.' She handed it to me to read during the trip. 'TERRE DES HOMMES, par Antoine de Saint-Exupéry,' I read. This was the first time I had heard of Saint-Ex and his now-famous *Wind, Sand and Stars*."

While leafing through the pages of the book, Phillips noticed a stocky man in a leather flying jacket standing close by and watching him. " 'Saint-Ex was once my boss,' he said, when our eyes met. 'He was very strict. Once when I was flying mail south, I saw him make a forced landing in the wilderness. I landed to see what was wrong—we didn't carry radios—but he greeted me with an angry, 'I fine you two hundred pesos, Rose, to teach you the proper respect for the mail you carry.' According to Saint-Ex I should have flown to my port of call, turned over my mail, and then reported his position instead of taking a chance myself.' "

When Phillips found himself in Algiers in 1944 and learned that Saint-Ex was there, he recollected the Patagonian incident, and decided to try and meet the man whose work he admired so much. He reports the following exchange on the telephone:

" 'Colonel,' I said.

" 'Major,' he corrected me.*

" 'Major de Saint-Exupéry. I would like very much to meet you. We have an old Argentine friend in common. . . .' "

"When I saw him, he was little more than a silhouette against the window in the early winter dusk. In profile the nose of this twentieth century Pico della Mirandola stood out with the mocking and insolent air that earned him the nickname of Pique la Lune."

The reporter also noticed the scar from the Guatemalan accident that "raised an eyebrow into a permanent look of inquiry," but otherwise Saint-Ex did not display any signs of "the many crashes which had broken practically every bone in his body."

They talked of the early flying days and of the great pilots such as Mermoz and Guillaumet. "I'm the last one," said Saint-Ex pensively, "and I can assure you it's a very strange feeling."

He went on to speak of his wartime experiences and of his accident with the Lightning. "But you don't ground a man for that," he added.

"The way he said 'ground a man' took on a terrible implication," Phillips reports. "It was then I asked him if he was writing. Saint-Ex shook his head.

" 'I can't,' he said. 'I have no right to say anything, as I'm not participating. Only those who participate have a right to speak.' "

Later, Saint-Ex told him, "I want to write, and I'll donate what I do to you, for your publication, if you get me reinstated into my squadron."

* In June 1943, Saint-Exupéry was promoted to Commandant, a rank almost equivalent to Major.

Determined that Saint-Ex should have this chance, and "incapable of imagining him sitting in a gloomy Algerian drawing room while men were struggling," Phillips proceeded to do all he could. As he was going on to Naples, he decided to approach Tex McCrary, then a colonel on the staff of General Ira Eaker, commander of the Allied Air Forces in the Mediterranean area, whose headquarters were at Caserta, near Naples. Colonel McCrary proved to be sympathetic to Saint-Ex's point of view and promised to speak to General Eaker. While waiting for a decision, Phillips went back to Algiers.

Saint-Ex was so eager that he returned to Naples with Phillips, who helped him pack. "I found that most of his belongings amounted to a huge pile of papers," the journalist wrote, "stacked up like a volcano on a low table. He also owned several fountain pens and asked me to carry his inkwell so it would not get lost."

Saint-Ex stayed in Phillips' apartment in Naples and passed the time watching Vesuvius erupt, reading Kafka, and playing chess. Colonel Chassin, who also gives an account of the Naples interlude, said that they spent considerable time telephoning, letter-writing, making appointments, and in the intervals discussing molecular physics with Professor Noetzlin, who had come especially to make observations on the volcano.

Finally, writes John Phillips, "I translated to McCrary his eloquent plea about how useful he would be as a writer if allowed to take further part in the war, and very reluctantly General Eaker cleared him to make five missions with his squadron. This squadron, the 2/33, was now incorporated into the Anglo-American Third Photo Reconnaissance Group, stationed at Alghero in Sardinia."

The journalist accompanied Saint-Ex to this base, where they were greeted by Captain Gavoille, commanding officer of the Group, whom Saint-Ex considered "the finest type France had produced," and who uncorked one of the best bottles of wine his mess offered to welcome his old comrade.

"Surrounded by his officers he looked like a triumphant hen," Phillips said of Gavoille. "But at briefings he volunteered his squadron, himself first, for the toughest missions. In return, partly in joke, he demanded butter and steaks as rations instead of margarine and Spam."

". . . Happy to be back with 'les camarades,' Saint-Ex covered every topic in monologue, turning conversation into a series of essays, which sounded like verbal soufflés to his spellbound listeners.

"He also kept us spellbound when his Lightning appeared over the field, especially after he convinced us all, including the ambulance driver who came roaring up, that he was going to land without his undercarriage. It wasn't only when he flew that I got palpitations; I also got them when he did not write. Like most authors, he got to work only when he had exhausted every pretext not to. Unlike most writers, however, he found fanciful excuses."

On the peaceful island of Sardinia, which the enemy had hurriedly left, some airfields had been laid out among the pinewoods, the forests of cork oaks, and the thinly cultivated farmlands. From these airdromes planes were sent out over northern Italy and would soon fly over southern France, where our armies were about to land. Group 2–33, which had remained in North Africa since the 1940 Armistice, was now established at the airfield just outside Alghero, a small town on the wild and rocky coast. Saint-Ex was quartered with seven other airmen in a remote cottage on the coast, where they slept and took their meals and enjoyed some relaxation between flights, talking hopefully of the day when, very soon, they would bring their planes down again on the soil of France.

When Saint-Ex arrived at the little house in Alghero, it was hard to say who rejoiced the more, his comrades or himself, but in any case it was a happy reunion. In addition Saint-Ex was greeted by the man he had mentioned in the first pages of *Flight to Arras*—the then-Lieutenant, now Captain Gavoille. It was during the German offensive and at the period of the "sacrificed missions." As they met again at Alghero they must have recalled that passage:

Yesterday, speaking to Lieutenant Gavoille, I had let drop the words, "Oh, we'll see about that when the war is over." And Gavoille had answered, "I hope you don't mean, Captain, that you expect to come out of the war alive?

Gavoille had not been joking. And yet here they were after that bloody campaign, still alive.

Hochedé was another old comrade encountered at Alghero, Hochedé whom Saint-Exupéry in the same book had called "a saint" and of whom he had said, "Hochedé made a total gift of himself to this war." But Hochedé was shot down while on a training flight in a Lightning, shortly after Saint-Exupéry's arrival.

"I encountered again," Saint-Ex said in the article in *Life* Magazine, "all those comrades of whom I had said that, under the trampling heel of the invading armies, they were not the vanquished but seeds buried in the silence of the earth."

Immediately the old fellowship was renewed, and Lieutenant Leleu, an eyewitness of this reunion, has described Saint-Exupéry's zest and enthusiasm. Another young lieutenant, Renoux, who met him there for the first time, recalled how amazed he was that, "despite his age, his fame and prestige, Saint-Ex was always the best sort of war comrade to us younger fellows." The "doyen of World War II airmen" praised the quality of these comrades in several letters, but though his zest had returned, there was not quite the enthusiasm of his earlier remarks on his comrades of the 1939–1940 campaign, when he had singled out Gavoille and Israël as having that "substance" he had found in Guillaumet. He could be gay again, and he had forgotten his broken vertebra and his gastric ulcer. Though he had suffered from the "gregarious life" at Oujda, he was glad to share the lives of his old Group 2–33 comrades. A few days after his arrival he celebrated the reunion by offering them a banquet for which ten sheep were slaughtered, the roast mutton being washed down with wine from a large keg broached for the occasion.

Again he was the center of life in his squadron, amazing the young flyers with his card tricks, entering into their games, inventing others. But they soon noticed that Antoine de Saint-Exupéry was a "bad loser" and, to tease him, they used all their cleverness, even to the point of cheating, to make him lose. But Jean Leleu tells us that, after having vented his anger in a few well-chosen words, "a game of chess or a few card tricks put him in a good humor again and brought back his beaming smile." [61] He still knew how to use that famous smile to be forgiven his moments of rudeness or ill-humor.

At the end of June the squadron was transferred from Sardinia to Borgo, south of Bastia, in Corsica. The summer sunlight burned hotly on the rocks, the pine trees were shedding their dry needles, which crunched underfoot. Saint-Ex changed to a lightweight American uniform which he wore untidily, collar open, blouse pockets stuffed with cigarettes, lighter, notebooks, odds and ends. His shirt was torn more often than not, and the frayed trousers were so big on him, now that he had lost weight, that they had to be held up by a wide tightly buckled belt.

Some commentators have said that at this time Saint-Exupéry was completely happy. There is no doubt that his life with the old Group, his feeling that he was again participating, gave him satisfaction. To his comrades he presented his customary aspect, now grave, now gay, at times joking, singing, amusing himself, discussing the problems most important to him, but always in realms of thought quite removed from the anxieties that had tormented him in Algiers. Toward the late afternoon, when the heat was less intense, he would join his comrades in a swim or would go out in a boat to fish with dynamite, delighted when he brought up a net full of fish. In appearance he was calm and happy. But the wound had not healed, and it troubled him at night, when he was alone. Even when flying he could not completely forget it or rid himself of the pain. Some of his letters reveal melancholy thoughts that were kept hidden from the men who shared his daily existence.

In one letter he said, "The idea that I may be shot down leaves me completely indifferent, I would die without any regrets." And again, "I don't mind at all if I die in a crash." To his most confidential friend, Madame X, he wrote, "I'm hurrying to finish this letter, for a plane is taking off this very minute and it's my last chance to reach you. The job I'm doing is difficult. On four missions I just barely missed returning to base, but I'm quite indifferent to what happens. . . ."

By this time he had exceeded the five missions that had been especially granted him by General Eaker. But Saint-Ex kept pleading for more and it was hard to refuse him "the favor." As he said to the young pilots, "You have plenty of time, but I must make up for lost time." And his comrades began to worry about him, for they knew, as Jean Leleu, the Operations Officer, put it, "his loss as a man would be infinitely more serious than his loss as an aviator." His old friend Chassin met him in Algiers where he was paying a short visit, the twenty-ninth of July, and remonstrated with him: "You've now made eight missions, that's enough, you ought to stop there. In three months you've done as much as the younger fellows have done in more than a year. You have the right to speak your thoughts now. And consequently you do not have the right to go on risking your life." To which Saint-Ex replied: "I can't stop. I must go on to the end, now. The end's not far off, I think. I'll stay with my Group to the end." (This recalls his reply to Werth, who had implored him in 1940 to stop fighting. At that time he had said it would be "an act of discourtesy" toward his comrades to stop.)

But he had deeper motives. Of these dangerous missions in 1944 he wrote to a friend, "I believe I'm paying my debt, and I believe I'm a good healthy carpenter." In *Wind, Sand and Stars,* he had described his friend Guillaumet as having "the quality of the carpenter face to face with his block of wood," meaning a very particular kind of courage. His main reason for wanting to continue flying may be found in his reply to Leleu when that officer and friend refused to do him the favor of sending him out on one more mission. "I need it," said Saint-Ex, "I need it physically and morally. . . ." And Leleu understood, for his own flying had fulfilled that longing, as he tells us in his tribute to Saint-Exupéry. It was a need to be alone for hours in the air high above the earth, "the sensation of living outside time, inert, almost dead, when the only links with life on earth were the whirring of the engines, the throbbing of one's heart, and the tug on the oxygen tank at each breath."

The Allied invasion of France was imminent, preparations were under way for a landing in southern France, and some of the officers knew the exact date, in the second week of August. There was a formal rule that anyone entrusted with this secret should not be allowed to fly over France, for the danger was great that a pilot might be captured, tortured, and made to reveal what he knew. In agreement with the American command, it was decided that on August 1, Saint-Exupéry should be entrusted with this secret.

But on the evening of July 30, 1944, he had no inkling whatever that a plot was being woven to ground him. He was thinking only of his ninth operational flight which he was preparing to make next day, over Annecy and Grenoble once more. That night the officers gave a dinner party, followed by a dance, to which some Corsican girls were invited. The dancing went on until quite late. These young girls who, a short time before, had enthusiastically welcomed their liberators, were glad to be in the arms of the heroic fellows whose lives were still in danger. And so they could not stop dancing. They seem to have paid scant attention to the tall officer with graying temples and an absent look in his eyes. He sat watching, but did not dance. "The only writer of our time touched by glory," as Léon Werth called him, always gave an impression of self-effacement, much to the surprise of younger members of the Group, who met him for the first time during this phase of his life. The attitude of diffidence was not a pose, it was genuine.

In *Flight to Arras* Saint-Exupéry tells frankly, without false modesty, about signing one of his books which Gavoille had bought for the farmer's wife with whom they lodged. He performed the operation while eating blood-sausage and drinking white wine. "I was not in the least embarrassed. I wrote in it with pleasure, to please them both. Gavoille sat scratching his leg. Israël was stuffing his pipe. The farmer's wife seemed pleased to have a book inscribed by an author. The kitchen was redolent of the sausage. I was a little tight, for the white wine was heady. I did not feel in the least strange, despite the fact of inscribing a book—a thing which in other circumstances has always bothered me. I did not feel at all out of place. Despite the book, I did not think of myself either as an author or as an outsider. . . . I was still one of them."

Léon Werth, speaking of Saint-Exupéry's natural diffidence, relates an incident he witnessed when seated with him in a Paris café a few weeks after his crash in the Libyan desert. They were suddenly approached by a well-known actress, who came toward them with arms outspread like two fluttering wings and said, in a voice that could be heard above the confusion, "All the women of France wept with me when you were lost. All the women of France rejoiced with me when you were found. . . ." Saint-Ex was very embarrassed, and when the woman had gone back to her table he leaned toward Werth and murmured, "Who is that silly goose?"

We must allow for Léon Werth's usual sarcasm. The scene may not have been as ridiculous as he describes it. But in any case, Saint-Exupéry was far from being touched by a demonstration which would have flattered most men. Indeed, he had a contempt for vanity, which he calls a disease in *The Wisdom of the Sands:* "I mused on vanity, which has always seemed to me not a vice but an ailment . . . Of all vain persons I would say that they have ceased living. For who can barter himself for something greater than himself, when he begins by insisting on receiving? Stunted for eternity, such men will never grow to human stature."

And so that night of the dance, July 30, 1944, the young Corsican girls did not especially notice Saint-Exupéry. After dinner, however, some of his comrades did persuade him to participate in the fun to the extent of performing a few card tricks. Then he discreetly left, returning alone to the villa where he and a few other airmen were quartered.

That night, the villa shone white in the moonlight. A warm breeze rustled the palm trees. Saint-Ex stood for a moment looking at the sea which, on the horizon, was a bright gleam, dissolving and fading as it came toward him, breaking into a myriad sparkling sequins at his feet, where little waves ebbed and flowed in a perpetual and sweetly melancholy whispering.

He entered the deserted villa. Everything that night was at peace in the silence. He had always loved silence; in all his books he praises silence, but nowhere more eloquently than in his last book, *The Wisdom of the Sands:*

> *I will indite a hymn to thee, O Silence! . . . In thy embrace I fold the city viewed from the mountain-top, when as night has stilled its rumbling wheels and clanging anvils and the tumult of its streets, and all things float becalmed in a bowl of shadows. For silence is God's cloak spread out upon man's restlessness, and in silence He steeps and soothes their fretful hearts. . . . I will hymn the silence of him who muses, gazing into the middle distance, receiving without expending, and distilling the elixir of thought. . . ."*

He went into the house and into his room. He lit a cigarette and spread out a map. Annecy. Grenoble. His mission tomorrow. He had already carried out flights in that region. He had asked Leleu to assign it to him, for this was a part of France he best knew and loved: Saint-Maurice was in that region, and Agay was practically on the way there. However, above that part of Provence he had twice had trouble, once with a stalled engine, another time with a leak in the oxygen tank, when he had almost fainted and had had to dive steeply to find a supply of breathable air. But he was not superstitious, and that evening as he studied the map, he was not thinking of danger any more than usual. Had he considered the two nearly fatal accidents as a warning? Or did he merely think it was time to provide for the dividing up of his property, material and spiritual? We will never know. But we do know that he opened the valise where he kept his manuscripts and notes—some of which have still to be deciphered. He lifted out the manuscript of *The Wisdom of the Sands,* held it in his hands a moment. For this book, he had told Pélissier one day, taking it brusquely from him, "is certainly my best work." And to Dalloz he had said, "Compared with this piece of writing, all my other books are but child's exercises." Tonight, Saint-Ex put the manuscript back among the others, then leafed through a notebook, after which he sat down at the table and drew forward his last operational flight order. Glancing at it absent-mindedly, he turned it over and wrote a few lines on the reverse side. In those lines he designated his spiritual legatee, the person to whom he bequeathed his manuscripts.

After undressing, he lay down on the bed, propped himself up on the pillows, lit another cigarette and smoked meditatively, staring for a long time at the ceiling, until drowsiness weighed down his eyelids. Then he plunged into his usual deep sleep.

When he reached the field next morning the sun was climbing into a clear, hot sky, and the strident song of the cicadas was filling the air. Saint-Ex asked Captain Leleu for his final orders. His plane, a 223, had just been tested by the mechanic. Captain Gavoille came up, they shook hands, and Gavoille helped Saint-Ex into his heavy and complicated high-altitude outfit. He needed always to be helped into it because of his stiffened shoulder.

As he fastened the innumerable buckles, he chatted, but Gavoille was unable to recall what they talked about, for as usual, at every departure of Saint-Ex on a reconnaissance flight, his friends were filled with anxiety. Gavoille checked everything, the oxygen tank, parachute, collapsible rubber boat and the apparatus to distill salt water in case of a crash at sea; the heated gloves, helmet, earphones, photographic equipment, countless gadgets. Gavoille was not merely seeing off a pilot but a close friend, who had acted as godfather at the christening of his infant son, named Christian-Antoine, only three days previously. Gavoille thought with relief that this would be the last mission. Next day Saint-Ex was to be let in on the secret—the date of the landing in southern France, and this would ground him. However, he was still worried as he helped Saint-Ex into the cockpit, always a difficult job, partly because of his awkward movements in the cumbersome equipment and partly because of the stiffened shoulder muscles that had resulted from the long-ago plane crash in Guatemala. To add to the torture that day, there was the summer heat. Saint-Ex groaned and grimaced. But once he had settled into his seat and was shut in safely, he recovered his usual smile, and as the engines began to roar and the machine to vibrate, his face lighted up, as if the machine's energy revived his own.

Saint-Ex then waved good-by and slowly opened the throttle. The Lightning started off, moved down the runway, and suddenly, under full power, it sped away in a cloud of dust, bounding up toward the luminous sky. Banking steeply it rose higher and higher, filling the air with its clamor of engines, a clamor that soon dwindled to a mere echo which was gradually drowned out by the cicadas' chant that had, for a moment, been arrested.

The snowy peaks of the Alps came into view, their whiteness looming up from a blur of gray-blue lands, and ahead of the pilot Lake Leman glittered metallically. Then Annecy could be glimpsed to the left, with its miniature lake, thirty thousand feet beneath him. He banked, and started up the apparatus controlling the camera.

"Operational flight to the east of Lyons" was what his flying orders specified. Lyons was somewhere down there, to the right. It was his birthplace, but he had not lived there for long and was bound to the city by no ties of affection. But nearer, beyond the dark forests, was Saint-Maurice-de-Rémens, invisible, that beloved old house which had given him so many memories; deep in his heart they had formed "that obscure range from which, as waters from a spring, are born our dreams." In moments of extreme danger, as when lost in the Libyan desert and when flying over the burning city of Arras, he had recalled that house, even addressing whole pages to the old housekeepers, Mademoiselle and Paula, who had surrounded his childhood with such anxious affection.

"Mission to the east of Lyons." Well, it was finished. Now, for the return. Once more he must leave this bright sky beneath which France existed in darkness. And as he glanced for the last time toward those mountains, valleys, towns, and villages where a nation of people, forty million hostages, had waited four long years for their liberation, he recalled their sufferings and was anxious over their future. There they were, beneath his wings. He had always thought of them with compassion. For almost eighteen years he had surveyed humanity from the heights to which his wings bore him, in silence and solitude, in storms over the Pyrenees and in Patagonia, above the burning sands of the desert or in the night skies hung with stars. For almost eighteen years he had meditated upon man's destiny. Like the camera registering the views, his mind had gathered up and registered these thoughts and impressions, then, returned to earth, he had studied and analyzed them as the technicians submitted the reel of film to stereoscopic examination. He had detected the virus that was arresting mankind's development.

Again Saint-Exupéry glimpsed the sea ahead of him, in the distance, guessed rather than glimpsed it, for the sun was approaching the zenith and blurred distant views. The horizon was almost invisible in the dazzling haze of sunlight. Then gradually the coastline of France asserted itself, and the sea, directly beneath him, became bluer, edging the shore with a white lace of foam. Saint-Ex leaned out slightly to get a last view of that Provence where his people dwelt and where, as a little boy, he had lived with his brother and sisters. Somewhere down there was the little château of La Môle, where Paula had walked with them in the park, leading tortoises by strings. Paula, who let herself be tyrannized and who knew such lovely stories to tell. She had gone back to her native Tyrol where she lived in a "chalet-barometer." And finally he was over Agay, where as a young man he had spent delightful hours with his sister Didi. And there was where he had married Consuelo. That was a little more than thirteen years ago. After the wedding, another cousin had asked him, "How old is your wife?" He had answered the question. "Why," the cousin had exclaimed, "just a minute ago she told the curé she was two years younger than that!"

> *God sent me that woman who lied so daintily, so simply, with a cruelty redeemed by the sweetness of her voice. I bent towards her as towards a cool sea-wind. . . . "Why do you lie?" I asked. She fell to weeping and her face was hidden by a veil of tears. . . . I heeded not the vain sound of her words, but only the struggle of the snared fox to free itself. . . . But now, O Lord, I see my error. . . . For if a little child's tears move you, they are windows opening on the vastness of the sea; for not those tears only, but the whole world's tears, are quickening your compassion. . . .*

Saint-Exupéry may have written those lines from *The Wisdom of the Sands* at Agay, for he often worked on it while visiting his sister at the Château d'Agay. But the Germans had destroyed the house in 1944; nothing remained of it but the foundations, which stood like the stem posts of a wrecked ship, lashed by the waves, stripped by the winds. Saint-Ex had heard of that destruction only a short time ago. Saint-Maurice had been sold; and now Agay, that second witness of his earlier and happier life, had been taken from him, this one forever. He had spoken of his distress in a letter to his mother, written at Borgo, a few days before this, his last mission.* She received it quite some time after he had been reported missing, and this is what she read:

> *Dear little mother,*
>
> *I so want to reassure you as to my health and safety. I am quite well. Only, I am so very sad at not having*

* The letters written by Saint-Exupéry in 1943–1944 were entrusted to some of his flying comrades, in the faint hope that they might be able to mail them. Several letters reached their destination after Saint-Exupéry disappeared.

seen you for such a long time. And I am anxious over you, dearest mother. How sad this epoch is! My heart was rent when I heard that Didi had lost her home. How I wish I could help her! Tell her to count on me in the future. When will we be able to tell those we love that we love them?

Mother, I send my tenderest thoughts to you; please send your tenderest thoughts to me.

—Antoine

In no other letter had Saint-Ex implored her loving thoughts; this was the first time he had asked for her love—the first and last time. Can it be, as with that "last will and testament" he had scribbled on the back of a flying-order form, that he had a premonition? Or was it merely a memory from his childhood, when his mother came upstairs to kiss her children good-night, bending over her "departing angels"?

Saint-Exupéry throttled down and began the descent. In a few minutes he would touch the airstrip, and a comrade would inscribe in the log book, "Mission accomplished." The log contains in brief the history of the air squadrons. Irony, drama, and even poetry exist there side by side, and it often makes absorbing reading. Sometimes the writing changes, if the man who had kept the log did not return from a mission. Then, after a long wait, another flyer took up the pen and wrote simply, at the end of the text that succinctly stated the mission of the day, "Not returned."

A month before this, on June 29, 1944, the log of the First Squadron of Group 2–33 contained the following description of a mission that had almost been Saint-Exupéry's last, but which had had a happy ending: "Alghero–Fertilio Field—good flying weather general, numerous missions over France. Commandant de Saint-Exupéry follows the C.O. on P.38 292 high altitude reconnaissance over Annecy region. . . . Still waiting for his return." June 29 was Saint-Exupéry's birthday and the Group members had ordered a special repast to celebrate it. Evening came, and they all waited anxiously at the table, where some superb lobsters and a birthday cake were the most tempting items. At last a message came to reassure them: their missing comrade had come down on the landing strip at Borgo. They later heard his account of this mission. While at 30,000 feet altitude over Annecy, his port engine stalled and he had been forced to turn back, flying at a lower altitude and with less speed through the Haute-Savoie valleys toward the sea. Suddenly he found he had taken a wrong turn, for he was surprised to see a wide plain opening before him, with numerous flying fields and at its center a large town. It was Turin, still held by the enemy. He dodged off and reached Genoa, also well surrounded by enemy airfields and from there managed to hop the sea toward Corsica. As soon as he reached the region he radioed the Americans on the ground, explained his difficulties somehow, for he still spoke little English, and was directed to Borgo, where he was obliged to land.

On the day after that almost catastrophic flight, he told Gavoille all about it. As Turin loomed ahead of him, he had anxiously glanced into his rear-view mirror and had seen "a great big black fly, a German fighter." He was at an altitude of only 2600 feet and was flying at only 140 miles an hour. He could not use his parachute. He flew on, expected the worst, but fortunately the German fighter had not spotted him. Jean Leleu also refers to this adventure, and says that Saint-Ex told him he was never very worried about enemy planes. "I have all I can do to pilot my plane, keep in touch with ground stations by radio, and work the camera. I'm not going to waste time looking out for the Boches." And Leleu adds, "We were alarmed at such foolhardiness."

Saint-Exupéry looked at his altimeter. It showed 15,000 feet. By keeping to the same angle of descent he would arrive directly on the Borgo field. The mission was virtually ended. From Borgo he could easily go to Corsica, which was that blurred line in the iridescent mist. He could relax now, and meditate as he was fond of doing, he could give himself over to the charm of the descent which already foretokened the repose ahead. The propellers were turning more slowly, they no longer battled against the pull of gravity, but merely aided his return to earth. All effort seemed abolished.

Saint-Exupéry did not see the two planes which, having flown over the west coast of Corsica, were now headed toward the north. They were a German patrol composed of a Messerschmitt reconnaissance plane escorted by a Focke-Wulf 190 "equipped for combat," and, having accomplished a reconnaissance mission over the region of Ajaccio, they were returning to the Luftwaffe base in the south of France.

The enemy planes had the sun behind them, so that Saint-Exupéry, even had he been on the alert, would not have seen them in the dazzle of the sunlight. This is a well-known tactic, often used by pilots of combat planes, to place themselves between the adversary and the sun; it had been especially effective in World War I, when planes had a far lower speed than modern aircraft. Saint-Ex himself had used the tactic in 1940, managing to escape six combat planes by placing his machine between them and the sun, as he recorded in *Flight to Arras*. But on that occasion he was at a high altitude, whereas on July 31, 1944, he was touching down, and had descended to an altitude at which the Focke-Wulf had the same speed as the Lightning. The Lightning could venture alone and unarmed over enemy territory because at an altitude of 30,000 feet and more it attained a maximum speed unequaled by any German plane at the time. But at an altitude of 9000 to 12,000 feet, the Lightning was, according to Gavoille, "an easy and inoffensive victim for the birds of prey." The pilot of the Focke-Wulf was aware of this; he recognized the two-engine plane and knew he could attack it without fear of an answering fire. In *Flight to Arras,* Saint-Exupéry had written: "Fighters do not fight, they murder." This is even truer when the fighter plane attacks an unarmed plane. But all is fair in war; assassination is not only allowed, it is recommended. The pilot of the Focke-Wulf, as he detached himself from his escort plane and headed toward the

Lightning, had no idea that he was about to assassinate one of the greatest men of his time. But had he known, he would have continued to aim at his target and when within shooting range to unleash death.

Like many of the pioneer airmen of his heroic epoch, both in war and peacetime, Saint-Ex had often faced death, sometimes coming so close to it that he had no hope of escape. In 1935 when he and Prévot crashed in the Libyan desert, the *Simoun*'s landing gear striking a high plateau at a tangent, he had one such glimpse of death, which he vividly described in *Wind, Sand and Stars:* "I am quite sure that in the split second that followed, all I expected was the great flash of ruddy light of the explosion in which Prévot and I were to be blown up together."

In 1926, when he began flying the mails on the Toulouse–Casablanca route, in dropping to 9000 feet he suddenly felt a violent shock and, as his plane became almost unmanageable, he thought it was breaking up and foresaw an inevitable tailspin. "I looked down at the fields where I was going to smash up, feeling a kind of astonishment," he said in a letter. "This was something new for me. I could feel myself growing quite pale and glazed with fear. A bottomless fear, but not odious. And a new, indefinable intelligence." All airmen who have experienced such an emotion will recognize the accuracy of this description. Death does not wear the grinning mask that literary men without much experience give it. "I had slipped into a world from which one does not often return to tell about it," Saint-Exupéry added, in this account of his brush with death.

Whenever he spoke of death—and he often did, for death often seemed near—it was with great serenity. He was not satisfied with merely accepting death as a natural consequence of life, but sought to understand its significance, even as he sought to understand the meaning of life. The young pilot of the Line saw death as a great repose, certainly, but the nature of that repose was still unfathomable. In *Southern Mail,* the small fort in the desert where Bernis spent his last night, leaving it to climb in his plane toward death, is described as a wharf, a moonlit threshold where nothing was quite real. In *Night Flight,* Fabien and his radio operator have disappeared. Rivière reflected that darkness would hide them, and nothing would be found until day dawned. "Then some humble peasants perhaps would come on two young bodies, their elbows folded on their faces, like children asleep amid the grass and gold of some calm scene. Drowned by the night."

In his later years, when writing *Wind, Sand and Stars,* having miraculously survived two serious accidents, and having long meditated on man's fate, Saint-Exupéry saw in death something other than repose. To the mature writer, death was the complement of life, the two equating each other: "It is only when we become conscious of our part in life . . . that we shall be happy. Only then will we be able to live in peace and die in peace, for only this lends meaning to life and to death. . . . Each life in turn bursts like a pod and sends forth its seed." This offers a glimpse of the direction which his concept of death was evolving, a concept that was to find its most complete expression in *The Wisdom of the Sands.* In his writings on the murderous campaign of 1939–1940 there is no allusion to death as a physical repose. "But who cares what happens to his body?" he asks himself in *Flight to Arras,* when his plane is the target of antiaircraft fire. "Extraordinary, how little the body matters." But recalling how, that very morning, his body had clung to the warmth and comfort of his bed, he says, "Like all men, I had given it a good deal of time, I had dressed it, bathed it, fed it, quenched its thirst. I had identified myself with this domesticated animal. . . . I had said of it, 'This is me.' And now of a sudden my illusion vanished. . . . The flames of the house, of the diving plane, strip away the flesh; but they strip away the worship of the flesh too. Man ceases to be concerned with himself: he recognizes of a sudden what he forms part of. If he should die, he would not be cutting himself off from his kind, but making himself one with them. He would not be losing himself, but finding himself. . . ."

A man who cherished such beliefs was understandably willing to run the risk of dying. However, Saint-Exupéry made an interesting distinction here: "the acceptance of the risk of death and the acceptance of death are very different," he declares in *The Wisdom of the Sands.*

His reflections followed a gradually ascending line, from the infinite repose of Bernis, through the sleep of Fabien and his radio operator "drowned in darkness," through the "pod that bursts and scatters its seed" to the "supreme exchange" and the abolition of the "cult of the flesh" which presupposes the permanence of the cult of the soul. "There was revealed to me," says the desert chief in *The Wisdom of the Sands,* another truth concerning man: "to wit, that neither his happiness, nor even self-interest, means anything to him. The only interest that stirs him to action is that of achieving permanence, of continuing." To a man who has reached the highest levels of thought, "there are no more things-in-themselves, but only aspects of that divine bond which binds things together."

Saint-Exupéry, who wrote so many lines such as these, charged with hope, had no faith. He was often heard to say, "If only I had faith, I would become a monk!" He meant, of course, Christian faith, resting on the word of Christ; the faith he had lost at the age of seventeen, while attending a Catholic school. As a child, his piety had never been great. His family were Catholics, but "religion seemed to him to be mainly a respectable family tradition, similar to holding royalist beliefs, for instance." [62] The procession that took place every evening at the Château de Saint-Maurice, from dining room to chapel, with Madame de Tricaud at the head, followed by her niece (Saint-Exupéry's mother), her grandnephews and nieces, with the servants bringing up the rear, apparently did not happily influence the young Antoine. However, all his life he had a kind of nostalgia for that lost faith. Not that he ever made an effort to find his way back—he had rejected dogmatic teaching. But he felt the need of faith. The materialistic ideas which he had had, it would seem, when he first started life on his own, could not satisfy him; he sought further and discovered Man. He who was not religious spoke and wrote as though there were a religion of Man.

Having rejected the Bible, he read Nietzsche. "I'm fond of that chap Nietzsche," he wrote from Spain to a friend, in the twenties. And later on, in *Southern Mail* and in *Night Flight* he speaks of the philosopher. In the latter book he wanted the protagonist, Rivière, to display "a Nietzschian energy."[63] Almost every page of *Wind, Sand and Stars* exalts the grandeur of man. But this book, a collection of articles written over a period of years, reflects his spiritual evolution, or rather, follows his search for God—although he does not yet name God.

Some have seen in the teachings of the desert chief in *The Wisdom of the Sands* an indication that the life of the desert had directed Saint-Exupéry's thoughts toward God, but I do not believe so. No doubt the desert's solitude, the immense void of earth and sky which man instinctively tries to fill, is more conducive than any other environment to meditation. But Saint-Exupéry was neither a Foucauld nor a Pisichari. In the desert he meditated more upon mankind than upon God. From Cape Juby he wrote to Renée de Saussine, "I'm going to lie on the sand and read Nietzsche." No, it would rather seem that he more nearly turned toward God in the skies of war or after one of his miraculous returns from a dangerous mission. Because of Man he had abandoned God; but it was through Man that he returned to God.

The final pages of *Flight to Arras,* all that portion preceding the "Credo" proper, but in fact a part of Saint-Exupéry's testimony of faith, are filled with the name of God. "I understand the origin of brotherhood among men," he writes. "Men were brothers in God. . . . As the inheritor of God, my civilization preached self-respect, which is to say respect for Man present in oneself. . . ."

That Saint-Exupéry ardently sought faith is evident in many pages of *The Wisdom of the Sands.* "Reveal Thyself to me, O Lord; for all things are hard to one who has lost touch with God." But his quest is imprecise, and the parables he employs make his thought still more difficult to grasp. Who is this God, likened now to a tree, now to "a huge block of black granite," a God who manifests Himself in silence, yet transfigures the seeker after faith by His very silence? The desert chief's prayer was not answered, but his despair gave place to an unlooked-for tranquility. We feel as bewildered as Saint-Exupéry was himself. Yet was not that God the same God depicted by Pascal as saying to the seeker, "Be consoled, you would not seek Me had you not already found Me"?

During the first two years of the war, the very numerous German fighter planes were a constant threat to the lives of our reconnaissance crews. Often the Luftwaffe planes pounced so suddenly that their presence was revealed only by the luminous spray of bullets. In *Flight to Arras,* Saint-Exupéry graphically describes these attacks by enemy pilots. "Having spotted you from fifteen hundred feet above you, they take their time," he writes. "They weave, they orient themselves, take careful aim. You know nothing of this. You are the mouse lying in the shadow of the bird of prey. The mouse fancies that it is alive. It goes on frisking in the wheat. But already it is the prisoner of the retina of the hawk, glued tighter to that retina than to any glue, for the hawk will never leave it now. And thus you, continuing to pilot, to daydream, to scan the earth, have already been flung outside the dimension of time because of a tiny black dot on the retina of a man."

This overwhelming description enables us to imagine the last moments of Saint-Exupéry's life. As he continued his descent toward Corsica, the northern shoreline emerged from the haze of sunlight, looming up like the prow of a ship out of the fog. In a few minutes he would touch down. In a few minutes he would be with his comrades again. At this moment the body relaxes, becomes emptied of the vibrations accumulated during the hours of flight; one experiences a kind of elation, which only gradually subsides, as one feels the solid earth again and hears clearly the shouts of the ground crew which at first come but faintly through the roar that still fills the ears. Soon he would say, "Gavoille, get the dice, we'll throw to see who pays for the drinks!"

The air was shattered by a burst of shells. The engine of the Lightning had been struck. From the hood of the engine, "the first tongue of flame rises out of the furnace fire." [64] Then came the inevitable descent toward the sea, the plane leaving behind it a sinister scarf of black smoke.

Was Saint-Exupéry wounded? Had he cut off the engine? We will never know. Alone in the immensity of sky and sea, beneath the dazzling summer sun, so near and yet so far from those who were waiting and hoping for his return, what were his thoughts in the last moment of consciousness? That is the final secret of all men who vanish without witnesses.

And while the body of Saint-Exupéry, almost integrally a part of the plane, came to the end of the vertiginous dive through the air and plunged into the depths of the sea, his soul climbed upward toward that Light it had so ardently sought.

Appendixes

1

The Disappearance of Saint-Exupéry

When Saint-Exupéry did not return at the expected hour on July 31, 1944, there was great anxiety among his comrades in the operations room. Some of them were sure that Saint-Ex, having exhausted his fuel supply, was grounded. But where? What had become of him? Had he been obliged to bring down his plane on occupied territory, and if so was he a prisoner of the Germans, or had he found refuge in some French home? Had a failure of the oxygen tank caused a blackout, and had he crashed in the Alps or been swallowed up in the Mediterranean? Or had an enemy fighter plane brought him down, and had he disappeared in the sea or mountains forever?

The projected landing of the Allies on the southern coasts of France would soon take place, and then perhaps these questions could be answered.

That night, the officer who kept the squadron's log book stared at the blank page reflectively awhile, then made the following entry:

A very sad event has occurred to dim the joy we all feel at the coming victory: Commandant Saint-Exupéry has not returned. Having left at 9 A.M. for the Haute Savoie on 223, he had not returned at 1 P.M. Unable to effect contact by radio. The radar posts, alerted, have searched in vain. At 2:30 A.M. there is no longer any hope that he could still be flying.

We lose in him not only one of the best of comrades, but a man who set us a fine example of cheerful faith. He had not come, despite his age, to share our risks in order to add vain glory to a career already magnificently fulfilled, but because he felt a real need to participate. We think of Saint-Exupéry as one of those men who achieved greatness because they are able to respect themselves.

Of course we have great hope that he will soon return; if it is humanly possible, he will find a way; he has 7,000 flying hours behind him and has survived some hard blows of fate. He may be grounded in Switzerland or camouflaged somewhere in the Savoyard maquis; or even if he is a prisoner, it will not be for long. But he will have been denied the joy of landing in liberated France with us.

When France was liberated, careful search revealed no trace of Saint-Exupéry or his plane. There were two theories about his fate: either he had crashed in the Alps and his remains would be found in a rarely visited ravine, or else—and this seemed more plausible and somehow more suitable to his destiny—he had been engulfed in the Mediterranean.

As always when the death of a famous man is cloaked in mystery, some rather wild rumors were circulated. According to one, Saint-Exupéry had committed suicide. According to another, stated in writing by a comrade, Saint-Exupéry's plane had been sabotaged at the instigation of General de Gaulle.

Years passed, during which the beacon light of Saint-Exupéry's life glowed ever brighter and his works enjoyed a constantly growing esteem. His books aroused renewed fervor in an epoch when men began to doubt their destiny, since the war had once again revealed the baseness of humanity. They also pleased many of the younger generation who had grown up during the war years and had an unquenched thirst for beauty. These young people refused to follow the shepherds of despair and woe.

In the spring of 1948, Saint-Exupéry's *The Wisdom of the Sands* was published, heralded and acclaimed widely. In literary circles everyone was talking about the posthumous work in which the airman–writer had expressed his most profound thoughts, giving the world a message rich in poetry and inspiration, from beyond the grave. Then, Gaston Gallimard, Saint-Exupéry's publisher, received a letter from Einbeck in Germany, dated March 15, 1948. It was from a man who had been a Luftwaffe pilot and in 1944 had been stationed at Lake Garda, his job being to scan intelligence reports on air operations over southern Europe. The letter, written in faulty French, said:

Dear Sir,

I have just read an essay on Antoine de Saint-Exupéry by Prof. W. Kellermann of the University of Göttingen in *Die Sammlung*, December, 1947, page 679 and following. Kellermann places at the beginning of his article a short biography of Saint-Exupéry, and in that I learned for the first time something factual about the death of the celebrated airman. He states that "*Am 31. Juli 1944 stieg er von einem korsischen Flugfeld zu einem Erkundungsflug über Südfrankreich auf. Von diesem Flug ist er nicht zurückgekehrt. Nie wurde eine Spur des Mannes oder seines Flugzeuges gefunden.*" (p. 680) *

After having read those lines, I scanned my agendas for 1944. I must tell you, sir, that I was, at that time, in the German Intelligence Service in Italy, specially detailed to sift reports of air operations. Among my papers I found, for the night of July 31–August 1, 1944, the following notation in [abbreviated] German: "Anr. Trib. K. Abschuss 1 Aufkl. brennend über See. Aufkl. Ajacc unver." ("Report by telephone from Capt. K. from region of Avignon: 'Destruction of a reconnaissance plane which fell in flames into the sea after combat. No traces found on later observation.' ")

You will notice that the exact time of the destruction is not given in this report, nor is the exact location and altitude of the combat, nor the type of plane brought down.

I am acquainting you with this, not because I believe it lifts the veil of mystery that hides the events of July 31, but merely to indicate a possible explanation for what happened that day over the Mediterranean. From that point of view, it is more by chance that my brief notes have been preserved. The sea was destined to receive that man, great both as airman and poet, who was venerated by many of the German aviators. Only a week or so ago I read *Wind, Sand and Stars* in the German transla-

* "On 31 July 1944 he flew from a Corsican airfield on a reconnaissance mission over southern France. From this flight he did not return. No trace has been found of the man or his plane."

tion. As with *Southern Mail* and *Night Flight,* I had already read it in the original French before the war. But alas, they are among my treasured books that are buried beneath the ruins of my house in Aix-la-Chapelle.

I am writing this to you, because I do not know to whom else I could convey this information and I hope that you can, without too much difficulty, pass it on to those who are interested.

After apologizing for his bad French, the correspondent signs his name, Hermann Korth.

Gaston Gallimard immediately communicated the contents of this letter to Saint-Exupéry's "spiritual heir" and good friend, Madame X. She at once got in touch with Hermann Korth to learn more. The German ex-aviator, after a period of imprisonment in Italy, had returned to Germany and was studying theology with a view to entering the Protestant ministry. There was an exchange of letters.

Soon everyone had heard of Hermann Korth's revelations. *La Bataille,* August 11, 1948, published the letter, announcing that "the mystery of Saint-Exupéry's death in the air has been cleared up by a German student." The author of the article, in speaking of the letter written by Hermann Korth to Gallimard, declared in substance: ". . . the German student, former chief officer of the Lüftwaffe headquarters in Italy . . . had consulted the military reports in his possession and found a note referring to the fact that a French plane had been shot down July 31, 1944, in the early afternoon, not far from the shores of Corsica. . . . Corresponding information has been checked. The only French plane that disappeared that day in the Mediterranean region was Saint-Exupéry's. One sole French plane, that day, had been shot down by the German fighters. The hour and the place of the combat correspond exactly to those of Saint-Exupéry's Lightning on the return flight."

So much for the information published by certain periodicals. The reporter rushes into print with any sensational news and is not bothered by scruples. The writer in *La Bataille* wanted to give more punch and versimilitude to his news; he wanted it to sound more or less official, and so did not hesitate to transform Hermann Korth into an important officer and his "notes" into "military reports." But worse still, he even gave the exact time and place of the supposed combat, whereas Hermann Korth lamented in his letter the lack of exact data on the subject. The German aviator had frankly declared that he did not feel he was lifting the veil of mystery from the events of July 31, but merely suggested that his information might prove useful. With no document other than this letter from Hermann Korth, the journalist declares that the mystery regarding Saint-Exupéry's death had been cleared up.

The first biography of Saint-Exupéry to be published after his disappearance was by René Delange (to which Léon Werth added, in the back pages, his own recollections). It appeared in 1949.* Delange was completing his book when news of Hermann Korth's letter reached him, and he at once wrote to the German pilot asking for more details without delay. From the information he received, René Delange believed it possible to conclude that Saint-Exupéry, when returning from his mission, had been shot down by a German plane "which attacked him when he was only a dozen or so kilometers away from the Borgo airfield and had begun his descent."

The publicity thus given by the periodical and the book to the revelations made by Hermann Korth brought him shoals of letters asking for more details and requesting interviews. Hermann Korth replied to all these requests as best he could. But it is curiously significant how influenced his correspondents were by preconceived notions. Korth wrote me: "I'm surprised at the different interpretations given to the suppositions I have expressed, and am surprised at the obvious difficulties resulting from the French translation made of a letter written originally in German." Later on, after we had had an interview, he wrote again on the subject: "I'm very grateful for your visit. To begin with, we were able, as much as possible, to reach a conclusion in our en-

* *La Vie de Saint-Exupéry*, by René Delange, followed by *Tel que je l'ai connu*, by Léon Werth. Editions du Seuil, 1949.

quiries regarding the death of Saint-Exupéry and were able to clear up many errors which have been circulated in both the French and German press as to that end and the role I have played in supplying a possible explanation."

Korth received letters not only from writers and journalists who wanted to know the exact circumstances of Saint-Exupéry's disappearance, but also from admirers who wrote to thank the German pilot for having shed some light in the darkness that veiled the last moments of a man they loved and venerated. The letter he received from a Madame Brodhéoux, a resident of Nice, obviously an impressionable and rather mystical person, brings us a revelation. It is dated August 15, 1951, and reads:

Dear Pastor,

Ever since I saw in a Paris newspaper the drawing you made on the subject of Saint-Exupéry's disappearance, I have wanted to tell you what I saw in July 1944—I cannot honestly state the exact day, but I know it was sometime between the 27th and the 31st.

My house, on Saint-Antoine hill, directly faces Corsica. One morning between 9 and 10 o'clock * I was on the balcony with my maid and her son. All of a sudden we saw two planes in combat: they were visible to the naked eye and not very high up.

I believe, from your sketch, that this was Saint-Exupéry under attack. And I have another reason for thinking this, a reason which you, as a man of God, may be able to understand.

None of my menfolk was in the Air Force; however, you can imagine the emotion I felt, for who could not be moved by such a spectacle! I sent up a prayer for those unfortunate men, but I seemed to hear within me the tolling of a bell for the death of some great human being.

I do not put forward this letter as an argument, naturally. But if the combat Madame Brodhéoux witnessed occurred on July 31, 1944, her statement is at least troubling.

The stream of letters and personal inquiries Hermann Korth re-

* Madame Brodhéoux may also not have recalled the exact hour but have been influenced by the hours on the sketch-map, which are, moreover, inexact—at least those hours purporting to be those of the presumed encounter of Saint-Exupéry with German fighter planes.

ceived obliged him to investigate further in order to clarify the hurried notes he had set down on the night of July 31, 1944. He spread out a map of the south of France and of Corsica—of that whole Mediterranean region he knew well from having flown over it often, and from his studies while he was in the intelligence service concerned with air operations in that theater of war. And in fact, he had once crashed there after a direct hit on his oxygen tank.

On the map he traced lines representing the probable routes followed by Saint-Exupéry, when returning from his mission, and other lines showing the routes usually followed by the German patrol on its way back to base in southern France. Then, with this map in mind, he made a sketch which he gave to a journalist, André Hurtrel, who came to interview him at the Wuppertal-Barman seminary in January 1951. This sketch—which Madame Brodhéoux obviously refers to—along with a photograph of Hermann Korth, was used to illustrate an article that appeared in the *Samedi-Soir*, January 20, 1951, entitled "The End of Saint-Exupéry."

This article recounts what Hermann Korth told the reporter about how he spent that evening of July 31, and about the comparable speeds of the Lightning at various altitudes and of the Focke-Wulf fighter plane at similar altitudes. For the first time, the theory of a surprise attack was advanced: the German planes had the sun behind them and Saint-Exupéry, dazzled, could not see them. But the article contains some errors on the route followed by the planes and the probable hour of their encounter. Aside from this, the writer quotes Korth as saying that he based his "certainty as to the hour and approximate place where Capt. de Saint-Exupéry was shot down upon the telephone call received at midnight. . . ." And farther on, after having given the translation of the message received by Korth, the journalist adds: "The exact time of the event is given in the following lines"—whereas we know that in his letter to Gallimard Korth had pointed out that he did not know the exact time or altitude at which the reported encounter took place. Korth has stated the same to others, and has reaffirmed it to me personally. But I shall return to this later. What is interesting for the moment is that André Hurtrel's article does not seem to leave him, or the reader, in any doubt of "the end of Saint-Exupéry," although he produces no proofs whatever.

Pierre Chevrier also corresponded with Hermann Korth, and even went to pay him a visit. Chevrier's book on Saint-Exupéry * recounts how the German officer received late at night on July 31, 1944, a telephone call from one of his comrades at the Istres airbase, and how he had noted down the message briefly in "his private notebook." And the author transcribes the telephone message—of which he gives a facsimile. Let us now examine it carefully. The letters within parentheses are those omitted by Korth; the abbreviations were sufficient to enable him to copy in his report made next day the full text of the message:

"*Anr.*[*uf*] *Trib.*[*un*] *K.*[*ant*] *abschuss I aufkl.*[*ärer*] *brennend üb*[*er*] *See. Aufkl.*[*ärung*] *Ajacc*[*io*] *unver*[*ändert*]."

Keeping in mind that *Tribun* is the code name of the German airbase at Istres, and that Kant is the name of the officer who transmitted the telephone message, the notation clearly reads: "Telephone call from Kant at Tribun reports reconnaissance plane brought down in flames over the sea. No change in Ajaccio patrol."

But Pierre Chevrier, in his biography of Saint-Exupéry, has translated the passage to read: "reconnaissance plane burning on the sea." This is incorrect. *Brennend* is the present participle of the verb "to burn" and *über* signifies "above" or "over." Had the plane been *on* the sea, the report would have used the word *auf*. There is a shade of difference here which is important. If the plane had been burning on the sea, then its pilot had been able to set it down; one of the engines having suffered a direct hit, the pilot had cut off the gas, to prevent the fire from spreading, and had set down the plane on the water. He could then have managed to get out. Although for years he had been hampered in his movements by a stiffened left shoulder, he always managed, on landing

* *Antoine de Saint-Exupéry*, published shortly after Delange's biography.

his plane, to get out of the cockpit unaided—and in this case could have used the lifesaving apparatus with which each pilot was equipped.

Chevrier's translation of *über* as "on" was kept by Georges Pélissier in his book on Saint-Exupéry.* And thus the error was perpetuated.

Whether the plane was in flames *over* the sea or *on* the sea is important. The day before Saint-Exupéry's disappearance, an American pilot flying a Lightning was shot down on a return trip, practically in the same spot and hour that Saint-Exupéry probably met his end. This pilot, Meredith by name, had radioed to base after being hit, the information that he was diving into the sea. He had first radioed, "I'm under attack" and almost immediately after, "I'm gettin' in"—which proves that he was engulfed by the sea. That is doubtless what happened to the plane brought down July 31, "in flames over the sea," and not "on the sea."

Pélissier believes it "improbable that within 24 hours at the same geographical point and at the same hour two planes could have been shot down in the same condition."

But once more it is important to note that Hermann Korth never mentioned either the exact hour or the exact place. When I questioned him on this lack of information in the message he had received by telephone, he replied: "The hours when such events occurred in the air did not interest us. We were given such data only in messages concerning the route followed by U.S.A. convoys in the Mediterranean area, and the time at which they could be expected at certain points on the course. In the case of the event under discussion, Kant *most certainly* would not state the time of day and I would most certainly not have asked for the information." (Korth himself emphasized the words I have underscored.)

Georges Pélissier, who was the first to call attention to the possible confusion of Meredith's plane with Saint-Exupéry's, refers to "Hermann Korth's certainty" as to time and place. But we must repeat: Korth, in his letter to Gallimard, expressly stated that he

* *Les cinq visages de Saint-Exupéry.*

realized his notes were too vague to clear up the mystery of Saint-Exupéry's death, and that he only hoped that what information he furnished *might* offer a possible clue to what happened that day over the Mediterranean.

My exchange of letters with Hermann Korth did not satisfy me, and I decided to go to Aix-la-Chapelle to meet the ex-pilot pastor. We had a long talk and studied the map on which he had traced all the probable air routes. I went through a large file containing newspaper clippings, queries, opinions, suppositions that Korth had received from correspondents, and his own replies. From all this I concluded that we have no eyewitness, and no radio witness (as in the case of Meredith) of Saint-Exupéry's death. We can only make deductions from the slight data at hand to determine whether the telephone message received by Korth referred to Meredith's plane, shot down over the Mediterranean on July 30, 1944, or Saint-Exupéry's plane, which disappeared the following day on the same route.

Could Hermann Korth have been mistaken as to the date? The whole question lies there. Pélissier, who interrogated him on this important point, writes: "Korth simply replied: '*über den Tod von Meredith hab ich schon gelesen. Doch besteht über das Datum des Anrufes kein Zweifel.*' Which is to say, he had read of Meredith's death. And he admits no doubt as to the date of the telephone call he had from Capt. Kant on July 31, 1944." Pélissier adds: "That is all." Those words fill the reader's mind with doubt. But a biographer is in duty bound to seek the truth and destroy doubt by every possible means. What precisely did Georges Pélissier ask Hermann Korth? As to the date, he replied clearly to the question with, "There is no doubt." Why was he so sure of this?

When Korth was grounded after his first accident, he had been appointed officer at Luftwaffe headquarters, second in command of the air fleet under Field Marshal Von Richthofen. He told me his job was to sift intelligence reports of air operations over the Mediterranean region. In his office, which was set up in a villa at Malcesine on the shores of Lake Garda, he received every night, by telephone, information on the operations of the day carried out by different aviation groups of the sector extending from the Avignon region to the Adriatic Sea. He transcribed this information in an agenda kept for the purpose.

When he received the telephone call from Captain Kant on July 31, 1944, it was very late, almost midnight. Captain Kant of the 2nd Air Division should have put in his call from Avignon sooner than this, and Hermann Korth waited in some irritation for his report, since he was supposed to attend a birthday celebration for one of the officers at a neighboring villa. Impatient to leave, he had cleared his desk and had put the agenda for reports in a safe. Alone in the calm night, he smoked a cigarette, waiting for the call. And he meditated upon this war that he had now been in for almost five years, serving first as gunner in the artillery and then as pilot in the air force which seemed indomitable. Now that force was weakening, was disintegrating. The Allies had landed in Normandy, in Sardinia, in Corsica, in southern Italy. Their powerful aviation dominated the German Air Force. The Germans no longer had many planes and were low on fuel; at several airfields, to economize on the precious gasoline, planes were moved by oxen. Hermann Korth had decided that if he came out of this war alive he would shed his fine aviator's uniform and would study for the ministry. But for the time being, the war went on, and he was waiting for that delayed telephone call, while his comrades not far away were enjoying a party.

Suddenly the telephone rang. Korth took up the receiver. A voice was announcing: "*Auruf Tribun . . .*"

It was Captain Kant at last. Korth reached for his pen and his diary, a loose-leaf notebook which was on the table. He kept it there for all kinds of jottings—his impressions, his thoughts, a poem of Rilke that had suddenly come to mind, and occasional sketches. In this notebook he wrote Kant's report in abbreviated form. And he jotted the report down on the page dated July 31st—which is important. At the end of every day's work, Korth was in the habit of writing the date of the next day at the top of each blank page. In his two-hour wait for Captain Kant's telephone call, he had already written on the next page the date of the following day: August 1. It was by sheer chance that, four years later, he found the notebook, just as it had been by sheer chance that he had originally written Captain Kant's message there rather than in the agenda kept for such reports. It was also fortuitous that he found it after reading of Saint-Exupéry's death, and concluded that the plane shot down on July 31 "might" be that of Saint-Exupéry.

When, in March 1948, Hermann Korth had run across the essay on Saint-Exupéry that had been published in the December 1947 issue of *Die Sammlung,* he was especially interested, for ever since 1939—when he had read *Wind, Sand and Stars* in the original French edition (*Terre des Hommes*)—he had been a great admirer of the French writer and airman. The book had been given him by a cousin, Paul Schenk, a pilot in the Lufthansa who had met some men of the Latécoère airline—among them Saint-Exupéry. The book had been a revelation, not only to the future pilot but to the future pastor. It had been among his most treasured books that had disappeared in the ruins of his house at Aix-la-Chapelle, destroyed by bombs in 1944. We can therefore imagine with what interest he had read the essay by Professor Von Kellermann, particularly the short biographical notice at the head of it. There, for the first time, the former officer at the Malcesine Luftwaffe headquarters learned that Saint-Exupéry, on an operational flight July 31, 1944, from a Corsican airfield over the south of France, had disappeared without leaving a trace.

He stopped reading, and began to reflect. So! The writer whose works he had read and admired so deeply had died not far from where he had been stationed. And Saint-Exupéry had been stationed, that summer of 1944, at one of those Corsican airfields which he, Hermann Korth, knew well: he had photographed them during reconnaissance flights, after the occupation by the Allies, on one of his last missions.

The young pastor got out of his chair and began looking for

a certain diary on the shelves where he was beginning to reassemble a library. He found it and opened it to July 31, 1944, read the communication received from Captain Kant: "a reconnaissance plane which fell in flames into the sea after combat." Could it have been Saint-Exupéry's plane? And so it was that he wrote to Saint-Exupéry's publisher, Gallimard, in Paris. (I noticed, when I had this issue of *Die Sammlung* in my hands, that the name Gallimard had been underscored with a blue pencil, and that beside the date a cross had been made with the same pencil.)

Any doubt of an error in dates being eliminated—that is to say, having ascertained that the message received by Korth had nothing to do with Meredith's plane—and since only one plane of the French Air Force in the Corsica–southern France sector had disappeared that day, it would seem to be useless to search for further proof. But we must examine every argument that has been put forward, no matter what its worth.

Two theories have been advanced. One concerns that phrase "after combat" which occurs in the translation of the message given by Hermann Korth to Gallimard. The former aviator had written in his letter, "destruction of a reconnaissance plane which fell in flames into the sea after combat." Now, the Lightning P–38 flown by Saint-Exupéry was unarmed, so there could have been no combat. However, in the original message, jotted down in German, the two words "after combat" did not appear. It was Hermann Korth who added them in writing to Gallimard, as he had added them on the official report he wrote next day in the agenda. He told me he did this since "aerial combat" was a phrase *always used* in such reports, even when the adversary had not fired but had only carried out defensive maneuvers.

In the instance of the attack on Saint-Exupéry's plane, there may not even have been "defensive maneuvers." Some of the great French aces, such as Guynemer, often attacked the enemy by surprise, without the enemy pilot's having been able to make a move in self-defense. But nonetheless the French government added a palm to the distinguished French aviator's *Croix-de-guerre* ribbon.

But no matter. It is very essential to keep in mind that the words "after combat" did not appear in the original message noted down in German.

The second argument is equally worthless. It is found in Georges Pélissier's summing up of the data which he had not thoroughly examined: "It seems improbable that within 24 hours at the same geographical point and at the same hour two planes could have been shot down in the same condition." Let us admit, for the sake of argument, that the hour and place were identical. They must not have differed markedly, since the planes accomplished daily the same mission, flying in opposite directions, and as Hermann Korth told me in a letter, the German fighters daily patrolled sea and land in the region of Ajaccio. "Then why," ask some, "why were there not more airplanes brought down in this sector?" This question is easily answered. To begin with, the planes had to be flying very close for the pilots to perceive each other: a few minutes' difference, and the point of encounter would no longer be possible. Then, the altitude at which they flew also played a part. And finally, the German patrol was comprised of two planes: an observer, unarmed—a Messerschmitt 109—and the fighter which it escorted, a Focke-Wulf, the two flying close together and separating only when the Focke-Wulf spied an enemy plane not too far off and made a surprise attack.

We know that Meredith was shot down sixty miles off the northern coast of Corsica. My belief is that Saint-Exupéry may have been shot down nearer the French coast, and that his Lightning may have been one of the "planes in combat"—that is to say, it was trying to elude the attacking Focke-Wulf plane—which Madame Brodhéoux saw one morning from the balcony of her house in Nice.

I have come to this conclusion because Saint-Exupéry, at the moment of being shot down, had not yet entered into radio contact with his base as Corsica, as Meredith had done. However, Jean Leleu, to whom I expressed this opinion, did not think much of it. "Your theory," he said, "is worth considering. But, absent-minded as he was, Saint-Exupéry would have been quite capable of not connecting up his radio until a minute before touching down on the field."

In addition to the mystery of his disappearance, Saint-Exupéry's literary remains raised some questions, doubts and contention. For many years he had been in the habit of keeping notes of his reflections, observations, meditations. Wherever he happened to be—whether in a café, on a train or plane—he covered pages of his notebooks with his often illegible handwriting. Wherever he moved, he carried these notebooks and manuscripts with him in a leather suitcase.

In 1944, shortly before his last flight, he asked his friend and superior officer Colonel Gavoille to hand over his personal effects to Dr. Pélissier, with whom he had lodged in Algiers from August 1943 to May 1944, in the event that Saint-Ex did not return from one of the dangerous missions he was at that time carrying out. On August 10, 1944, two weeks after his last mission, Captain Gavoille had the personal effects of his "comrade, Saint-Exupéry," as he put it in the accompanying note, sent to Dr. Pélissier. Among these effects was the suitcase containing the notebooks and manuscripts. "None of his things," Colonel Gavoille added, "has been sent to the military depot; I am handing everything over to you, although it's not exactly according to the rules, but I feel I can do this much for Saint-Ex." (The quotation is from Pélissier's book on Saint-Exupéry.)

In January 1945, when Nazi Germany, at last vanquished, was about to collapse, the squadron to which Saint-Ex had belonged happened to be at Nancy. With the squadron was Captain Leleu, who had been one of the last to see Saint-Exupéry before he took off from the Borgo airfield in Corsica on his last, fatal flight. Captain Leleu recalled this, of course, when his general entrusted him with a confidential mission: he was to fly to Algiers and retrieve from Dr. Pélissier the missing aviator's personal belongings and the manuscripts which Colonel Gavoille had left with him. On this mission Captain Leleu was accompanied by a young flyer who was to play the part, more or less, of a process-server and handle the signing of the necessary papers in the transfer of Saint-Exupéry's effects.

Arrived at Dr. Pélissier's residence in Algiers, they were met with a categorical refusal. Pélissier would not turn over the effects that had been entrusted to him, although, except for the famous suitcase containing the notebooks and the manuscript of *The Wisdom of the Sands,* they were of no value. Captain Leleu had to insist and was obliged to return several times and to remain a week in Algiers before he finally obtained possession of Saint-Exupéry's belongings.

In Pélissier's book, *Les Cinq Visages de Saint-Exupéry,* we find only a few lines devoted to this affair, and they were obviously written in an effort to justify his behavior, by mentioning the necessary legal formalities in the transfer from one trustee to another objects that had belonged to a man who had disappeared but who had as yet not been pronounced "legally dead."

Did Dr. Pélissier, against all likelihood, consider himself as the spiritual heir of Saint-Exupéry? When he handed over Saint-Exupéry's belongings to Pélissier, Colonel Gavoille had written, "You must certainly have had some instructions in this matter," referring to the suitcase of manuscripts. Pélissier says nothing on this score in his book. Yet it would have been surprising if Saint-Ex had never given him such instructions. They lived in the same house at Algiers for eight months, and although Saint-Ex was careless about his material possessions, he attached deserved importance to his manuscripts, especially to *The Wisdom of the Sands.* And it is still more surprising that he would have requested Gavoille to deposit his belongings with Pélissier without having previously discussed the matter with Pélissier himself.

Colonel Gavoille, in his letter, had instructed Pélissier to sort out and make an inventory of Saint-Ex's effects. Did Pélissier, in making that inventory, discover certain writings which he thought too unpleasant to certain people to allow publication until death should have "reduced us all to ashes"? We shall never know, since Dr. Pélissier, who wrote those lines in his book on Saint-Exupéry, is no longer among the living. Besides, his whole book is written in a cryptic style which seems to exaggerate the importance of its contents.

What was important was the retrieving of Saint-Exupéry's manuscripts, and this alone justified the mission of Captain Leleu. But who was the "spiritual heir" of this poet, philosopher, moralist, and writer of fiction? His wife claimed the title. But the woman who had been his friend, his Egeria, also claimed it. Legally, the manuscripts would go to his relatives, that is to say, to his mother—who apparently remained outside all the proceedings and heated arguments involving this matter. Shortly before his death, it would seem that Saint-Ex had written, on the back of a military order, a kind of will, which turned over the manuscripts to his close friend who had been the first to read the whole manuscript of *Citadelle*. But the will was neither dated nor signed, and would therefore have been contested had the dispute reached the courts—a painful eventuality that was fortunately avoided. And so, at last, the precious documents came into the hands of the person best fitted to comprehend their value, in conformity with Saint-Exupéry's wishes. For although Dr. Pélissier maintained silence about any instructions from Saint-Exupéry as to who was to fall heir to the manuscripts, I have a first-hand testimony that he expressed in conversation many times during the last months of his life the wishes that he scribbled on the back of that military form.

That "spiritual heir" of Saint-Exupéry has known how to play the part he expected of her. Slowly and carefully she is deciphering the notebooks and already has had some portions published. Aside from this, she has written (under a pen-name) a rather important study of Saint-Exupéry, though it cannot be considered a complete biography because of her quite natural bias and concealments. No matter how honest the wife or mistress turned biographer, there is always too much stress laid on the qualities of the hero, while the defects are scarcely mentioned. The bonds of affection are too strong, and in their books the hero is seen but dimly through eyes clouded with love. These biographers do not enjoy the independence and objectivity that a good biographer must have. Even so, Madame X's work is an admirable document, and provides a detailed chronology which is of great help to the biographers who have followed. I would classify it among the three or four worthwhile books on Saint-Exupéry that have appeared thus far, and since his death more than fifteen have been published in the French language alone.

Another friend who was deeply affected by his disappearance was Léon Werth, who had returned to liberated Paris after existing in concealment for four years during the German occupation. At long last, he had the satisfaction of living in his own home again in the Rue d'Assas. But he was overwhelmed with sadness and felt a great loneliness, for his young friend was no more. Saint-Exupéry's last flight had been made not quite a month before the Allied armies entered Paris. He had given his life for the liberation of the Hostage, of all the hostages. Werth deeply felt the loss of his companionship: "Oh no," he said, "he couldn't do this to us. . . ."

Two years later he was asked to collaborate with several other writers on a special issue of the magazine *Confluences,* which was to be devoted exclusively to articles on Saint-Exupéry. He hesitated a while, still unable, he said, "to separate him from myself." Later on he added fifty pages to René Delange's biography, entitling them, "Saint-Exupéry, as I knew him"—*Tel que je l'ai connu.* He shows us the real Saint-Exupéry, in whom "the sublime was not distinct from the everyday and natural," and in a few lines he draws a portrait with a sureness and clarity that demonstrate unerringly his profound knowledge of the man. "Saint-Exupéry was the most limpid and at the same time the most troubled of men," he writes. "As he went through life he unleashed a joy which seemed deeply established in him. Faithful to everything but unfaithful to every happiness. Aside from the perfect hours—which he so often created—he was everywhere imprisoned yet never at rest. His was not a vain agitation. He mistrusted himself to such an extent that he often tried out the resonance of his writings on heads not more worthy than that of Molière's servant-maid. No matter what person served him, at times, as a wall against which to bounce the ball." And again, referring to Saint-Exupéry's chronic restlessness: "An uneasy mind often surrounds itself with tenebrous shadows; in former times the restless seeker was confounded with the hero rapt in Byronic gloom.... But in Saint-Exupéry this restlessness was less a play of shadows than a perpetual movement of reflections."

Until the last hours of his life, which flickered out in December 1955, at the age of seventy-eight, Werth maintained a flawless devotion to his vanished friend. Once, at a meeting of the "Association of the Friends of Saint-Exupéry" (an association that did not survive Werth), this "cantankerous man" took a violent stand against some remarks made by Gide, who was never checked by scruples and was incapable of comprehending certain kinds of grandeur—and who, moreover, had never had Saint-Exupéry's real friendship. Perhaps it was this scene that alienated some members of the Association from him. Be that as it may, Jean Lucas was the only one among them to attend the funeral of Léon Werth. And while the flames of the crematorium consumed the aged body which the soul had just left—that soul in which Léon Werth did not believe—Lucas reflected upon Saint-Exupéry who had given so much to so many men, but who had bestowed upon this slighted and forgotten man his rarest gift: true friendship.

2

An Open Letter to Frenchmen Everywhere
by Antoine de Saint-Exupéry, an article published in *The New York Times Sunday Magazine,* November 29, 1942.

First of all, France! The German night has swallowed up the country. For a time we were still able to know a little about those we love; we could still send them words of affection, even if we could not share the wretched bread on their tables. From afar we could catch their breathing.

All that is over now. France is nothing but a silence; she is lost somewhere in the night with all lights out, like a ship. Her mind and spirit have been absorbed into her physical being. We shall not know even the names of the hostages who tomorrow will die before the German rifles.

It is always in the cellars under a tyranny that new truths are born. Let us not play the part of braggarts. There are 40,000,000 people over there in France who must endure their slavery. We shall not be carrying any fire of the spirit to those who are already nourishing the flame with their life's blood—like the wax of a candle. They will deal with French problems better than we can; they have all the right to deal with them. Our talk about sociology, politics and art will carry no weight with them. They will not read our books, they will not listen to our speeches. Perhaps our ideas may make them sick.

Let us be infinitely modest. Our political discussions are the discussions of ghosts; ambitions among us are comic. We do not represent France; all we can do is to serve her. And whatever we do, we shall have no just claim for recognition. For there is no common measure between freedom to fight and bearing the crushing weight of the darkness. There is no common measure between the métier of the soldier and the métier of the hostage. The people over there in France are the only true saints. Even if we have the honor of taking part in the battle, we shall still be in their debt. There, in the first place, is the fundamental truth.

Men of France, let us be reconciled in order to serve!

I shall say a few words about the quarrels which have divided Frenchmen in the hope of doing something to remove them. For there has been a grave spiritual disorder among French people. The souls of many among us have been torn; these have need of peace of mind, and they should find it. By the miracle of American action in North Africa, all our different roads have led us to the same meeting-place. Why now should we get bogged down in the old quarrels? It is time to unite, not to divide, for opening wide the arms, not for exclusions.

Were our quarrels worth the hate we wasted on them? Who can ever maintain that he alone is absolutely right? Man's field of vision is minute; language is an imperfect instrument; the problems of life burst all the formulas.

We were all in agreement as to our faith. We all wanted to save France. France had to be saved both in flesh and in the spirit. Of what use is the spiritual heritage if there be no heir? What good is the heir if the spirit be dead?

All of us hate the idea of collaboration. Some of us accused France of real collaboration while others saw only a ruse. Let us think of Vichy as a trustee in bankruptcy, negotiating with a greedy conqueror for delivery to France of a little grease for railroad cars. (France can no longer get gasoline, or even horses, to bring food to her towns.) The officers of the Armistice Commission will one day tell us about this persistent and atrocious German blackmail. A quarter-turn of the key—delivery of any less grease than required—and a hundred thousand more French children would die in the next six months.

When a single hostage is shot, his sacrifice shines forth. His death is the cement that binds French unity. But when the Germans, by merely holding up an agreement on grease for cars, kill a hundred thousand hostages of 5 years, where is the compensation for this slow, silent hemorrhage? What is the acceptable fixed price for dead children? What would have been the tolerable limit of Vichy's concession in its attempt to save them? Who can say?

You are aware that French denunciation of the armistice terms would have been equivalent to a return to a state of war. It would have justified the conqueror's seizure of all adult males as military prisoners. This blackmail lay heavily over France. The threat was plainly set forth. German blackmail is no jest. The rot of German prison camps yields only corpses. My country was thus threatened, purely and simply, with utter extermination, under legal and administrative pretense, of 6,000,000 men. France was armed only with sticks to resist this slave hunt. Who is in a position to say for certain what should have been her resistance?

Here at last is the seizure of North Africa by the Allies within sixty-six hours to prove, perhaps, that in spite of blackmail and in spite of two years of pressure, Germany has failed seriously to encroach upon this North African territory. Somewhere, then, there must have been attempts at resistance. Perhaps the victory in North Africa has been won, at least in part, by our 500,000 children who have died. Who would dare say that the number is insufficient?

Frenchmen, if we could reduce our differences of opinion to their true proportions, that would be enough to make peace among us. We have never been divided except on the question as to the weight to be attributed to the Nazi blackmail. On the one hand, some said, "If the Germans are determined to wipe out the people of France, they will wipe them out, whatever the French do. This blackmail ought to be despised. Nothing should make Vichy take such and such a decision or give this or that promise."

On the other hand, other people thought: "It is not merely a case of blackmail but of blackmail unique for cruelty in the history of the world. Let France, refusing all capital concessions, employ every sort of ruse to delay the menace from day to day. The tone of the official utterances shows that when a Ulysses or Talleyrand is disarmed, there remain to him only words with which to deceive the enemy."

Do you believe, Frenchmen, that these diverse opinions as to the rigors of the Nazi blackmail or as to the real intentions of this circumscribed government really ought to make us hate one another still? (When the English and the Russians fight side by side they leave to the future disputes which are grave enough.) Our divergences of opinion do not touch our hatred of the invader, while at the same time we are all indignant, as are all the people of France, at the surrender of the foreign refugees, a violation of the right of asylum.

Well, these quarrels of the past have no longer any point. Vichy is dead. Vichy has carried with it to the grave all its inextricable problems, its contradictory personnel, its sincerity, its ruses, its cowardice and its courage. Let us leave for the time being the role of judge to the historians and the courts-martial after the war. It is more important to serve France in the present than to argue about her history.

The German occupation of all France has settled all our quarrels and brought appeasement to the drama of our consciences. Men of France, are you willing to become reconciled? There is no longer even a shadow of a reason for argument among us. Let us abandon all party spirit. Why should we hate one another? Why should we be jealous of one another? There is no question of positions to be won. There is no question of any race for offices. The only places open are soldiers' places—perhaps some quiet beds in some little cemetery in North Africa.

The military law of France binds all men up to 48. From 18 to 48 we ought all of us to be mobilized. There is no question whether we wish to enlist or not. It is demanded of us, in order to turn the balance of war, that we take our places in the scale—altogether and quite simply.

Although our old quarrels are now merely quarrels for the historians, there is another danger of disunion among us. Let us have the courage, men of France, to surmount this danger.

Some among us trouble themselves about the name of one leader as against another, of one form of government as against another. They see the phantom of injustice rising on the horizon.

Why do they thus complicate matters? There is no injustice to fear. None of our personal interests is going to suffer in the future. When a mason devotes himself to the building of a cathedral, the cathedral cannot injure the masons. The only role expected of us is a war role. I myself feel wonderfully safe against any form of injustice. Who could do me an injustice since I have only one idea—namely, to rejoin in Tunis my comrades of Groupe 2/33 with whom I lived through nine months of the campaign and then the brutal German offensive, which took two-thirds of our number, and finally the escape to North Africa on the eve of the armistice? Let us not dispute now about precedence, about honors, about justice, or about priorities. There is nothing of all that offered to us. They are only offering us rifles—and there will be plenty of these for everybody.

If I feel so much at peace now it is because again I find in myself no leaning toward the position of a judge. The group of which I become a part is neither a party nor a sect, it is my country. I am not interested in who will command us. The provisional organization of France is an affair of state. Let us leave it to Britain and to the United States to do the best they can. If our ambition is to press the trigger of a machine gun we shall not be worried about decisions that will seem to us secondary. Our real chief is France, now condemned to silence. Let us hate parties, clans, divisions of any kind.

If the only desire we formulate (and we have the right to formulate it, since it unites all of us) is to obey the military leaders rather than the political leaders, it is like the military salute which honors not the soldier who is saluted but the nation which he represents. We know what General de Gaulle and General Giraud think about authority: they serve; they are the first servants. That should be enough for us, since all the quarrels which weakened us yesterday are now resolved or absorbed in the present.

Here, it seems to me, we stand. Our friends in the United States should not get a false picture of France. Some regard Frenchmen as a little like a basket of crabs. This is unjust. Only the controversialists talk. One does not hear those who keep still.

I suggest to all those Frenchmen who have up to this time been silent that they emerge from their silence just once to reassure Cordell Hull as to the true state of our spirit. I suggest that each of these send to him some such telegram as the following:

> We ask the privilege of serving in any way whatever. We desire the mobilization of all Frenchmen in the United States. We accept in advance any organization that may be deemed the most desirable. But, hating any spirit of division among Frenchmen, we ask simply that the organization be outside politics.

The State Department will be astonished at the number of Frenchmen who will take their stand for unity. For, despite our reputation, most of us at heart know only love of our civilization and our country.

Frenchmen, let us become reconciled! When we find ourselves one day together in a bomber fighting five or six Messerschmitts, the thought of our old fights will make us smile.

During the war, in 1940, when I came back from a mission with my plane shot full of holes, I used to drink an excellent Pernod at the squadron bar. I often won my Pernod throwing dice, sometimes from a Royalist comrade, perhaps from one who was a Socialist, or perhaps from Lieutenant Israël, the bravest of our crew, who was a Jew. And we all clinked glasses in the greatest friendliness.

Notes

1. *Wind, Sand and Stars* (tr. Lewis Galantière; New York: Reynal & Hitchcock, 1939).
2. *Ibid.*
3. In *Confluences,* No. 12–14 (1947), a special issue devoted to Saint-Exupéry.
4. *The Little Prince* (tr. Katherine Woods; New York: Reynal & Hitchcock, 1943).
5. *Lettres à sa mère.*
6. *Ibid.*
7. See Migeo, *Henri Guillaumet.*
8. For a description of this desert tragedy, see the account in *ibid.*
9. J.-G. Fleurey, *La Ligne.*
10. This letter is quoted in Gide's preface to *Night Flight* without any mention of the person to whom it was written, thus giving the mistaken impression that he was the recipient.
11. In *Confluences.*
12. Dubourdieu, in *Forces Aériennes Françaises,* No. 34 (July 1949).
13. Quoted in Didier Daurat, *Dans le Vent des Hélices.*
14. In *Forces Aériennes Françaises.*
15. Quoted by Pierre Chevrier, *Antoine de Saint-Exupéry.*
16. *Ibid.*
17. This and other portions of the newspaper articles not found in *Wind, Sand and Stars* are from the quotations given by René Delange in *La Vie de Saint-Exupéry* (1949).
18. In *Confluences.*
19. *Ibid.*
20. In *Forces Aériennes Françaises.*
21. Léon Werth, *Tel que je l'ai connu.*
22. In *Confluences.*
23. *Ibid.*

24. Georges Pélissier, *Les Cinq Visages de Saint-Exupéry.*
25. *Le Voltaire,* No. 102 (January 30, 1937).
26. Georges Altman in *Franc-Tireur* (December 16, 1955).
27. In *Confluences.*
28. *Antoine de Saint-Exupéry, Poète, Romancier, Moraliste.*
29. These notes on education were incorporated almost word for word in *The Wisdom of the Sands* (tr. Stuart Gilbert; New York: Harcourt, Brace & Company, Inc., 1950).
30. *L'Humanisme cosmique de Saint-Exupéry.*
31. *Ibid.*
32. *Science et Humanisme.*
33. Lewis Galantière, "Antoine de Saint-Exupéry," *Atlantic* (April 1947).
34. Published in *Le Figaro Littéraire* (July 27, 1957).
35. *"Lettres de guerre a un ami"* (1940) in *ibid.*
36. *Ibid.*
37. Pierre Dalloz in *Confluences.*
38. *Tel que je l'ai connu.*
39. "Letter to General X.," *Le Figaro Littéraire* (April 10, 1948).
40. In *Forces Aériennes Françaises.*
41. In *Confluences.*
42. Galantière, "Antoine de Saint-Exupéry."
43. Quoted by Pierre Chevrier, *op. cit.*
44. In *Confluences.*
45. *Atlantic* (April 1947).
46. *Ibid.*
47. Quoted by Mary Lecomte de Noüy, *Lecomte de Noüy.*
48. *Ibid.*
49. Galantière, "Antoine de Saint-Exupéry."
50. *Ibid.*
51. In *Confluences.*
52. Chevrier, *op. cit.*
53. *Confluences.*
54. Léon Werth, *Tel que je l'ai connu.*
55. In *Confluences.*
56. *Ibid.*
57. Pélissier, *op. cit.*
58. Robert Bordoz in *Forces Aériennes Françaises.*
59. General Chassin in *Confluences.*
60. Simon & Schuster, Inc., 1959.
61. In *Forces Aériennes Françaises.*
62. Abbé Jean Goffaerts, *Itinéraire Spirituel de Saint-Exupéry.*
63. Luc Estang, *Saint-Exupéry par lui-même.*
64. *Flight to Arras* (tr. Galantière; New York: Reynal & Hitchcock, 1942), p. 325.

Bibliography

1. Books by Antoine de Saint-Exupéry

Courrier Sud. Preface by André Beucler. Gallimard, Paris, 1928.
Southern Mail. Translated by Stuart Gilbert. Harrison Smith and Robert Haas, New York, 1933.

Vol de Nuit. Preface by André Gide. Gallimard, Paris, 1931.
Night Flight. Translated by Stuart Gilbert. Reynal & Hitchcock, New York, 1931. Penguin Books, London, 1939.

Terre des Hommes. Gallimard, Paris, 1939.
Wind, Sand and Stars. Translated by Lewis Galantière. Heinemann, London, 1939. Reynal & Hitchcock, New York, 1939).[1]

Pilote de Guerre. Gallimard, Paris, 1942.
Flight to Arras. Translated by Lewis Galantière. Heinemann, London, 1942. Reynal & Hitchcock, New York, 1942.

Lettre à un Otage. Gallimard, Paris, 1944.
Letter to a Hostage. Translated by Jacqueline Gerst. Heinemann, London, 1950. Also translated by J. Rodker. Hogarth Press, London, 1944. Quotations for this book translated by Herma Briffault.

Le Petit Prince. With illustrations by author. Gallimard, Paris, 1946.
The Little Prince. Translated by Katherine Woods. Reynal & Hitchcock, New York, 1943. Heinemann, London, 1945.

Citadelle. Gallimard, Paris, 1948.
The Wisdom of the Sands. Translated by Stuart Gilbert. Harcourt, Brace & Company, Inc., New York, 1950. Hollis and Carter, London, 1952.[1]

Oeuvres Complètes. One vol., illustrated. Gallimard, Paris, 1950.

[1] The French and English texts of these books are not identical, the English texts being sometimes cut, sometimes including additional material.

Airman's Odyssey (contains *Night Flight; Wind, Sand and Stars;* and *Flight to Arras*). Harcourt, Brace & Company, Inc., New York, 1943.

2. Articles by Antoine de Saint-Exupéry

"L'Aviateur" (pages from an unfinished novel, *L'Evasion de Jacques de Bernis*). In *Navire d'Argent,* April 1, 1926, Paris.

Report on May Day in Moscow, 1935, in *Paris-Soir,* May 14, 1935.

Reports on Spanish Civil War, in *L'Intransigeant,* August 16, 19, 1936; *Paris-Soir,* June 27, 1937, July 3, 1937, August 3, 1937.

Essay on War and Peace, in *Paris-Soir,* October 2, 3, 4, 1938.

"Reflections on War," translation of above, in *Living Age,* November 1938.

"Crash in the Desert," *Atlantic Monthly,* July–August 1938 (excerpt from *Wind, Sand and Stars*).

"An Open Letter to Frenchmen Everywhere" in *The New York Times Magazine,* November 29, 1942. (Original version, in French, in *Le Canada,* November 30, 1942.)

"Lettre au Géneral X." In *Figaro Littéraire,* April 10, 1948.

3. Letters and notebooks, published posthumously

Carnets Gallimard Paris 1953

Lettres de Jeunesse Gallimard Paris 1953

Lettres à l'amie inventée, presented by Renée de Saussine, Plon, Paris, 1953.

Lettres à sa Mère. Gallimard Paris 1955

"Lettres de Guerre à un Ami," *in Le Figaro Littéraire,* July 27, 1957.

4. Prefaces by Antoine de Saint-Exupéry to:

Grandeur et Servitude de l'Aviation, by Maurice Bourdet. Corréa, Paris, 1933.

Le Vent se Lève (French version of *Listen, the Wind*), by Anne Morrow. Corréa, Paris, 1939.

Pilotes d'Essai, by Jean-Marie Conty. Ed. Spes, Paris, 1939.

La France que J'aime, by Helen Mackay. Ed. Variétés, Montreal, 1944.

5. Books and articles about Saint-Exupéry and books in which he figures

Albérès, R.-M. *Saint-Exupéry.* Nouvelle Edition. Paris, 1946.

Anet, Daniel. *Antoine de Saint-Exupéry, Poète, Romancier, Moraliste.* Corréa, Paris, 1946.

Baratier, Jacques. "Retour d'Amérique Saint-Ex nous dit." In *Nouvelles Littéraires,* March 11, 1939.

Barjon, Louis. *Saint-Exupéry et Gide.* Etudes. Paris, 19 . . . ?

Bordaz, Robert. "Témoignages," in *Forces Aériennes Françaises,* July 1949.

Bougerol, R. P. Guy. *Ceux qu'on n'a jamais vus.* Arthaud, Paris, 1943.

Chevrier, Pierre. *Antoine de Saint-Exupéry.* Gallimard, Paris, 1949.

Confluences No. 12–14, 1947. A special issue devoted to Saint-Exupéry, with articles by Blaise Cendrars, Roger Caillois, General Chassin, Richard Aldington, August Anglès, Guillain de Benouville, Louis Barjon, Louis Dumont, Pierre Dalloz, Hélène Froment, Léon-Paul Fargue, Pierre de Lanux, A. R. Métral, Georges Mounin, Jean Leleu, Jules Roy, Léon Werth, Simone de Saint-Exupéry, Roger Stéphane, Francisco Giner de Los Rios.

Crisenoy, Marie de. *Antoine de Saint-Exupéry, Poète et Aviateur.* Ed. Spes, Paris, 1948.

Daurat, Didier. *Dans le vent des hélices.* Le Seuil, Paris, 1956.

Delange, Réné. *La Vie de Saint-Exupéry* (Includes *Tel que je l'ai connu* by Léon Werth). Ed. du Seuil, Paris, 1949.

Dubourdieu, article on Saint-Exupéry in *Forces Aérienne Française,* July 1949.

Estang, Luc. *Saint-Exupéry par lui-même.* Ed. Le Seuil, Paris, 1956.

Fleury, Jean-Gérard. *La Ligne.* Gallimard, Paris, 1942.

——— *Chemins du ciel.* Nouv. Ed. Latine.

Galantière, Lewis. *Antoine de Saint-Exupéry. Atlantic,* April 1947.

Gascht, André. *L'Humanisme cosmique d'Antoine de Saint-Exupéry.* Bruges, 1947.

Goffaerts, Abbé Jean. *Itinéraire spirituel de Saint-Exupéry.* Brussels, 1952.

Huguet, Jean. *Saint-Exupéry ou l'enseignement du désert.* Colombe.

Kessel, J. *Mermoz.* Gallimard, Paris, 1938.

Las Vergnas, Raymond. "Action et littérature" in *Nouvelle Littéraires,* May 8, 1947.

Leleu, Jean, "Recollections of Saint-Exupéry," in *Forces Aériennes Françaises,* No. 34, 1949.

Massimi, B. de. *Vent debout.* Plon, Paris, 1949.

Migeo, Marcel. *Henri Guillaumet.* Arthaud, Paris, 1949.

Notice généalogique sur la famille de Saint-Exupéry. "A Paris, chez Jouaust, 338, rue Saint-Honoré. Edition de 1878, tirée à 150 exemplaires."

Pélissier, Georges. *Les cinq visages de Saint-Exupéry*. Flammarion, 1951.
Phillips, John. *Odd World*. Simon & Schuster, Inc., New York, 1959.
Roy, Jules. *La Vallée Heureuse*. Gallimard, Paris, 1946. (Tr. by E. O. Marsh: *The Happy Valley*. Gollancz, 1952.)
——— *Passion de Saint-Exupéry*. Gallimard, Paris, 1951.
Simon, Pierre-Henri. *L'Homme en Procès* (Malraux, Sartre, Camus, Saint-Exupéry). Neuchâtel, 1950.
Zeller, Renée. *L'Homme et le navire*. Alsatia. 1951.

About the author

The son of a French provincial family, Marcel Migeo is descended from the poet and philosopher Antoine Migeot, a disciple of Malebranche and d'Alembert. Destined like his father for a civil-service career, Mr. Migeo escaped this conventional fate by going into aviation. While training at Strasbourg he first met Antoine de Saint-Exupéry, also a student pilot. Like his subject, Migeo developed a passion for flying and for the African desert, where he was stationed. Back in civilian life, Migeo maintained his interest in aviation by lecturing, amateur flying, contributing to air magazines, and writing a series of books on aviation and noted airmen. For his *Saint-Exupéry* he spent ten years researching all available documents, interviewing living witnesses, and retracing the great writer-pilot's footsteps. Mr. Migeo is now working on a novel about the French airmail service and on a biography of Didier Daurat, the airman who inspired Saint-Exupéry's *Night Flight.*